AN ENVIRONMENTAL HISTORY OF FRANCE

Making the Landscape, 1770–2020

Peter McPhee

BLOOMSBURY ACADEMIC

LONDON · NEW YORK · OXFORD · NEW DELHI · SYDNEY

BLOOMSBURY ACADEMIC
Bloomsbury Publishing Plc
50 Bedford Square, London, WC1B 3DP, UK
1385 Broadway, New York, NY 10018, USA
29 Earlsfort Terrace, Dublin 2, Ireland

BLOOMSBURY, BLOOMSBURY ACADEMIC and the Diana logo are trademarks of Bloomsbury Publishing Plc

First published in Great Britain 2025

A catalogue record for this book is available from the British Library.

A catalog record for this book is available from the Library of Congress.

ISBN: HB: 978-1-3502-6779-4
PB: 978-1-3505-2385-2
ePDF: 978-1-3502-6780-0
eBook: 978-1-3502-6781-7

Typeset by Deanta Global Publishing Services, Chennai, India
Printed and bound in Great Britain

To find out more about our authors and books visit www.bloomsbury.com and sign up for our newsletters.

For my *compagne de voyage* Charlotte Allen

CONTENTS

PLATES

FIGURES

ACKNOWLEDGEMENTS

In the centuries after the European invasion in 1788, the unique landscape of much of my home country of Australia has been radically altered, mostly in a destructive way, by industrial practices of land clearing, urban settlement and mining. Landscape, and who uses and regulates it, is at the heart of public policy and expressions of identity by those who live in 'the bush' or 'the outback' or 'on country'. From the time that I first went to France as a young student, I was struck by the physical contrasts, although I soon realized that control over the use of landscape (*paysage*) was just as fraught an issue as in Australia. I came to appreciate this foreign landscape and to understand why *paysage* has much the same cultural resonance as 'the bush' in Australia. And, as this book reveals, changes to the French landscape since 1770 and to the values people inscribe in it have been no less dramatic than those in my own country, although less obvious on the surface.

Making sense of 250 years of landscape history has been a challenging project. My intellectual debts are obvious from the bibliography at the end of this volume. Along the way, specific assistance has been offered by many individuals, among them Caroline Ford, Kit McPhee, Kieko Matteson, Karine Rance, André Mir, Carine Renoux, Baker Schmitz, Richard Serle at the Baillieu Library in Melbourne, Véronique Despine-Faure at the Musée de la Révolution française in Vizille, and the many archivists and librarians whose repositories I used. In particular, the reflections of my partner, Charlotte Allen, have been a constant source of insight.

ABBREVIATIONS

AD	Archives départementales
AN	Archives nationales
AHR	*American Historical Review*
AHRF	*Annales historiques de la Révolution française* (Note: the AHRF changed from volumes to individual issue numbers from 1977)
CNRS	Centre national de la recherche scientifique
CTHS	Comité des travaux historiques et scientifiques
FHS	*French Historical Studies*
JMH	*Journal of Modern History*
PUF	Presses universitaires de France
SÉR	Société des études Robespierristes

MAPS

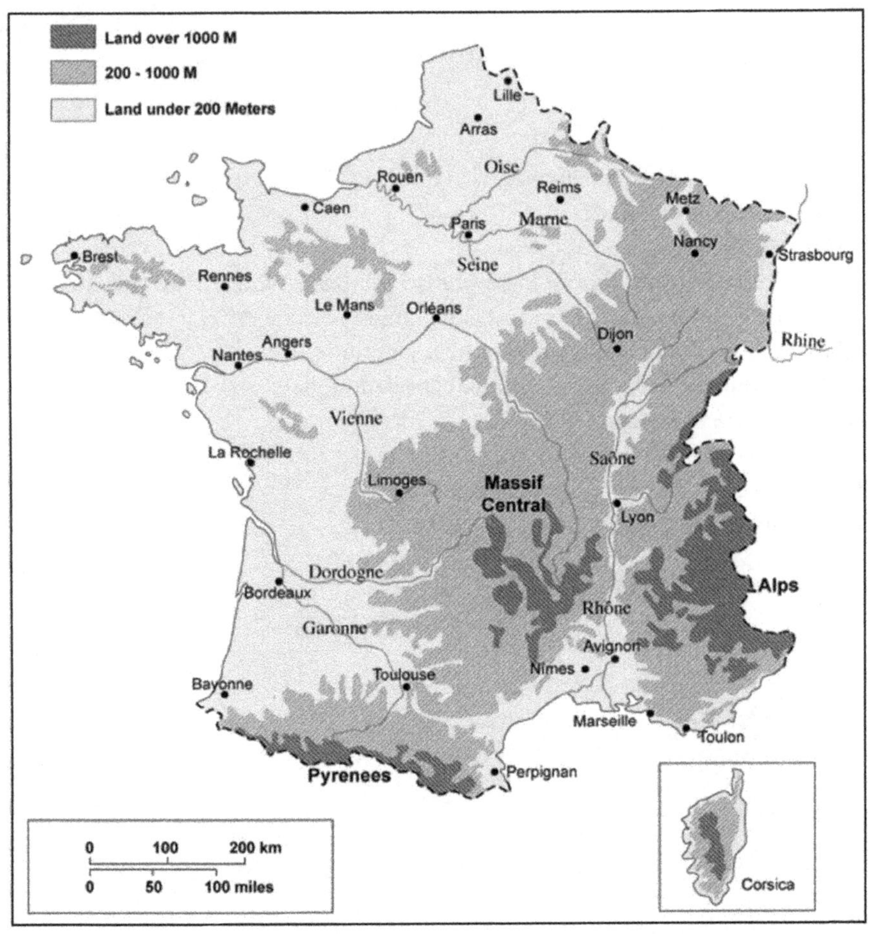

MAP 1 The physical geography of France. Graphic Design, University of Melbourne.

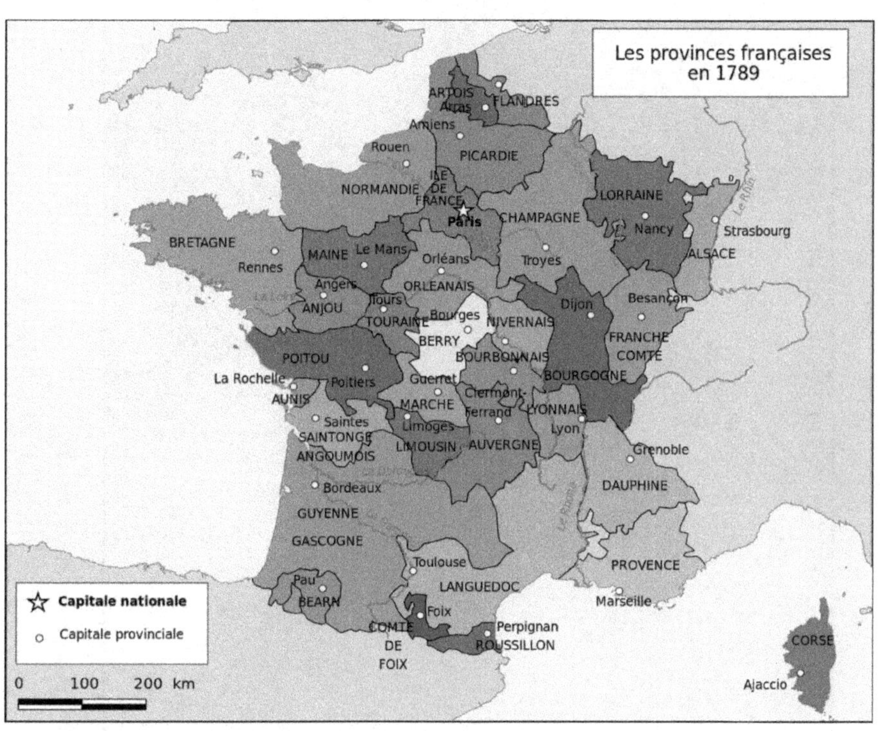

MAP 2 Provinces. Licensed under the Creative Commons Attribution-Share Alike 4.0 International license.

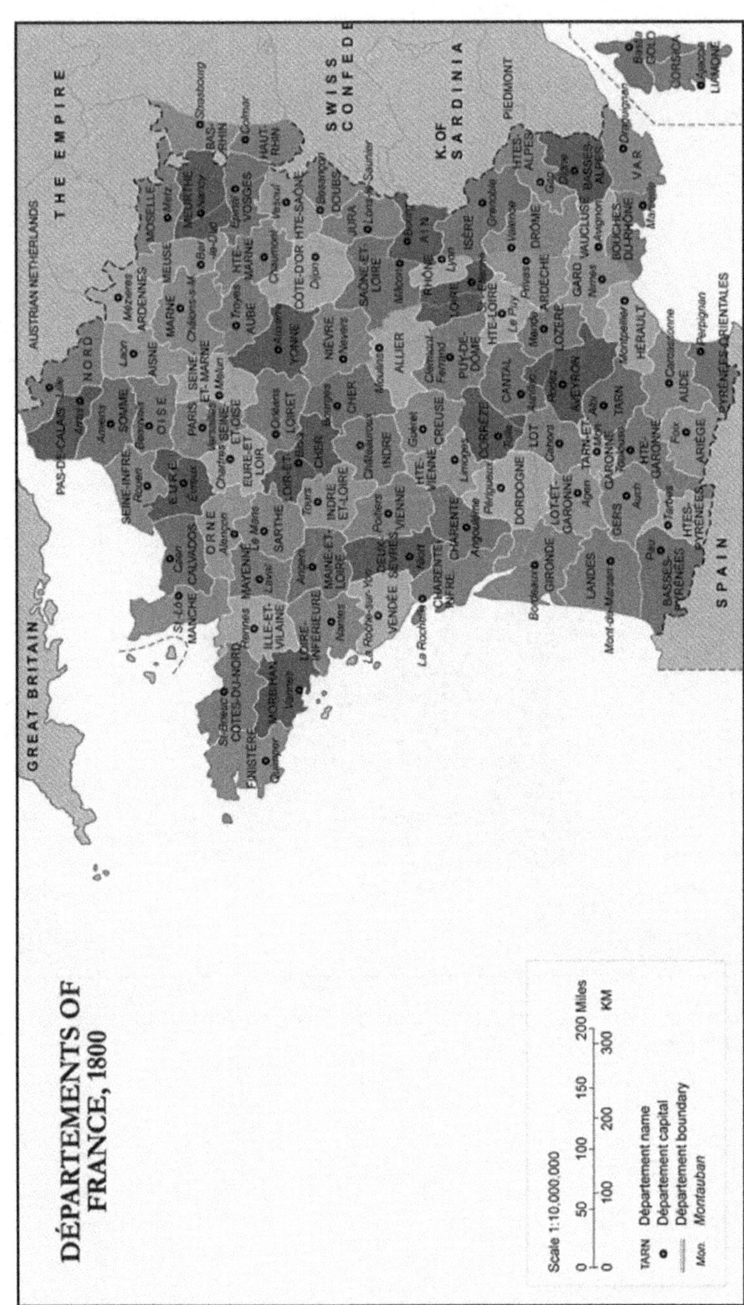

MAP 3 Departments. Graphic Design, University of Melbourne.

INTRODUCTION

Every year, almost ninety million tourists flood into France, the most popular travel destination in the world. While the most visited places are the Louvre and the Eiffel Tower, high on the list are provincial sites such as Mont-Saint-Michel and the *châteaux* of the Loire, serviced by buses and guided tours. Millions of tourists make their trips to other provincial attractions, preferring to travel by car, bicycle or train to experience the pleasures of rural France, studded as it is by picturesque villages and small towns across a rich and varying landscape.

International visitors as much as tourists from France's cities delight in the seemingly endless variety of landscapes, from the rolling farmlands of the southwest and the Île-de-France to the sharp peaks of the Alps and Pyrenees, from the sweeping sandy beaches of Languedoc and Landes to the rocky promontories of Brittany and Corsica, from the gorges of the Tarn and Verdon rivers to the slow sweep of the Loire. Many others relish these landscapes vicariously each year through watching the Tour de France or documentaries. There are few landscapes anywhere to rival for beauty the pastures of the Charolais and the croplands of the Limagne, the mountain landscapes of the Vercors and *pays* Basque or the vineyards of Saint-Émilion and the Côte Vermeille south of Perpignan (see Figure 0.1, Plates 1 and 2 and Figure 5.6). Many visitors find less attractive the overbearing intrusion of nuclear power plants and wind farms, the sprawl of commercial and industrial zones into the countryside and the endless traffic roundabouts.

A plethora of websites induce visitors to discover the joys of France's most beautiful villages, regions and gardens.[1] The assumption underpinning such experiences is that tourists will have a taste of 'eternal France', that the bucolic countryside through which they travel is the 'authentic' France beyond the noise and bustle of motorways and suburban sprawl, that the rural world they first observe is the remnants of a hitherto unchanging countryside, a world slowly being lost. French people are no less immune to such assumptions.

In France itself, the ideal of landscape (*paysage*) has a special cultural depth of a similar resonance in national identity as 'wilderness' in the United States or 'the bush' or 'the outback' in Australia and perhaps more so than 'the country' in England. The etymological links of French terms for 'land', 'peasant' 'landscape' –

FIGURE 0.1 The famous vineyards of Saint-Émilion (Gironde), east of Bordeaux, evoke ideas of an unchanging French landscape but have been created and transformed by centuries of human labour. Charlotte Allen.

pays, paysan, paysage – point to the deep resonance of the physical environment in cultural identities and French history.[2]

But what do we mean by 'landscape'? Each of us sees a landscape in our own way. There is not a uniform relationship between the viewer and the object. A geographer, a geologist, an artist and a farmer will perceive a landscape in distinctive ways, and this holds true for all of us. Landscapes are not simply creations of 'nature': they are perspectives from different points of view.[3] The pioneering Australian environmentalist George Seddon (1927–2007) at various times held university chairs in English, Geology, History and Philosophy of Science, and Environmental Science. In one of his earliest books, fifty years ago, he noted that

> an environment becomes a landscape only when it is so regarded by people, and especially when they begin to shape it in accord with their taste and needs. Nature may offer the raw material of scenery unaided, but to transform it into landscape demands the powers of the seeing human eye and the loving human hand.[4]

Similarly, although prosaically, the 2000 European Landscape Convention defined landscape as 'an area, as perceived by people, whose character is the result of the action and interaction of natural and/or human factors'.[5] In France itself, the meaning of *paysage* has been multiple and contested despite the influence of the great tradition of history and human geography exemplified by Marc Bloch, Fernand Braudel, Lucien Febvre, Roger Dion, Georges Duby, Emmanuel Le Roy Ladurie, Gaston Roupnel, Olivier de Serres and others.[6]

As the philosopher and sociologist Henri Lefebvre argued, 'every social space has a history, one invariably grounded in nature, in natural conditions that are at once primordial and unique'. There may be conflict between the 'lived space' of the users (*le vécu*) of the landscape and the conceived landscape (*le conçu*) of engineers, public utilities and others.[7]

This identification of landscape as both a human construct and a product of the imagination has been echoed by Alain Corbin, who has written brilliantly of the history of emotional responses to the natural world. For Corbin, 'landscape is a way of reading and analyzing space, of representing it for oneself . . . to give it an aesthetic appreciation, to fill it with meaning and emotion'. A purely geographic or 'scientific' analysis of the history of a landscape empties it of cultural and emotional meaning. A history of landscape must therefore be multidisciplinary and respect the history of its meanings, including sound and smell. In Corbin's words, 'the environment is a set of data that one can analyze, that one can catalogue, independent of any aesthetic appreciation; it's not the same as the landscape'.[8]

If every landscape is a representation – by those who live and work in it, by artists or engineers – then this book is a historian's perspective of the landscape as layers of time. It is a book about the modern 'making' of the French landscape, a complex and engrossing story linking human geography, history, agriculture, politics and culture. It understands the countryside in which people live and work and through which they travel as a complex human creation across 250 years in an environment which was already far from 'untouched'. It understands the landscape as a creation of humans who not only used its resources but also negotiated and sometimes fought openly for control of it. As Marcel Roncayolo expressed it in a collection of essays on 'places of memory' in France, landscape for the historian is 'a source of knowledge, an archive of material and living things: land use and development contain the traces of a distant and eventful history'.[9]

There are very few areas of France – only the most inaccessible mountain regions – that could possibly be described as 'wild' or 'wilderness', and the most profound cultural affinities are with landscapes that are nurtured and tended. From the time when the Barbizon school of art in the 1850s popularized images of human landscapes of villages, fields and forests, the deepest appeal to national identity in this increasingly urbanized society has been that of rural harmony. Some of France's most celebrated painters captured the landscape in distinctive ways at specific times, including Gustave Courbet, Jean-François Millet, Claude Monet, Rosa Bonheur, Jules Breton, Jules Bastien-Lepage and the Fauves. Proposed infrastructure work on a grotto on the Lison River made famous by Courbet in

1864 led to the foundation of the Société pour la Protection des Paysages de France in 1901, the law of 21 April 1906 on the protection of natural sites and monuments, and finally the first international congress on the protection of landscapes, held in Paris in October 1909.[10]

Like these painters, some of France's best-known writers, such as Honoré de Balzac, George Sand, Gustave Flaubert, Alain-Fournier, Émile Zola, François Mauriac, Marcel Pagnol, Colette and Julien Gracq, created evocative descriptions of specific areas of the countryside, but so did people who were of peasant background and knew the land directly through their toil, such as Martin Nadaud, Eugène Le Roy, Émile Guillaumin and Pierre-Jakez Hélias.

The cultural resonance of *paysage* remains powerful. In June 2021, a new film starring Catherine Frot, *La Fine Fleur* ('The Rose Maker' in English), had its cinema release. It is ostensibly a heart-warming light comedy about a famous but traditionalist rose grower who has fallen on hard times in the face of large, corporate producers and who saves her business with the help of some unskilled workers on employment schemes. But one of the key 'actors' in the film is the landscape, in this case the rose garden and its environs at Montagny, northwest of Lyon, since 1828 in the hands of the Dorieux family. The subliminal appeal of the film is not only the ideal of good-hearted social solidarity but also the ideal of traditional, non-industrial farming techniques in an eternal and paradisiacal landscape. This is *la France profonde.*

*   *   *

Of course, the French landscape in 1770 was already many millennia in the making, and today's countryside is studded with physical evidence of that, such as the more than 2,700 aligned *menhirs* (standing stones) erected 4,500 years ago at Carnac in southern Brittany or the floating market gardens (*hortillonnages*) of Amiens and its hinterland along the Somme, which date back to at least the thirteenth century and today are primarily maintained for tourism purposes (see Figures 0.2 and 0.3).[11] The 3,000 surviving ponds (*étangs*) of the Sologne region between Orléans on the Loire River and Vierzon on the Cher had mostly been constructed by religious orders from the thirteenth century to drain a vast area of marshes created by the impermeability of its soil, a mixture of sand and clay. The Dombes region east of Lyon had a parallel history.

The most spectacular remnant of the past is the Pont du Gard, an aqueduct bridge constructed over the river Gardon in the first century CE to carry water over 50 kilometres to the Roman colony of *Nemausus* (Nîmes). After the Roman Empire collapsed and the aqueduct fell into disuse, the Pont du Gard continued to function as a toll bridge, maintained by local lords and bishops. It began to attract tourist attention starting in the eighteenth century. But the surrounding area is home to less obvious human creation of the landscape dating from the

FIGURE 0.2 The floating market gardens (*hortillonnages*) of Amiens along the Somme, *c.* 1914. The gardens date back to at least the thirteenth century and were still intensively cultivated by hundreds of workers until the 1950s. AD Somme 8FI 4764.

same period, such as the terracing around Cavaillon to the west of Nîmes. Further south along the Mediterranean, between Narbonne and Béziers, the extraordinary thirteenth-century drainage works that produced the Étang de Montady are dominated by the bluff on which was situated the sixth-century BCE Roman hill town of Ensérune, overlooking what was then a lake.

Mediterranean France, in particular, has been 'designed and redesigned by humans' for almost 8,000 years.[12] Many of the hillside terraces so distinctive of southeastern and southern France may be dated as far back as the first millennium CE, although most were constructed in the medieval and early modern periods (*c.* 1100–1600 CE) and maintained since.[13] Most were used for the cultivation of cereal crops and vegetables, with terracing providing soil stability on denuded slopes. In the upper valley of the Tarn towards Pont-de-Monvert, for example, there are still remnants of terraces up to 1,300 metres above sea level which were fashioned for growing chestnuts and for crop production. In the eastern Pyrenees, there are remains of ancient terraces on slopes of up to 75 per cent gradient in the valleys of the Têt, Tech and Ariège rivers, constructed for vegetables and cereals along the slopes exposed to the south called 'soulanes'. Inevitably, those drystone terraces still in use, particularly in winegrowing areas south of a line from Biarritz to Strasbourg, have required constant maintenance across many centuries right up to the present.

Despite the evidence of millennia of human impact on the landscape, this book argues that the last 250 years have seen a dramatic acceleration in human impact

FIGURE 0.3 The *hortillonnages* of Amiens supplied the city with vegetables until rapid motor transport in the 1970s and are now primarily maintained for tourism purposes. A small number of market gardeners still provide vegetables to the *marché sur l'eau* (water market) in Amiens. Peter McPhee.

on the rural environment and that this impact is inscribed on the landscape we see today. Changes to population, farming techniques, modes of travel and sources of energy have combined with public policy to create a landscape that is particularly vulnerable to human action, with positive and negative outcomes.

But why 1770? The question is important, for it takes us to a central question about historical awareness and to the work of France's greatest historian. Fernand Braudel spent much of his life studying and living in other countries, commencing with *The Mediterranean and the Mediterranean World in the Age of Phillip II* (1949). When he completed his subsequent three-volume masterpiece *Civilization and Capitalism, 15th–18th Century* in 1979, aged seventy-seven, he decided to turn his attention at last to his greatest passion, his own land. He left his great work on *The Identity of France* until last, as he said in its opening passages, like a peasant savouring his white bread. The two volumes he completed before his death in 1985 were both intellectually captivating and deeply affectionate. While insisting that he would 'try to keep my feelings out of it', he admitted that 'I love France with the same demanding and complicated passion as did Jules Michelet; without distinguishing between its good points and its bad.'[14]

Braudel's approach to the history of the interaction between the peoples of France and their environment reflected the *Annales* school of historical writing founded in the 1920s by his colleague Lucien Febvre, which abandoned the history of the privileged world of institutional politics and the detailed analysis of specific historical moments for the study of the very long term, the *longue durée*, and the geographic, climatic and resource structures of the environment. For the *Annalistes*, such structures underpin the slow but perceptible rhythms of the 'conjunctures' of economic systems, states, social structures and forms of warfare. Last – and certainly least – of the three layers is the world of 'mere events', of individual actions to which historians, like the actors themselves, mistakenly accord significance.[15]

The structure of the analysis in Braudel's survey of the making of France replicates the layers of analysis in the works of the *Annales* school: from geography and the environment to population and production in the two volumes of *The Identity of France* to the state, culture and international relations in the two other volumes he never got to write. Over the last millennium, he argued, the great transformation has been the collapse of peasant society, in his words, 'the spectacle that overshadows all others'. The creation of contemporary France – capitalist, urbanized, mechanized – was for him a heroic saga, for here was a veritable tidal change, sweeping all before it.[16] While Braudel recognized that rural France had undergone significant changes beforehand, for him the disappearance of the landscape of peasant France really only happened with the mass mechanization of agriculture after 1945 and with it the capacity for production to be the work of a fraction of the previous rural workforce.[17] The consequences would be felt everywhere with the collapse of village life: there were fewer people with employment, and fewer rural trades as automobiles made cheaper, larger urban stores accessible.

Braudel conveyed his infectious love and deep knowledge of the French landscape and its making by thousands of years of labour. He, more than anyone else, was equipped to comment on the ways in which economic change – particularly since 1945 – has reduced the variety of fauna and flora, polluted waterways and undermined the vitality of rural cultures. But so wedded was he to the inexorability, even desirability, of economic transformation that he could only occasionally bemoan the loss of the world he knew as a child before the First World War, as when he recalled the ancient rural lanes now disappearing under autoroutes and ploughs: 'with their uneven cobbled surfaces and the hawthorn trees lining the way, how lovely they can be in springtime!'[18]

Unlike Braudel, this book argues that it was from the late-eighteenth century rather than the Second World War that the forces were felt that would destroy

France as a primarily agrarian, peasant and subsistence land. The landscape that is familiar today to French people and their foreign visitors has been 250 years in the making. The great tidal change of mechanization that Braudel saw as turning after 1945 did indeed sweep all before it, but a long series of waves of environmental change since the 1770s had fundamentally but slowly transformed both the landscape of France and the experiences of the people who created those waves. There have been political decisions whose consequences for the landscape have been of far more significance than just froth on the waves of change.

But there is a far more important reason why 1770 is an appropriate starting point for this book. In 2000, Paul Crutzen and Eugene Stoermer proposed using the term 'Anthropocene' or the age of humanity for the current geological epoch to emphasize the central role of humankind in geology and ecology. For the first time, climate change had predominantly human or 'anthropogenic' origins, together with the assumption that humans are capable of mastering nature through control of the power over its resources, an assumption which underpins the unintended consequence of creating a geological age where such actions have altered the balance between humans and nature.[19] At the same time, there were always voices – now a crescendo – expressing horror at what was seen to be reversible devastation.

Crutzen and Stoermer argued that the Anthropocene had commenced with the Industrial Revolution in Britain in the 1780s because glacial ice cores have revealed a growth from that point in 'greenhouse gasses'. Since then, scientists supportive of the term 'Anthropocene' have identified a 'Great Acceleration' since 1945 or have favoured the atomic bomb testing during the 1950s as a more decisive turning point.[20] The latter date was accepted in May 2019 by a working group of the International Commission on Stratigraphy, which resolved that the Anthropocene should indeed be listed as a new epoch. Others have argued that the roots of the crisis have more to do with capitalist economic imperatives than humanity per se and have proposed 'Capitalocene' as a more pointed identification.[21]

As a result, in the words of Australian historian Tom Griffiths:

environmental history has turned out to be far more radical than it first seemed four decades ago. It does not merely add nature to the categories of historical analysis; in the epoch of the Anthropocene, it also questions the very separability of culture and nature. In the twenty-first century, the binary that was the foundation of history has collapsed, and the fate of humanity has become inextricably bound up with that of nature and the Earth.

We now have to understand history as the *interaction* between humans and their environment as well as the traditional form of history as the *actions* of humans within their surroundings.[22]

So this book begins in the 1770s, not because the French landscape was unchanging or 'authentic' at that time, but because these were the years which marked the beginning of the transition from timber to coal as the primary source of energy, as evidenced in the beginnings of industrial coal mining in the east of Languedoc after 1770. It is bookended by the closure of the last coal mine at La Houve in Creutzwald on the border with Germany in 2004.

*   *   *

As well as the very rich scientific literature and local historiography of environmental change, the book draws on selected archival sources for case studies of landscapes which have been created by human interaction, from the *bocage* and its clearing in western France to the *garrigues* and erosion of the Corbières in the south.[23] Such landscapes include those transformed by particular military campaigns: in the northeast during the First World War (the Chemin des Dames) and in Normandy in 1944 (the Bataille des Haies). Every region and department of France has its own extensive list of 'monuments historiques' and, while these are dominated by the cathedrals and *châteaux* of provincial cities, there are many which deliberately recall rural life, such as the massive grain-mill on the Seine at Andé in Normandy, the eighteenth-century farm buildings at 'Domaine Planon' in eastern France and the 1930s farm near Lyon, the 'Ferme du Champ bressan'.

The book begins with an overview of the French countryside in the 1770s, the last years in which there were controls over agrarian resources which we might call seigneurial or even aristocratic, when timber was the source of fuel and when there was a clear dominance of the imperatives of subsistence polyculture in most rural areas. It then examines the protracted upheaval of the French Revolution of 1789–99, when social divisions within rural communities and peasant antipathy to the survival of seigneurial property resulted in an intense period of extreme pressure on the rural environment, reflected in angry debates about landscape degradation. Revolutionary governments also legislated a radical transformation in the nature of the state and its legal framework for property relations and the economy. A new conception of the meaning of property would ultimately reshape the relationships between humans and their rural environment.

Succeeding chapters examine the *moyenne durée* of the nineteenth century. As a consequence of population increase and more extensive cultivation (from about 16 million hectares in 1789 to 20.6 million in 1840), great strain continued to be placed on the environment. This was particularly the case in forests and on uncultivated land which sustained bird and animal life. The greater freedom of owners to use their forests for commercial purposes, such as for charcoal for forges, accelerated tree-felling. In steep river valleys, this aggravated erosion and caused serious lowland flooding. On cultivated land, however, peasant polyculture was attuned to the local ecology and carefully conserved resources. Virtually all human and animal waste was returned to the soil as fertilizer, and plant sub-species and local farming practices continued to flourish.

The decline in the population of upland communities after 1850 and large-scale reforestation following laws passed in 1860 permitted the gradual recovery of mountain ecologies. Some areas had been so denuded over the centuries that they were never to recover. Coastal and inland swamp-draining and the bringing into cultivation of 'wasteland' were, usually, to the detriment of the rich fauna and flora of delicate ecologies now 'reclaimed' for human use and destroyed ancient pastoral economies and their peasant cultures. After 1880, and especially after 1945, the transition to specialized agriculture in lowland areas, now starting to use chemical fertilizers and pesticides, was to create long-term problems of soil and water degradation, whereas peasant polyculture had generally been reliant on human and animal manure. While the increasing uniformity of provincial cultures across generations of national market structures was to erode the distinctive agricultural and cultural diversity of the countryside, new signifiers of provincial landscapes and identity were developed in the form of *appellations* of key produce from 1905 and tourist marketing campaigns.

The book concludes with an analysis of current issues in the French countryside, in particular the tension between environmentalism, 'clean' food and water, and remediation of degradation (including the reintroduction of wolves and Pyrenean bears) on the one hand and industrial-scale production, chemical fertilizers and pesticides, and measures against 'noxious' pests and animals (such as wild boars) on the other.[24] Equally significant today is the 'hollowing out' of rural settlements as commercial centres on the outskirts replace shopping centres in old neighbourhoods and the countryside becomes silent (except for the hum of engines) and villages empty (except as dormitories if close to towns). The immediate hinterland of towns, even small regional centres, is increasingly marked by 'peri-urbanization', the spread of residences and shopping malls across the immediate countryside surrounding older centres. The intriguing paradox is that some of those changes – notably the stark population decline in particular regions of the countryside – have permitted some degraded environments, particularly in upland areas, to slowly recover while at the same time making them more vulnerable to the fiery consequences of climate change.

Fernand Braudel described forests as 'the jewel among properties' as well as the most contested natural resource in the modern history of France. Forests exist in public consciousness as nature's finest raiment, their presence a tangible gauge of our fragile hopes for a sustainable future. For these reasons, French environmental history has concentrated on the history of forests and their protection.[25] Basic to the common story of France's forests has been the *légende noire* of the French Revolution, seen to be a time of unchecked peasant pillage of forest resources until stemmed by the new forest code of 1827 and slow but triumphant reforestation after 1860. This book instead focuses as much on agricultural landscapes as on forests and contests the assumption that the desire to protect the landscape has been a virtue of the state and scientific elites confronted with a rapacious rural population. The human history of the French landscape is far more complex and interesting.

1 THE PRE-INDUSTRIAL LANDSCAPE OF THE 1770S

Fernand Braudel once quipped that 'France is diverse to the point of absurdity'.[1] Along the southern flanks of the Montagne Noire north of Carcassonne, for example, within a few kilometres the traveller passes from the rolling cereal plains of the Lauragais to the highland forests and pastures of the Cabardès and then to the classic Mediterranean *garrigues* of the Minervois. Along the way, every community has its own distinctive human geography: indeed, geographers have identified no fewer than 600 distinct agricultural micro-regions across France's 40,000 communes. Such diversity is found in every region and is at the heart of the experience relished by travellers.

How might we begin to make sense of such diversity? One of the first attempts was made by Arthur Young (1741–1820), the son of a Suffolk clergyman and an enthusiastic agriculturalist (albeit an unsuccessful farmer). He is most famous as a traveller and diarist, having made three trips to France (May–November 1787; July–October 1788; June 1789–January 1790), after which he published two volumes of his observations across travels of eighteen months and 12,000 kilometres. Young's affectionate but acidic commentary reflected his certainties that large-scale, enclosed farming as practised in England was the imperative for progress, but he was an eager student, sympathetic to the conditions of the peasantry. His descriptions of the landscape reflected his prejudices, but they are a precious witness. So he admired the country around Boulogne – 'the country improves, more enclosed, and some parts strongly resembling England' – while pitying the 'hungry, sandy gravel' of 'the *triste* Sologne', which would be 'highly improvable, if they knew what to do with it'.[2]

Young was no geologist or soil scientist, but he was acutely aware of the fundamental equation underpinning the varied landscapes through which he travelled: the dynamic relationship between soil, climate and human labour. Indeed, in his 'general observations', he divided rural France according to its seven soil types: rich loam, heath, chalk, stony soils, mountains, various loams and gravel. The first of these predominated in the north and east, but in travelling north from Clermont-Ferrand in central France, he traversed another rich landscape, that of the Limagne. This is a great undulating plateau 90 kilometres long and 15–40 kilometres wide between the chains of the Forez mountains to the east and the volcanic *puys* to the west, a black soil plain marked by *buttes* of ancient lava flows. Young was dismissive of the 'execrable ploughing' and 'ignorance' of the farmers, but he praised their gardens and orchards and noted that the land was never in fallow and was highly sought after, 'by far the most fertile district in all France' despite its modest rainfall. The great challenge for its farmers was that the volcanic subsoil was impermeable and that the region, studded with ponds and marshes, was vulnerable to persistent flooding after occasional heavy rain.[3]

Young's attempt to make sense of the variety of the French landscape was among the first in a long series by geographers, agronomists and geologists. This is a variety they have commonly found bewildering, no matter whether they have approached it by generalizing about types of soil, agricultural practices or climate. A more common model than Young's begins with four great river valleys (the Seine, Loire, Garonne and Rhone) surrounded by the sea and the mountain chains of the Pyrenees, Alps, Jura and Ardennes (see Map 1). Certainly, these four broad valleys have been the arteries of food production for millennia. The great southern corridor linking the Atlantic and the Mediterranean along the River Garonne and the Canal du Midi was already the granary for much of the south and beyond. The Massif Central is at the heart of the country with its great limestone massifs to the south, bisected most spectacularly by the gorges of the Tarn, Ardèche and Verdon. Only in the northeast and east are there few natural barriers with neighbours; not surprisingly, at times this has been the point of entry for enemy armies. In the centuries since 1770, invasions have occurred from the east in 1792–4, 1814–15, 1870–1, 1914–18 and 1940–4.

Drawing on the great French tradition of historical geography created by Roger Dion, Gaston Roupnel and Marc Bloch, Robert Specklin simplified this model still further, arguing that there were three fundamental distinctions of landscape across France: the *finages* or communal territories of the south, with their irregular plots of land; the *bocages* of fields marked by hedges and trees in the west; and the *campagnes* or open field of the north and east, often enclosed. While there were many internal contrasts reflecting local topography, soils and climate, these distinctions were also mirrored in broad differences in rural housing, especially roof types.[4] Centuries of change since 1770 have not obliterated the durable physical evidence of these regional contrasts.

First, much of the south was dominated by the presence of substantial, clustered villages surrounded by a patchwork of fields, often separated by drystone walls or terracing. In upland areas, there were sharp contrasts between the intensively cultivated plots near waterways and thinly vegetated hillsides, often known to the administration as *vacants* or *terres en friche* (wastelands) and to the locals as *communaux* (commons) or *garrigues*. The landscape was home to an extraordinary range of activity, evident in the feudal dues payable to the bishop of Béziers, seigneur of Gabian in Languedoc. Among the dues were 100 *setiers* (a *setier* was about 85 litres) of barley, 28 *setiers* of wheat, 880 bottles of olive oil, 18 chickens, 4 pounds of beeswax, 4 partridges and a rabbit. Reflecting Gabian's ancient role as a market between mountains and coast, it also had to pay 1 pound of pepper, 2 ounces of nutmeg and 2 ounces of cloves. The arable land was dominated by hundreds of small plots of vegetables, grain crops and grapevines; the hillsides were covered with sheep producing wool for nearby textile towns. A century later, the landscape would be a sea of grapevines.[5]

The second broad type, particularly in the west and northwest, was fields separated by hedgerows on earth mounds, commonly called *bocage* ('small wood'). The vegetation, which could be low bushes, fruit trees or more substantial trees, served many purposes: to hold livestock, particularly cattle; to provide fruit and fuel; to serve as windbreaks; and to provide protection for small game such as rabbits. Their precious function in preserving biodiversity would become far more apparent with their uprooting in subsequent centuries. While most common in the northwestern provinces of Normandy, Brittany, Poitou, Anjou and Maine, there were also areas of *bocage* further south, in Berry and parts of the Massif Central long distinguished by timber and cattle industries. The village of Chanzeaux in Anjou, for example, was characterized by its *bocage* landscape, where high hedgerows across the undulating landscape kept cattle enclosed and bordered a maze of narrow tracks. Suitable land was also used to grow vegetables, wheat or rye, but from eye level, the region appeared like a vast forest. The village skyline was dominated by a new *château* completed on the ruins of an old manor house in 1769. But this would be destroyed during the French Revolution, and today the skyline is dominated by its grandiose replacement, constructed in the 1840s in 'style troubadour', an excessively ornate homage to medieval romance.[6]

Third, much of the north and east was characterized by open field farming, with large, enclosed fields around small villages dominated by substantial courtyard farmhouses. Today, Artois and Picardy are studded with small villages with names ending with 'court' (Hébécourt) or, less commonly, 'mesnil' (Briquemesnil), meaning farmhouse or rural mansion; in Normandy, the proliferation of villages ending in 'ville' (Monneville) denoted a similar settlement dominated by a large farm.[7] One example, about 20 kilometres northeast of Amiens, is the tiny, ancient village of Vadencourt, its current population of about one hundred much the same as in the late eighteenth century. Then as now, the village was dominated by the lord's *château*, then restored around its courtyard but dilapidated now (see Figure 1.1). The landscape is dominated, as in the eighteenth century, by open fields, with about one-fifth in forest. Whereas today much of the human activity on the landscape is of locals commuting to and from Amiens, then it was labourers toiling on the lord's vast estate.

A fourth, final distinction might be added. While much of the coastline of France is rocky or lined by cliffs, there are major exceptions, especially the great

FIGURE 1.1 Two centuries of warfare and economic change have radically altered the landscapes of parts of the northeast. Most of the great farmhouses and *châteaux* around their 'courts' which had dominated the landscape were destroyed in the First World War. One which survived is at Vadencourt (Somme). Peter McPhee.

deltas of the Somme in the northeast, the Loire in the west and the Rhône in the south. The last – the Camargue – is today a large natural reserve famous for its birdlife and horses, but in the eighteenth century it was intensively cultivated as well. The delta was a tapestry of channels and streams cultivated in time with the seasons. While inundated with river water much of the time, during summer a contemporary described it as 'almost a desert':

> The soil was parched and cracked . . . A stranger coming across the land would think he was in the midst of the steppes of Asia or America rather than in a country where science, industry and the arts have reached such a high degree of perfection.[8]

West of the Camargue, the Étang de Berre (today dominated by petrol refineries) was the first of a chain of lagoons extending hundreds of kilometres almost to the Spanish border. Mosquito-ridden and sandy, much of this coastal land was used by fishers and shepherds, whereas today it is studded with beach resorts.

Whatever the specific features of the landscape across France's regions, everywhere the presence of timber was of primordial importance. It is difficult today to envisage the dependency of pre-industrial society on wood, but its products accompanied humans from the cradle to the coffin. It was the key form of domestic fuel for heating and cooking: Paris alone consumed two million tonnes of firewood yearly. Timber was the basic raw material for industries ranging from winemaking, building and furniture to modes of transport and fortifications. Charcoal was equally important, for heating and for the iron industry which was mostly rural in location. Its by-product, potash, was essential for textile and glass industries. The demands for timber by the royal navy were primary, even on private land. Over the century before 1770, the monarchy had asserted the primacy of its own military needs, and the 1669 forest decrees of Louis XIV's First Minister, Jean-François Colbert, had served to stabilize the balance between supply and demand, at least in state forests. Nevertheless, the pressures on timber resources were inexorable, in particular the constant need to clear land for growing cereals for an increasing population, the often unregulated grazing of livestock in woodlands and expanding industrial fuel consumption. Between 1760 and 1789, the price of firewood increased by about two-thirds.[9]

The demands of the royal navy at a time of almost incessant warfare were at least as responsible for the depletion of forest resources as were the needs of the peasantry. After the humiliation of the loss of its colonies on the North American mainland during the Seven Years' War (1756–63), the monarchy had embarked on an ambitious programme of rebuilding its navy to rival Britain's. The Marine Royale was to play a crucial role in the defeat of the British at Jamestown in 1781 and in rivalry with Britain in the Indian Ocean. The strain on the wooded environment in France was accentuated. The most common navy vessel of seventy-four cannon required 2,800 century-old oaks for its construction, and forty-seven such vessels (as well as thirty-seven frigates) were built in the 1780s. Another twelve of these and ten frigates were under construction in 1789.[10]

Not surprisingly, trees dominated the work of the few landscape painters of the second half of the eighteenth century. Their themes reflected the influence of their master, Antoine Watteau (1684–1721), in the ways in which they envisioned rural France. Bucolic, idyllic splendour was used to capture the expression of emotions triggered by the power of the natural elements through windswept forests and forbidding mountains rather than attempting to mirror landscape detail. The brilliance of the sumptuous brushstrokes in the work of Watteau's nephew, Louis-Joseph Watteau, and Nicolas Fragonard composed fantastic natural backgrounds to capture an air of frivolity and aristocratic luxury. François Boucher preferred quaint images of dilapidated rural buildings as details within his evocations of stormy skies and forests, while for Hubert Robert, the ideal landscape environment was studded with classical ruins to the point that his nickname became 'Robert of the ruins' (*Robert des ruines*). He had spent eleven years in Rome. Occasionally, painters sought to capture rural landscapes in detail, as did Nicolas Lépicié and Jean-Baptise Lallemand (see Plate 6), but one of the few painters who depicted the pervasive poverty of the rural world, Louis Gabriel Moreau, contrived to do so in a sentimental way. The power of stormy skies and wild seas was altogether a more attractive subject than the precise details of the rural world.[11]

Only the work of Lallemand, the son of a tailor from Dijon, can evoke the stark contrasts between the eighteenth-century landscape and that of today. The polarity between earlier mixed, subsistence agriculture and contemporary agricultural specialization is only one contrast. It is difficult to imagine a landscape in which the tallest structures were the parish church and the lord's *château* rather than the water tower and electricity pylons; in which almost all transport was along narrow, unmade roads; in which the loudest sounds were of church bells and livestock; and in which there was no artificial lighting other than candles and torches made of twigs, bark or vine cuttings. The skies were dark except on moonlit nights across landscapes that were far less timbered than today but far more crowded with animals and humans.[12]

A traveller from today would have been struck not only by the absence of made roads but perhaps more so by the presence of humans in the rural landscape, everywhere tilling the soil, carrying water and fuel, and tending livestock. Although France's population of 65 million today is more than twice that of the 1770s, ten times as many people inhabited France's villages and farms as do today. If we define an urban community as one with more than 2,000 people, then only two people in ten lived in an urban centre in the eighteenth century. The great majority inhabited 60,000 rural parishes with, on average, about 450 residents. And more people were seeking to extract a living from the soil than ever before. Despite the ever-present threat of harvest failure, after 1750 a long series of adequate harvests disturbed the demographic equilibrium of births and deaths; the population had increased from perhaps 24.5 million to 28 million by the 1780s.[13]

Much of the housing which studded the rural landscape in the eighteenth century – whether in clustered villages, in scattered hamlets or on isolated farms – has survived into the twenty-first century. Most houses were constructed from stone cut in local quarries and therefore blended into the local landscape. The use of external roughcast (*crépi*) only became common in the twentieth century. But the poorest housing has mostly long disappeared. In the second half of the eighteenth century, population growth created a large and increasing rural proletariat of landless labourers, often called *brassiers*. In some areas of Burgundy, 60–80 per cent of the population were labourers, often living in drystone shelters (*cabanes*) or huts made of thatch (*chaumières*), which were to disappear in the nineteenth century.[14]

A traveller in time from today would have been equally struck by the diversity of economic strategies which sought to meet the needs of the household within a regional or micro-regional market. Almost everywhere, the rural landscape was a patchwork of intense and varied cultivation, alternating with fallow. The rural economy was essentially a peasant economy, that is, household-based agrarian production which had a primarily subsistence orientation. This complex, polycultural system sought to produce as much as possible of a household's consumption needs, including clothing, and produce was grown which today has disappeared from specialized agriculture finely tuned to local soils and climate.

A great historian of rural France, Emmanuel Le Roy Ladurie, estimated that, between 1715 and 1789, agricultural production increased by about 40 per cent, roughly the same as population growth. The landscape was densely populated and intensively cultivated, and, in Le Roy Ladurie's words, it was 'a veritable ocean of rural misery'.[15] The increasing population of a rural society marked by mass poverty left its mark on the landscape in parts of the countryside. Around Saint-Flour in the Auvergne, the 'terres froides' – too cold for easy cultivation – were usually common lands used for pasturing, but population pressure impelled the poorest peasants to seize small plots despite the opposition of livestock owners and the authorities. They quickly planted hedgerows or erected drystone walls to express their 'ownership'. Burning the grass in the enclosure might have provided enough nutrients for intermittent crops or vegetables. Today, these tiny enclosures on the most marginal hillsides have long been abandoned to uncultivated land (*friches*) but the outline of walls is still visible in places, witness to a past landscape.[16]

Rudimentary roads and population density were two reasons why the landscape was also polycultural everywhere in a way that would be unrecognizable today. While particular regions had their own specialized products – for example, olives in Provence, fruit in Normandy – agricultural staples, in particular cereal crops and wine, were produced almost everywhere. The lowlands of Languedoc and Roussillon, which would be a sea of vineyards a century later, were in 1770 largely devoted to production of grains for local consumption and to winter pastures for millions of sheep from the highlands.[17]

This polycultural landscape was evoked by Nicolas Restif de la Bretonne, born in 1734 in the village of Sacy, on the border of the provinces of Burgundy and Champagne. Restif, who moved to Paris and became notorious for his ribald stories in *Le Paysan perverti* (1775), wrote of his recollections of Sacy at mid-century in his voluminous memoirs *Monsieur Nicolas* (1794). He recalled the suitable and happy marriage his relative Marguerite was making to Covin, 'a great joker, well-built, a vain country-bumpkin, the great local storyteller':

> Marguerite had about 120 livres' worth of arable land, and Covin had 600 livres' worth, in meadows as well as vineyards and arable land, some under vines, and some fields dispersed in the grasslands; there were six parts of each type, six of wheat, six of oats or barley, and six fallow . . . as for the woman, she had the profit of her spinning, the wool of seven or eight sheep, the eggs of a dozen hens, and the milk of a cow, with the butter and cheese she could extract from it. . . . Covin was also a weaver, and his wife had some domestic work; her lot in consequence must have been pleasant enough.[18]

Across the centuries, the nobility and Catholic clergy had etched their eminence onto the physical landscape through the construction of *châteaux* and churches, recalling the duties of commoners to labour, pray and defer to their betters. The remnants of the topography of power in the eighteenth-century countryside are still omnipresent through the built heritage of *châteaux* and churches, which then were congruent with power in a way that has since disappeared. While aristocratic lords (*seigneurs*) were less likely to reside on their country estates by the 1780s than earlier in the century, preferring to inhabit Paris or other major cities, they continued to exercise a maze of prerogatives reinforcing the community's subordinate position, whether by reserving a pew in the parish church, wearing a weapon in public, or controlling farming routines. Everywhere, the use of the landscape was dictated by who controlled the land as much as by climate and soil. The peasantry owned outright about one-third of all land, but their agricultural practices were restricted by enforced agreements about the form in which they were to pay feudal dues to the lord and tithes to the church.

Where peasants rented land, often as sharecroppers, from the church, the nobility or bourgeois property owners from a local town, contracts were highly restrictive about land use. Pierre Reynes and his son Mathieu rented a large farm – about 30 hectares – near the southwestern town of Villefranche-de-Lauragais from the 'high and powerful seigneur' the Marquis d'Hautpoul.[19] The farm produced about 100 *setiers* of wheat (20 *setiers* would feed a family of five for a year) and a wide array of livestock, vegetables and other produce. Under this annually reviewed sharecropping contract, the seigneur took 20 *setiers* in advance – whatever the volume of the crop – and half of the rest; after setting aside seed for the next year, the Reynes would be left with 15 *setiers*, less than their family needed. They were rigidly tied to a three-field system (maize and vegetables, wheat, fallow) and, while the proceeds from livestock were also divided, any extra forage had to be provided by them. They were to buy young pigs, though the seigneur's agent was to have half; in addition, they were to provide 108 chickens and capons and 600 eggs yearly.

Villefranche-de-Lauragais had the commercial advantage of being on the Canal du Midi, linking the Atlantic with the Mediterranean between Bordeaux, Toulouse and Sète. Arthur Young was stunned by the 'magnificence' of the canal, 'a noble and stupendous work' completed in 1681 (see Plate 3). Indeed, about 1,000 kilometres of canals had been constructed, including those of Orléans (1691), Loing (1724) and Picardie (1738). That of the Centre, which linked the Loire to the Saône river and the north of France to the south, would be completed by 1792.[20] Even though some of the roads Young used were similarly impressive – near Tours, Limoges and Narbonne – in fact, his travels were severely limited by the paucity of roads which were paved for use in all seasons. Even if improvements after 1765 meant that no major city in France was more than ten days' travel from Versailles, most of the kingdom south of the Loire only had roads which connected major towns. Coaches could in five days take people the 470 kilometres from Paris to Lyon, France's second-largest city. It took five days to reach Strasbourg or Nantes from Paris, six to reach Bordeaux, and eight to arrive at Toulouse or Marseille.[21] But there were thousands of communities in the Massif Central, Pyrenees and Alps for which news of events at Versailles took weeks to arrive.

The inscription of power on the landscape was everywhere apparent, for example, in the village of Bruère-Allichamps between the towns of Bourges and Saint-Amand-Montrond. The village is one of seven in the area claiming to be at the exact geographic centre of France, its proud boast made on a plaque on a third-century Roman column still standing in the centre of the main road. Far more imposing, south of the village along the river Cher, is the twelfth-century Cistercian Abbey of Noirlac. The great days of the abbey were long past, back in the thirteenth century, when it had landholdings in twenty-seven parishes. There were just seven monks in Noirlac in the 1770s, living on the abbey's revenues of 10,800 *livres* (pounds) from rents from its eight farms, produce from its forest, a range of minor charges on peasants, and sales of produce, including walnuts and acorns. The abbey had had extensive refurbishment in the mid-eighteenth century, and the religious were lodged in very comfortable accommodation. They were able to employ eleven servants and farmhands at the abbey itself. Since its sale as a national property in 1791, the abbey has variously been a porcelain factory, a camp for refugees from the Spanish Civil War, a hospice and, since 2007, a tourism and cultural centre.[22]

In the south of the kingdom, in particular, a crowded and stressed landscape was undergoing a dramatic change, with consequences still visible today. Population pressure and mass poverty were two of the reasons why the government of Louis XV sought to bring what it regarded as 'wastelands' into productive use. These uncultivated lands were almost everywhere across the kingdom, known according to the region as *terres vaines et vagues, vacants, gastes, garrigues, landes, biens hermes, flégards* or *wareschaix*. They were often unsuitable for crops but vital for pastures and often hotly contested between rural communities and their seigneurs. A *Mémoire sur les défrichemens* by the marquis de Turbilly in 1760 had recommended that land clearing be encouraged and was reflected in royal decrees which offered fiscal inducements to those who cleared land which had not been cultivated for at least forty years.[23] Then royal edicts of 1766 and 1770 offered tax concessions on all state taxes and tithes for fifteen years for land cleared and duly reported to the authorities. The decree stipulated, however, that Colbert's forest code of 1669 remained in force, outlawing the clearing of wooded terrain, riverbanks and hillsides. In the decades after 1750, some 800,000 *arpents* (an *arpent* was approximately one acre) of France were cleared, some 3 per cent of the total surface area.[24]

West of Avignon, in the foothills of the Alps, is a remarkable vestige of the *défrichements*. The tiny settlement of Les Savournins, just outside the village of Gordes, is a collection of twenty-eight drystone dwellings known as *cabanes*, now called incorrectly *bories* (a *borie* is the French word for the Provençal *bori* or farmhouse). The village dates back to the land clearing and cultivation that took place following the royal edicts of the 1760s (see Figure 1.2). The prospect of clearing the *garrigues* without paying tax led to a rush of legal and illegal clearances,

FIGURE 1.2 The tiny village of Les Savournins, near Gordes (Vaucluse), is a collection of drystone dwellings known as *cabanes* or *bories*, dating back to the land clearing and cultivation that took place following the royal edicts of the 1760s. Licensed under the Creative Commons Attribution-Share Alike 4.0 International license.

and the mass of limestone being removed from the ground to make way for fields was ideal for building drystone walls and huts. The huts were typically what is now called the 'Gordoise nave' with its distinctive pointed roof: barns used for seasonal dwellings, storage of grain, sheep shelters, and winemaking.[25]

This 'village des bories' at Gordes is the most dramatic vestige of a phenomenon which has left traces throughout the Mediterranean backcountry. Nowhere was this land clearing as extensive as in Languedoc, especially in the regions of Carcassonne and Narbonne, and the official figures in these dioceses do not take account of land cleared illegally or of communities where officials failed to complete formal reports (one parish in twelve).[26] Few regions of France are so beloved of tourists than this Mediterranean backcountry between the Rhône and the Spanish frontier, and few regions have changed their appearance so much since the 1770s. Today, the landscape is dominated by a patchwork of vineyards and *garrigues*, limestone hillsides covered in thickets of small kermes and holm oaks and wild herbs such as sage, thyme, rosemary and lavender (see Plate 4). The scrub fires that afflict this dry region reveal in their aftermath that the *garrigues* are also laced with ancient pathways (often called *drailles*) dating back many hundreds of years, when shepherds established patterns of transhumance from lowland regions such as the Corbières and the Crau in the winter up to the Pyrenees and Alps in the summer. The existence of these pastures, and of the paths linking them, is also marked by the common presence today of abandoned drystone shelters (called, according to the region, *capitelles*, *bories*, *barraques* or *cabanes*) built by shepherds and peasants. Shepherds often lived outside the village in these small shelters, with a drystone enclosure for the sheep and often a huge stable (*bergerie*) for the sheep during winter. In the 1770s, the stony hills of this huge region were swarming with millions of sheep and, to a lesser extent, goats: in the Corbières alone, there were almost a million sheep.[27] Similarly, the Aubrac in the southern Massif Central drew on huge flocks which wintered further south in Languedoc. In the region around Rodez, there were an estimated 580,000 sheep as well as 78,000 cattle and 22,000 goats late in the century.[28]

These massive flocks provided the wool for a vigorous and ancient textile industry centred on bustling towns such as Montpellier, Narbonne, Carcassonne, and Bédarieux, and smaller woollens workshops and tanneries in large villages such as Saint-Chinian, Lagrasse and Fabrezan. Paradoxical as it may seem for a region which is today visibly dominated by winegrowing and tourism, this was one of the most industrial regions of the kingdom.[29] The industry produced woollen cloth destined mostly for the Middle East. The sheep were not only raised for wool; there was a constant movement of lambs and older sheep along the paths to the abattoirs. The flocks were also vital to other aspects of the rural economy: with goats, they provided milk, cheese and occasional meat for rural people, and they provided essential manure for the thin soils they grazed.

Like much of Languedoc, the mountains of the Cévennes in the 1770 would be unrecognizable today, covered as they were by flocks of thousands of sheep providing wool to the textile factories of Nîmes, Alès, Clermont-de-Lodève, Sommières, Anduze, Lodève and elsewhere. The size of the flocks was declining, as it became more profitable to plant mulberry trees for the silkworms providing thread for workshops as far away as Saint-Étienne, Lyon, Tours and Paris. That was not all. Travelling through the Cévennes in 1770, the Norman entrepreneur Pierre-François Tubeuf was startled by the richness of the coal deposits in the Alès basin and the possibilities of their large-scale exploitation in place of the eighty 'foxhole' diggings operated seasonally by peasant families.[30]

The attractions of coal were obvious: 100 kilogrammes of iron could be produced with 600 kilogrammes of coal rather than the 25 tonnes of timber needed for the requisite charcoal.[31] In 1773, Louis XV granted Tubeuf an extensive thirty-year concession around Alès, but his plan to concentrate the existing small mines into three major enterprises was always thwarted by conflict over access to land and resentment by the operators of the tiny mines. Although Tubeuf was forced to sell his concession and mines a decade later, the concession would mark the beginnings of the major transition from a wood-based economy to one based on fossil fuels, in the first instance coal. There had been small-scale extraction of coal here and in the north of the kingdom for centuries, but now the developing technologies in Britain and Germany would facilitate industrial-scale extraction. The coalminer would replace the charcoal burner.

The inexorable pressures of overgrazing on hillsides were observed closely by the mining engineer Antoine de Genssane. In 1766, he was commissioned by the royal administration in Languedoc to do a report on coal reserves. His report was to highlight the increasing importance of coal for domestic heating and in the silkworm industry and led him into the question of forest reserves, which he claimed were being depleted at three times the rate of new plantings.[32] When he published his five-volume report in the late 1770s, Genssane reported of the Corbières region south of Carcassonne:

> It is astonishing that these mountains, so suitable for producing beautiful forests, are covered only in bushes and scrub, and that one cannot see a single tree suitable for use in building. . . . We noticed in these areas three unforgiveable abuses . . . 1. three iron forges which are unsuitable in a land stripped of wood; 2. the habit of the common people of stripping the bark from oaks . . . 3. the huge flocks of goats which are allowed to graze at random.

It was not only educated individuals such as Genssane who were horrified by threats to the landscape. Louis XV's decrees encouraging land clearing were soon to be the target of widespread peasant criticism of the degradation of local environments, although we have very few statements from rural people in the eighteenth century of how they judged the landscape in other than purely material terms. One example is from the communities of Maron, Messein and others near the eastern city of Metz, which regretted that the nearby forests 'are going to be devastated and will result in this province, formerly so beautiful because of its woods, being totally devoid of them'. On the other side of the kingdom, the Breton parish of Coulier near Quimper assured the king that they would maintain the trees properly if they had the responsibility: 'you would see as a result the land embellished and decorated with trees'.[33]

These rare comments exist as items on lists of grievances (*cahiers de doléances*), which the 60,000 rural parishes across the kingdom were required to compile as part of the established process before a meeting of the Estates-General. The body was representative of the three orders of society and was convened by Louis XVI to meet in May 1789 at Versailles to advise the king on a path out of the kingdom's financial crisis. The king's request to rural parishes to submit their grievances unleashed a torrent of complaints about how the agents of the royal state, grasping religious orders and nobles, and avaricious industrialists were stripping the landscape of its bounty.

These documents, predominantly the voice of the prominent farmers and artisans in rural communities, offer us an unparalleled glimpse into how working people viewed their landscape and its health. Environmental historians have argued that the second half of the eighteenth century was a time of transition in elite intellectual perceptions of the 'natural' world. Rousseau especially has been identified as in some sense the 'founder' of western environmental sensibility, notably because of his appreciation of the emotional power of mountainous landscapes in his novel *La Nouvelle Héloïse*.[34] Instead, the *cahiers* of 1789 reveal that there was also a widespread popular understanding of the vulnerability of the landscape, born of the practice of agriculture across centuries.

Cahiers from southern regions were often studded with complaints about the impact of Louis XV's decrees, which had intensified existing pressures on resources. In the Médoc region north of Bordeaux, the decrees of the 1760s had been seized upon by hundreds of landowners large and small to clear hillsides for cereals and vines. Their clearances were often bitterly opposed by owners of livestock, for whom these uncultivated slopes of *padouëns* (common lands) were a vital resource for grazing. One large landowner in Saint-Médard-en-Jalles complained that owners of flocks had made life impossible for those who had cleared his land: 'to the point of meeting at night, filling in ditches and uprooting what has been planted or sown'.[35]

The consequences of the clearances led the flock-owners of Montlaur, near Carcassonne, to complain in their *cahier* that

> By digging up the ground . . . to make it arable, the woods are being destroyed so much that in a few years there will no longer be an oak-tree in this part of the Corbières; the tanneries and the lime kilns contribute a good deal to these depredations . . . we have no hesitation in stating that the wool that [the sheep] produces in this region is as fine as that of Spain or England. The ruin of the forests is making the production of this commodity impossible.[36]

Cornillon was one of scores of communes in the neighbouring *sénéchaussée* (bailiwick) of Nîmes, which identified the ecological impact of Louis' encouragement of clearances. These

> deprive us for ever of the wood which would have grown there and of pastures for livestock which produce the manure for other cleared land; in addition, these same cleared lands are situated on the slopes of mountains and hills; rainstorms carry off the good soil and leave only gravel.[37]

From the *sénéchaussée* of Cahors came a chorus of complaints about the decline in soil fertility across the previous forty years. Such had been the extent of clearances on the hillsides that the best land along the river Lot was now carried off in storms rushing down ravines caused by erosion; even vines were regularly washed away. As it was put by the parish of Ségos, 'erosion has already taken half our crops, and there is no hope for the future, for the soil has been completely stripped from the mountains and so there is nothing but rocks and huge ditches'.[38] The inhabitants of Le Montat, in the hills of Quercy south of Cahors, were equally grim about the consequences of more intense pressures caused by the clearing of land:

> Formerly the farmer had a surplus (*superflu*), and with this surplus he paid his taxes; but today, the population having increased with the greater extent of cleared land and crops having diminished in proportion to the deterioration of the soil, there is no longer any surplus. . . . there used to be immense forests where were fed a large number of flocks, the basis of fertility; most of these forests have been cleared, there are far fewer flocks, most land has gradually lost its fertility, whether because of lack of manure, or by the nature of things, or from the storms which have desolated and ravaged our mountains and valleys.[39]

In eastern France, the proliferation of wood-fuelled extractive industries was the focus of peasant ire such as that demonstrated in the widely repeated article of the *cahiers* of the *bailliage* of Amont, which urged that forges and furnaces should only be permitted where the proprietor owned sufficient private supplies of wood.[40] Near Metz, the village of Altwiller complained that there were 'in German Lorraine too many wood-fuelled factories'; here, as in the *cahiers* from scores of surrounding villages, the royal saltworks at Dieuze, Moyenvic and Château-Salins were especially singled out for criticism because they consumed vast quantities of wood to produce salt, which was in any case more expensive than sea-salt.[41] In this area, the *cahiers* were virtually unanimous in their condemnation both of the impact of such industries and of the complicity of forest owners and royal administrators in supplying wood to industry at the expense of the poor. It was this, argued the commoners of Guébestroff, which forced the poor to damage forests further by illegal cutting of trees.[42] The imposing neo-classical structure of the royal saltworks at Arc-en-Senans, near Besançon, designed by Nicolas Ledoux and completed in 1775, consumed vast quantities of wood in extracting salt from local spring-water.[43] Around Quimper and Tréguier in Brittany, it was instead seigneurs and large landowners who were singled out as primarily responsible for a shortage of wood. Peumérit-Cap complained that 'our countryside is almost bare; forests are visibly receding; seigneurs and landowners totally neglect to plant'.[44]

By the late 1780s, the landscape of France had never been so populated with people and their livestock. Its arable areas were a mosaic of polycultural agriculture, and its wooded slopes scarred by the multiple demands of construction, heating and fuel. Pressures on the environment were mediated through a political filter of social relationships between those who worked in the landscape and those who extracted their wealth from it through the labours of others. In 1788, when Louis XVI requested of his subjects that they formulate and submit their grievances as part of a process through which he intended to strengthen his finances and his authority, he instead unleashed waves of expectation and resentment which his regime could not contain.

The most common rural grievances (*doléances*) concerned the taxation exemptions of the privileged orders and the weight of indirect taxes, but trenchant also were grievances pertaining to control over and protection of the environment. Across the kingdom, parish assemblies focused on grievances about common lands, the claims by seigneurs to control of the commons, pasturing rights, access to and ownership of forests, land clearances, erosion and flooding.[45] As the regime of Louis XVI stumbled into crisis in 1789, the competing claims to control over the landscape would explode into open conflict. The resolution of those grievances was to result in an intense period of friction and violence in the countryside, which would transform the landscape forever.

2 THE ENVIRONMENTAL CRISIS OF THE FRENCH REVOLUTION, 1789–99

By the summer of 1788, Louis XVI and his government were embroiled in a profound political and financial crisis.[1] Within a year, the crisis involved every section of French society, evident from the impassioned statements of grievance and hope in the *cahiers* drawn up across the kingdom in March–April 1789 prior to the meeting of the Estates-General. These remarkable documents reveal that a fundamental issue across most of rural France was that of access to resources and the claims of the privileged orders over the product of those resources.

The bold claim of commoner deputies to the Estates-General on 17 June 1789 that they were a 'National Assembly' was reinforced by armed insurrection by working people in Paris. News of the storming of the Bastille on 14 July startled a hungry countryside, crackling with rumours of imminent aristocratic manoeuvres to destroy ripening crops by way of revenge. The ensuing rebellions would become known as the Great Fear (*Grande Peur*), the largest insurrection in French history. It was the most spectacular moment in a decade of upheaval, which was to lay the foundations of dramatic change across the landscape.

From an historian's perspective, the French landscape had always been a stage on which people had negotiated and contested who had the right to use its resources and in which ways. From 1789, this competition became open, even violently so, as the rules of ownership changed. The French Revolution was one of those rare periods of history in which it was the control of the landscape and its uses which for a decade was the great social question. Extensive illegal tree-felling and land clearing after 1789 generated a debate about the environmental consequences of unchecked clearances, which was remarkable for its anger and intelligence.

The pre-industrial landscapes of France had borne the physical imprint of an ancient social and economic framework. These were landscapes hundreds of years in the making. Now that framework was to be shaken to its foundations by a series of shocks: the abolition of the seigneurial system, the accelerated felling of forests, radical changes to land ownership and its use, and a new institutional environment which would facilitate continuing change to the landscape.

While *châteaux* and parish churches would continue to be the dominant structures in the rural landscape, the material substance of that architectural presence was hollowed out forever. The Assembly responded to the *Grande Peur* on the momentous night of 4 August by abolishing 'servile' dues, such as the hunting privileges of seigneurs. The National Convention finally abolished all harvest dues without compensation in July 1793. Tithes paid to the Catholic Church were also ended, and the Assembly assumed the obligation of paying the clergy (and Protestant pastors) from taxation revenue.

At the heart of the deputies' vision of the regenerated kingdom in 1789 was a revolutionary recasting of the concept of property, now understood to be a foundational right along with liberty, security, and 'resistance to oppression'. The Assembly asserted in its Declaration of the Rights of Man and Citizen that property was an 'inalienable', individual right and that it could only be appropriated after just compensation. This was a radical notion in a world in which claims of individuals, religious corporations and other bodies to own property outright had co-existed with overlapping claims of seigneurial rights over peasant property, the right of the Catholic Church to levy tithes, and formal and informal claims by rural communities of collective rights in forests and on harvested land. Now all property was to have a sole owner – an individual, a municipality or the state – and the only other legitimate claims were to be those of the state to levy taxes on all privately- owned property.[2]

This was a seismic shift in the meaning of ownership of property, which was to have profound implications for custodianship of landscape. In the short term, however, many of the king's subjects took advantage of the collapse in the structures of public authority to seize any advantage. Among the first targets of rebels were the contested resources of the countryside. The most basic elements of the rural ecosystem were now vulnerable to angry social conflict. The French countryside was about to experience the most intense period of human pressure in its history.[3]

The insistence of rural people in the *cahiers* that forest resources be sustainable was not commonly matched by sympathy to the fauna which inhabited them. Seigneurial privileges in hunting and fishing, and the maintenance of dovecotes and rabbit-warrens, had been among the most common grievances of rural parishes. For example, one-third of the parishes around Amboise on the Loire River had complained in their *cahiers* of 'wild beasts' – rabbits, pigeons, deer and boars – eating their crops.[4] Fauna seems to have been understood as either 'useful' or 'noxious': the issue was who had the right to kill animals, not whether there were some species to be protected despite being 'wild'.[5] The August 1789 decree on feudalism stipulated that no longer could seigneurs alone keep dovecotes and hunt the pigeons which feasted on peasant crops: 'all hunting preserves, under whatever denomination, are equally abolished'. Now individuals could kill pigeons on their own land, as well as rabbits and other game.

The abolition of hunting monopolies unleashed a massacre of wildlife. As Arthur Young travelled between Avignon and Aix at the end of August 1789, he was indignant that

I have been pestered with all the mob of the country shooting; one would think that every rusty gun in Provence is at work, killing all sorts of birds; the shot has fallen five or six times in my chaise and about my ears. . . . [and] has, I am everywhere informed, filled all the fields of France with sportsmen to an utter nuisance.[6]

The frightened priest of Tournissan, near Carcassonne, inquired whether 'brigands' were now allowed to shoot at pigeons at random, including one of his which had landed on his window-sill.[7] Far away, 60 kilometres north of Paris, Pierre Delahaye, the schoolteacher in Silly-en-Multien (today Silly-le-Long), happily detailed in his diary the unchecked killing of the game on the nearby estate of the Prince de Conti and the delight of his fellow villagers that they could hunt as they wished, 'just as the Prince used to'. Conti had fled France after the storming of the Bastille on 14 July. On 21 November, Delahaye recorded that 'we hunted the whole day in the Chaalis forest. . . . I brought home 18 pounds of meat'. Well into the winter of 1789–90, he was recording that 'hunting is still going on; we're hunting everywhere'.[8] A hunting law of 28 April 1790 gave property owners the right to forbid it on their land, and it was made illegal to hunt across fields before harvests, but royal land remained vulnerable. The Grand Parc at Villepreux near Versailles was spared the massacre of game in the summer of 1789 as the king's private possession, but a year later thousands of poachers descended on the domain.[9]

Fish were not spared. The elderly marquise de Créquy was caustic about the damage done to one of her ponds on her estate near Orléans. On the pretext that the Assembly had abolished the hunting privileges of the nobility, instead of buying the fish, 'four or five bands of people from roundabout, led by their mayors in their tricolour sashes' forced her guards to take refuge and 'everyone helped themselves to our fine fish and carted off what they could. It had been sixty years since this pond had been drained. . . . All of them went off gaily, shouting . . . Vive la nation! Vive l'Assemblée nationale!'[10]

Other issues erupted, particularly those of control of state and private forests and the commons owned or controlled by the former privileged orders. From 1789, governments issued a maze of legislation regarding land use based on individual property rights, including a reformed forest code and a general rural code, laws on the subdivision of commons and on illegal land clearances. Decrees sought to protect forests, to outlaw unauthorized clearing of common land and to manage the subdivision and sale of church land and commons. There was a widespread refusal to listen or obey.

By 1790, there were reported to be about 6.7 million hectares of forested land. The crown, the church and communes each owned about 15 per cent, individuals the other 55 per cent. Forests covered about 14 per cent of the kingdom, possibly a decline of 10 per cent over the previous century.[11] Despite the fevered attempts of revolutionary governments to protect them, the forests were to experience unprecedented pressure from the summer of 1789. Reports poured into Paris of seizures of land belonging to the state and to former lords and of unchecked felling of trees. Marginal, uncultivated land and even forested land was being seized and cleared by the rural poor. Half of all the districts in France experienced conflict over forests by 1793.[12] On 1 September, Arthur Young reported acidly of his visit to the estate of the Baron of La Tour-d'Aigues, north of Aix, where he saw 'the venerable woods, park, and all the ensigns of family and command, and even the lives of the owners at the mercy, and trampled on, by an armed rabble. What a spectacle!'[13]

On 2 November, the National Assembly placed forests under the protection of 'the Nation', but in general, this order was simply ignored. On 11 December, the deputy Barère de Vieuzac, himself from the Pyrenees, complained to the Assembly that 'the devastation of forests has reached its limit everywhere in the kingdom. These precious resources of the navy, of construction, of workshops, of manufactures and of all the necessary arts, are almost annihilated.' Barère's hyperbole succeeded in having his proposed decree passed, placing forests under the protection of the law and public authorities, but this decree was to receive as little respect as the others.[14] While promising a thoroughgoing revision of Colbert's forest code of 1669, several times in 1790 the Assembly had to respond to the urgent appeals of the forest administration by warning that forest incursions would be punished 'with the greatest rigour'.[15] It was an empty threat.

Distressed reports continued to flood in, such as when, in December 1790, the municipal council of Bourg in the Bresse region of eastern France received a report that 'the forests around the town of Bourg have been completely devastated by different individuals, the guards appointed to ensure the conservation of the said woods were insufficient to prevent the damage'.[16] In April 1791, the king's foresters of Bouzonville on the eastern border begged the National Assembly to re-establish order and 'complained that they can no longer prevent the depredations without number which people are committing in the forests'.[17]

There was a similar crisis on common lands. We do not know the extent of the commons at the beginning of the French Revolution, but it was considerably greater than the 9 per cent remaining in 1846, when a completed cadastral survey allowed for reasonably accurate national statistics. They were particularly important, often covering well over one-quarter of the surface, in the upland areas of the eastern third of France, from the Ardennes to the Alps; in the Pyrenees and southern Massif Central; and in Brittany and Corsica.[18]

The commons were the focus of social tensions wherever they existed. They had often been under the control of lords who had levied a charge on their use for grazing livestock or had used a feudal right to alienate and enclose one-third. The commons – often referred to as *vacants* or 'wastelands' – were now placed under extreme pressure as the poorest members of the rural community rushed to seize the opportunity to clear and cultivate a plot. Instances of illegal seizure and division of common lands occurred in 30 per cent of all districts, especially along the lower slopes of the Pyrenees and on the lowlands of Languedoc; in the north of the Massif Central; and in parts of the northeast.[19]

The news of the seizure of such land, often with the full support of village councils, outraged the Assembly and local authorities. Some municipalities responded to the damage being done to commons by urging the National Assembly to allow them to divide them between the inhabitants so that individual families would take better care of them. For others, it was too late. The municipality of Grospierres (department of Ardèche) bemoaned the impact of the royal decree of 1766, which had encouraged people to clear land; its repeated requests to divide the commons legally had been ignored to the point where 'the woods have continued to be ravaged, to such a point that there is no longer anything to be found there'.[20] Everywhere, however, there were vested interests seeking to preserve the status quo, and, in the upland areas of the Alps, Pyrenees and Massif Central, most households were clear that the pastoral economy required the maintenance of collective grazing rights on the commons.[21]

The alacrity with which some in the rural community seized on the ambiguity of the revolutionary decrees or simply chose to take advantage of the collapse of authority horrified others. Landowners from the village of Grouches (Somme) complained that 'the inhabitants of their commune, by interpreting decrees as they wish, are clearing the hills on our territory, even though these slopes, very steep and dry, cannot produce anything'.[22] Similar reports were being received from all over the country, but they were particularly agitated from Mediterranean hinterland areas with huge areas of stony pastures on the *garrigues*.

In response to anxious reports from many regions, the National Assembly sought, in a decree of April 1791, to resolve the issue of ownership of the commons. The Assembly had difficulty in resolving the tension between its principles of private ownership and ancient popular assumptions of multiple rights of usage. The legislation was clear that former seigneurs no longer had the right to appropriate the *vacants*: they were henceforth to be communal property (*biens communaux*) unless the seigneur could demonstrate legal acquisition before 1789, either by having put them to productive use at least forty years beforehand or 'by virtue of the laws, customs, statutes or local usages then existing'. Even where former seigneurs could justify this ownership, however, communal rights of usage – for grazing animals and collecting wood in particular – were to be respected.

The legislation inevitably generated further confusion and contestation over what constituted adequate proof of prior ownership. Tensions emerged within many communities between the poor, desperate for a cultivable plot for growing foodstuffs, and the larger landowners who dominated local political power and who also possessed the largest herds of livestock. In the northeastern department of Aisne, where there was a very high percentage of landless or near-landless farm labourers, the division of the commons (here called *usages*) was seen as a partial solution to land-hunger. Near Château-Thierry, for example, a group of villages simply took it upon themselves to divide their commons in 1790–1.[23]

The concerns expressed in many *cahiers* about the link between land clearance and erosion now became more agitated. At the local level, as well as in the National Assembly, there was an impassioned debate in the years after 1789 about the impact of land clearances on the environment. In January 1791, Raymond Bastoulh, the exasperated senior administrator of the department of Aude, reported that

> people are complaining on all sides about the misguided greed of peasants who are spending every day clearing the woods and the uncultivated land on mountainsides, without realizing that this soil will only be productive for a year or two. . . . This pernicious clearing has accelerated since the destruction of the feudal régime because the people of the countryside imagine that the communes have become the owners of the *vacants*, that the former seigneurs were stripped of them at the same time as they were of judicial power, and that they have no other formalities to complete other than to inform the secretary of the municipality of the land they intend to clear.

It was already obvious, he stated, that gravel and stones were being washed down by storms into streams, congesting their beds and causing them to spill over onto the best land. The departmental authorities decided, in the interests of the hillsides and pastoralists, to ban clearances altogether, but in vain.[24]

In Paris, governments were horrified by reports of environmental damage in many parts of the country. But they oscillated between their commitment to the sanctity of private property and recognizing peasant attachment to collective customary rights. This was evident in two key pieces of legislation passed in September 1791. First, on the 28th, the Assembly voted a rural code, in which it tried to balance the rights of individuals to enclose pastures and forests with ancient collective rights, for example, to graze sheep on common or fallow land. The contradiction would prove impossible to resolve.[25] Next day, the Assembly passed its long-awaited forest code, essentially a restatement of the major provisions of Colbert's 1669 code asserting state control of forests but with an insistence that privately owned forests were fully at the owners' disposition, 'to do with as he wishes', whatever the traditional rights of access by peasants.[26]

The Assembly's hopes that the decrees would put an end to law-breaking in forests and friction over the exercise of customary rights were soon dashed. Despite regular missives from Paris reminding municipalities of laws protecting forests dating from 1669 and now reinforced, illegal woodcutting went on unchecked.

The forest code was ignored, in part because forests in private hands were assumed to be – and often were – the property of enemies of the Revolution. In April 1792, five hundred people invaded the *château* at Le Mercou, near Le Vigan (Gard), and made such an intense bonfire of its furnishings that the stone walls cracked. They also felled avenues of chestnuts, laurel trees and an orchard of pear trees.[27]

The conflict over common lands would prove just as difficult to resolve as that of control over forests. Finally, on 10 June 1793, the National Convention passed a detailed, radical and contentious law, which, together with the final abolition of seigneurial rights on 17 July, was the most ambitious attempt of the revolutionary government to meet the needs of the rural poor. The June legislation empowered a municipality to convene a general assembly of all inhabitants in order to debate the division of non-wooded common land into equal plots. It required communes to proceed to a division if this was the wish of one-third of adult men; the land was then to be divided on the basis of an equal share to every man, woman and child.[28]

Debates about the substance of the decree polarized many communities. Only a minority of communities possessed commons, and where they did exist many people did not want them divided. In the department of Somme, only 31 communes out of 958 finally divided their commons and in Ardèche just 5 of 334.[29] In general, the law had little application outside regions north and northeast of Paris and parts of the south. Sometimes the areas involved were tiny, but the battle over the commons could be bitter even when the stakes were small. Thirty kilometres north of Paris, twenty-seven poorer inhabitants of Seugy (Seine-et-Oise) demanded in 1791 the division of commons and were hotly opposed by their wealthier pastoralist neighbours. The division escalated into a political division between republicans and conservatives. When the poor finally won the day in August 1794, the 331 lots were just 25 square metres each.[30] In some areas, the impact on the appearance of the countryside was dramatic. In the southwest near Montauban, in Verdun-sur-Garonne, the land was divided between the 681 adults. In the northeast, too, some communes convoked a meeting of all citizens to divide the commons by head: Bayonville divided its commons into 223 sections of 'mountain' and 196 sections of 'slopes', with 446 inhabitants receiving a little of each.[31] What had been unfenced commons used for grazing became tiny private plots.

Upland areas were largely untouched because rural communities realized that partition of the slopes would be ruinous for the topsoil as well as for the pastoral industry. In the Corbières region of the department of Aude, where illegal land seizures had been endemic, the flock-owners succeeded in keeping much of what remained of the commons as pastures: Ornaisons decided to keep about 275 hectares for pasture and to divide the remaining 95. In the department of Gard, similarly, only 18 of 361 communes used the law of June 1793 to partition the land, with almost all deciding that the stony *garrigues* were best suited to grazing village livestock in common. In many communes, however, the poor had already seized parts of the commons to eke out a subsistence, in defiance of the law and of wealthier locals.[32] Only the law of 29 February 1804 (9 Ventôse Year XII according to the new revolutionary calendar), the last of more than forty laws on the commons since 1789, ended the uncertainty, at least legally. Revolutionary sales of common land were regularized, 'irregular' sales could be made good, while illegally seized land had to be returned to the community.[33]

Everywhere, debates on the commons revealed the anger of local administrators as well as revolutionary legislators at the environmental damage in many parts of France as the poor cleared and cultivated these 'wastelands', especially on hillsides. In a report from the southern department of Aude on 8 December 1793 (18 Frimaire Year II), the Jacobin official Cailhava fulminated:

> It is enough to drive you into a holy rage when, under a burning sky, you see destroyed in one minute the parasol that nature has spent fifty years perfecting. . . . The terrain of the municipalities that make up the district of Lagrasse were once covered with wood thickets, mostly holm oak; but, in the Revolution, each individual used them up as though they were cabbages from his garden. Moreover, coal having become highly expensive, the charcoal-burners used their neighbours' possessions all the less sparingly for that; the villagers who remove the bark from the holm oak in order to sell it to the tanners were no more sparing; add to that the shepherds who prefer to take their herds to the youngest thickets, and who fell the tall trees so that their animals can enjoy the tender leaves that grow on the stalks, and you will agree that it takes much less than this to destroy the largest forests.[34]

Nothing was spared. The Ancien Régime monarchy had long encouraged the draining of marshes as a way of increasing the land available for cereal production. Now a decree of 4 December 1793 (14 Frimaire Year II) declared that not only marshes but all *étangs* (lagoons and ponds) would be drained. The measure appealed to the government as a part of the *levée en masse* of the nation's resources; moreover, most *étangs* had been church or noble property. Local populations, more aware of the benefits of the ponds than the government, objected to what the measure would mean for fishing, irrigation, the milling of grain, and the availability of reeds for roof-thatching, but close to Paris and in the Dombes region east of Lyon, many ponds were indeed drained. It was 'a conspiracy against the carp', mocked Georges Danton in the National Convention.[35]

So deep were the hostilities during the Revolution's great military crisis of 1793–4, with foreign armies on French soil and a vicious civil war in the west of the country, that conflict over environmental resources inevitably became embroiled with political and social divisions. So from Condé-sur-Sarthe (Orne) came the complaint in December 1793 that a battalion of army volunteers from Argentan, 45 kilometres to the north, was camped on the property of the *émigré*

Vaucelles and 'every day cutting huge quantities of all kinds of trees, walnuts, oaks, elms, alders, plums'.[36] The exigencies of war after 1792 exacerbated the pressures on forests. Just as shipbuilding needs of the royal navy had expanded considerably since the humiliation of losing the Seven Years' War in 1763, after 1792 the army would add to this demand for timber for its fortifications. State forests in the Ardennes, Alps and Pyrenees were stripped of mature trees.

Elsewhere, the landscape of the west was to be not only the location but also a contributing factor to the greatest bloodshed of the Revolution. The region was characterized by its distinctive *bocage* landscape, where high hedgerows across the undulating landscape kept cattle enclosed. The Revolution was resented for having destroyed a religious culture inseparable from life itself without having done anything for those who rented farms and therefore who had few seigneurial obligations.[37] Once conscription of young men was introduced in February 1793, the region south of Nantes erupted in violent rage at the prospect of its young men being forced to fight in unpopular wars on the other side of the country. The *bocage* terrain suited guerilla-type ambushes and retreats and exacerbated a vicious cycle of killing and reprisals by both sides, convinced of the treachery of the other. 'The Vendée' was to cost the lives of 170,000 locals and 30,000 troops.

While war raged along the borders and civil war engulfed the west, by the summer of 1793 the rest of the countryside was a different environment, and not just because of land clearing and felling of trees. It was now quiet as well. The young men of 18–25 years were all conscripts in the army or hiding in the forests. On 23 July 1793, the Convention decreed that parishes could have only one bell: the metal from others was to be used for weapons or, if unsuitable, for coinage. Fewer than half the churches were open anyway. In many parishes, the removal of bells was angrily contested. Near Le Mans, at Marolles-les-Braults, 250 soldiers with artillery were needed to take down the two bells in October 1793. Nationally, up to 100,000 bells from 60,000 church towers were melted down.[38] By Easter 1794, when only about 150 churches openly celebrated mass, the countryside must have been disconcertingly quiet, devoid of the sound of bells and the call to worship. It would be years before the familiar aural sensations of the countryside were restored.[39]

The Revolution also generated a phenomenal volume of artistic creativity, from a democratized portraiture to political caricature and lithographed images which circulated in huge numbers. Relatively little of this artistic explosion focused on the landscape as such. Where it did, as in some of the work of the little-known Claude Michel Hamon Duplessis, it was as a backdrop to scenes of military camps on the outskirts of villages. Pro-revolutionary painters such as Alexandre-Hyacinthe Dunouy and Jacques-François Swebach celebrated edifying acts of courage and acts of patriotic sacrifice by ordinary rural citizens in transporting provisions for the army without the assistance of horses. More commonly, however, landscape painters such as Louis Gauffier and Pierre-Henri de Valenciennes preferred to continue the tradition of neo-classical depictions of famous Italian sites. Once the military crisis had been surmounted in 1794 and the months of crisis government had been labelled as 'the Terror', others used landscapes as allegories of disaster and survival. Jacques-Antoine Vallin depicted a *Scène de naufrage* (Shipwreck Scene) in 1795 to illustrate a few survivors emerging from a wild sea as a warming sun broke through the storm clouds.[40]

The regime of the Directory (1795–9) had no more success than its predecessors in regularizing access to forests and commons. In these years of incessant warfare, rampant inflation and precarious resources for policing, illegal tree-felling and large-scale theft often went unpunished. By then the evidence of clearances and woodcutting, especially in the south, had become of national importance. In a series of reports, the agronomist Jacques-Michel Coupé argued that the hillsides of southern France were now as denuded as other parts of the Mediterranean coast from Spain to the Near East. He reported indignantly that the Narbonnais, 'which the Romans called their province and Italy itself, no longer offers anything but arid mountains for the most part':

> Even in living memory, people believe that the climate has changed; vines and olives suffer from frosts now, they perish in places where they used to flourish, and people give the reason: the hillsides and peaks were formerly covered with clumps of woods, bushes, greenery . . . the greedy fury of clearances arrived; everything has been cut down without consideration; people have destroyed the physical conditions which conserved the temperature of the region.[41]

What was the overall impact of the Revolution on the rural environment? Certainly, the revolutionary years exacerbated long-term pressures on forests and common land: by the end of the decade, perhaps one-quarter of France's forests had been felled illegally, and by then the forested area of France had fallen to 10–12 per cent, compared with about 20 per cent a century before, or more than 30 per cent today.[42] In many regions, vast areas of commons had been cleared for agriculture, whether through illegal seizures or legal division. The clearers were unrepentant. When a committee of farmers from Lagrasse in 1795 had to choose two recipients of an award for 'industry', it decided on two poor peasants:

> these men . . . who formerly had not the tiniest little parcel of land, are presently harvesting abundant foodstuffs; with no other help than their own hands, with no other tool than their spades, with no other means than labour, these individuals have cleared little plots of dry, arid, stony ground, according to public opinion useful only for growing scrub.[43]

Such had been the extent of post-1789 land clearances and tree-felling that a durable view quickly took hold that the Revolution had unleashed the rapacious attitudes of peasants towards their environment, that the Revolution was an ecological disaster.[44] Once Napoleon seized power in 1799, such a view suited his image as the 'saviour' of France. The comments of Napoleon's senior administrator (*préfet*) of the department of Vaucluse in 1808 were echoed everywhere along the Mediterranean: 'after having cleared the plain, the hillsides were cleared, then even parts of the mountains were cleared; the remainder of the woods perished later under the axes of crime and greed, or under the teeth of flocks'.[45] Perhaps one-fifth of the surface of the department of Aude had been cleared, mostly illegally, after 1789, and the Prefect, Baron Trouvé, claimed that unchecked land clearances had wreaked environmental damage:

> In this region, people have always complained about the fury of land seizures and clearances. Decrees and laws were made to repress it. The storms of the Revolution having released this brake, now powerless against anarchy, seizures multiplied, clearances became an almost general calamity; and a region, formerly covered with pastures and flocks, suddenly found itself threatened with losing the raw material for its manufactures, the principal source of its wealth. . . . bushes and trees have been uprooted; and the fields on the hillsides, formerly so fertile and useful, were no long held together by the tree-roots and were washed into the streams which they have blocked and forced to overflow on to the river-flats, and to cover them with the gravel and stones with which their beds were obstructed.[46]

However, the degradation after 1789 had only intensified the land clearing encouraged by decrees issued by Louis XV after 1760. These decrees had exposed hundreds of thousands of hectares of hillsides to overuse and the effects of erosion. While there is no question that the Revolution of 1789 had unleashed a dramatic, sustained period of human stress on the environment, the imputation that the battered landscape was the result of revolutionary 'excess' alone was wide of the mark. Well before 1789, the administration and conservation of forests were under great strain because of increased pressure from an increasing population and rising wood prices, shipbuilding and more commercial attitudes from owners of forest resources.

Another agronomist, Jacques Rougier de la Bergerie, who despaired at the environmental degradation across much of France during the Revolution, was insistent that it had initially been unleashed by the monarchy's encouragement of land clearances in the 1760s and the vested interest the church and seigneurs had had in seeing land come into production of crops and hence of more lucrative tithes and harvest dues.[47] Some of the other prefects who reported to Napoleon on the state of their departments shared this longer-term perspective. Amans-Alexis Monteil, in his brilliant report on Aveyron, noted that people were in general better-off than before the Revolution but bemoaned the environmental impact of decades of neglect:

People were already complaining about the degradation of forests before the Revolution: since that time, most of them have been razed. What little is left will soon accede to the pillagers' axes, the murderous teeth of animals, and the greed of the new owners.[48]

The Revolution also had a significant impact on the ownership of the countryside. Even more important in scale than legal and illegal seizures of common land were the sales of *biens nationaux* – church and later *émigré* property nationalized and sold at auction. The most detailed estimate is that 8.5 per cent of land changed hands as a result of the expropriation of the church (about 6.5 per cent) and *émigrés*. In all, there were up to 700,000 purchasers: about one family in six bought some land. The sale of *émigré* property benefitted the peasantry more, since it was subdivided into small lots and could be paid off in instalments. Overall, peasants bought up perhaps 1.5 million hectares of nationalized land: by 1800 peasant holdings had increased from perhaps one-third to two-fifths of the total.[49] Many noble families survived with their lands intact, but some 12,500 – one-half of all families – lost some land, and a few virtually all. About one in five noble families were effectively expropriated.[50]

Despite this transfer of land, most people worked the land in 1800 just as they had in 1770. The nature of their work – manual, skilled and repetitive – remained the same. France remained essentially a rural society dominated by small farm units, on which households used ancient methods and techniques to produce mainly for their own survival. The production of wine, wheat and cloth involved the same techniques: with few exceptions, agricultural production remained at similar levels in 1800 as before the Revolution. As in 1770, the countryside in 1800 was a busy, crowded landscape of manual and animal labour. Across much of the country, this polycultural and subsistence orientation of agriculture would persist well into the nineteenth century.[51]

Peasant landowners were among those who benefitted materially from the Revolution, and the dominant feature of the landscape – small-scale, intensively worked farms – was to endure almost until our own times. Decisions taken by successive assemblies in 1792–3, under massive peasant pressure, to finally abolish compensation due to seigneurs for the end of feudal dues and to make *émigré* land available in small plots at low rates of repayment encouraged small owners to stay on the land.[52] Inheritance laws in 1790 and 1793 dividing deceased estates equally between children ensured that farms would be constantly threatened by subdivision. But those peasants who owned their own land were the substantial beneficiaries of losses by the nobility and the church, for their land was now free of seigneurial dues and tithes.

But the seeds had been sown for further, sweeping change. In some areas, the retention of a greater share of produce by peasant landholders facilitated the contemplation of the risks of market specialization.[53] Profit-oriented farm enterprise was enabled by a series of legislative changes and the relative consistency with which successive regimes after 1789 upheld the primacy of private ownership and control over claims of collective, community practices. Except where sharecropping contracts specified what tenants were to produce, peasants were now free of the stifling constraints over land use imposed by payments of tithes and harvest dues in kind, especially grains; now landowners were able to use their land for their own purposes. Only the strength of the attachment to communal lands in many regions prevented a thoroughgoing change to total private control of rural land.

There are few built reminders of the Revolution in the rural landscape. There are very ancient 'liberty trees', perhaps dating back to 1792 or even 1790, at Tamniès (Dordogne) and Villardebelle (Aude). The Revolution was celebrated in a carved stone image of the Bastille above a door in Camps-sur-l'Agly (Aude) and in a stone from the Bastille purchased in 1790 by the village of Saint-Julien-du-Sault in Burgundy. Surviving from opposition to the Revolution is a tiny chapel in ruins just across the border in Spain from Coustouges in the eastern Pyrenees. More recent commemorations include the reconstruction of the windmill overlooking the plain on which the first great revolutionary victory was achieved at Valmy in September 1792 (see Figure 2.1). Some of the reminders are present in destroyed buildings, most famously the partial demolition of the massive Benedictine monastery at Cluny, northwest of Mâcon, once it was sold as a national property. Many churches across the country never repaired external statuary damaged by anti-clericals during the war with the European coalition.[54]

The Revolution had other permanent effects on the landscape, both in physical appearance and in entitlements to its control. The starkest reminder may still

FIGURE 2.1 Inscribing politics in the landscape: the monument to General Kellermann at Valmy (Marne) was erected on the centenary of the first great triumph of revolutionary armies in 1792. It dominates the surrounding plain. Licensed under the Creative Commons Attribution-Share Alike 4.0 International license.

FIGURE 2.2 The pressure of centuries of grazing by huge flocks of sheep in Languedoc has in places left its mark on eroded hillsides, as here at Pradelles-en-Val (Aude). Peter McPhee.

be seen in the hills of the Corbières south of Carcassonne, where the fears of administrators and local communities about the impact of clearances on hillsides were realized in spectacular examples of erosion still visible today (see Figure 2.2). By the turn of the nineteenth century, the countryside looked rather different in some regions than it had a decade earlier. In coastal Languedoc and elsewhere, much of the 'marginal' land, such as the *garrigues* formerly used for pasturing animals, had been seized and cleared, often for vineyards. There were fewer sheep and goats. In many regions, forests had been further thinned or even felled completely. In regions close to large towns, there was less polyculture and more specialization as rural producers had slightly more margin for risk in meeting market demand.

The most durable impact of the Revolution on the countryside lay in the institutional structures surrounding France's rural ecosystem. From 1789, there was a series of institutional and legal changes creating the environment within which specialized agriculture would later thrive. Here, the Revolution had a profound impact. Gone were the myriad of claims by seigneurs of 'rights' over rural property, the right of the Catholic Church to levy tithes, and the assertion by rural communities of collective rights over private property.[55] Now all property was to have a single owner, an individual, a municipality or the state, except where communes had kept their commons.

The profound impulse of revolutionary governments to make institutional structures and regulations uniform in the new nation created the terrain on which the resources of the countryside could be freed from 'feudal' constraints on their use. The free enterprise and free trade (*laissez-faire, laissez-passer*) legislation of the Revolution guaranteed that manufacturers, farmers and merchants could commit themselves to the market economy, secure in the knowledge that they could trade without the impediment of a multitude of law codes. The uniformity of administrative structures was reflected, too, in the imposition of a national system of weights, measures and currency based on new, decimal measures. The nation was now measured by a single system of metres, francs, litres and grams. These evident benefits to commerce were accentuated by the abolition of all internal customs houses. The institutional structures had been created which would slowly unravel the patchwork of economic, cultural and ethno-linguistic diversity of early modern France. In the long run, the impact on the landscape itself would be profound.

*　　*　　*

The countryside and control of its resources were at the heart of the Revolution. The battles were played out in the landscape. After 1789, social divisions within rural communities and peasant antipathy to the survival of seigneurial property had resulted in an intense period of extreme pressure on the rural environment. Illegal tree-felling and land clearances across this decade of revolutionary upheaval horrified revolutionary administrators. In turn, their reports generated a durable *légende noire* of destructive peasant atavism after 1789, even though the environmental pressures after 1789 were essentially an intensification of actions unleashed by royal legislation in the 1760s.

The Revolution also had a powerful but paradoxical juridical impact on the landscape. On the one hand, the triumph of landowning peasants in freeing themselves from seigneurial controls and levies had ensured that rural France would continue to be dominated by small farms. The sale of church and *émigré* property had enabled peasants to extend their holdings even though most noble estates had remained intact. On the other hand, radical changes had been made to the legal and economic context that would also ensure rapid change to the landscape. In particular, the revolutionary change to the concept of 'property' itself, whereby all land was controlled by a single owner, meshed with the creation of a unified national system of laws, currency, weights and measures to facilitate market-oriented specialization. The Revolution was an epochal shift in the nature of the state and its legal framework for property relations and the economy, which was to reshape the relationships between humans and their rural environment and ultimately the landscape itself.

3 'CRISS-CROSSING THE KINGDOM', 1800–50

On 15 July 1801, First Consul Napoleon Bonaparte signed a Concordat with the Papacy, and on Easter Sunday 1802 the bells of Notre Dame in Paris rang out in celebration of a new alliance of state and altar. This was the signal for unchecked and joyful bell-ringing from church steeples across the nation wherever bells still existed. Napoleon subsequently used plebiscites to have himself appointed First Consul for life in 1802, then in 1804 as Emperor. His imperial mission in Europe would be matched by his internal campaign against 'disorder', not least in the use of natural resources.

Napoleon and his administrative elite had a distinctive *mentalité* which combined the authoritarian assumptions of Louis XIV with the zeal of French revolutionaries for national unity, institutional vigour and uniformity. It was a world view which understood the landscape as a palette for economic initiative and national grandeur, as resources to be measured and used.[1] In September 1807, the Emperor commissioned a cadastral survey of all property in every commune. This massive undertaking, which occupied legions of engineers and technicians until 1850, assumed that, apart from public property, all land was a privately owned and used commodity.[2] Gone was the pre-revolutionary feudal concept of multiple claims over land and those who worked it. The cadastral surveys imposed an urban and bureaucratic concept of ordered, taxable space onto a reality of local arrangements and customs.

Cadastral officials and local notables first had to agree on the boundaries of 40,000 communes before measuring every parcel and pathway. How were officials to decide whether a path was communal or private property? What if it went through private land? And how could laws extinguish ancient collective rights to enter private, communal and national forests or to glean on harvested fields? On Corsica, for example, how could ancient agreements (and feuds) about transhumance between mountain villages be captured by a model based on private property? Only about 40 per cent of the island had been surveyed by 1843.[3]

Napoleon was also determined to reimpose obedience in the imposition of controls on resource use. Between 1789 and 1799, successive governments had issued a maze of legislation pertaining to land use, ranging from a reformed forest code to a general rural code, laws on the subdivision of commons and laws on illegal land clearances. Of particular importance were scores of decrees seeking to protect forests and decrees outlawing unauthorized clearing of commons and state-owned land. Most of these laws and decrees had simply been ignored or sidestepped. Now the new regime was determined to have its powers respected.

Most urgent for the new Bonapartist administration after 1800 was the reassertion of state control over forests. The regime's forest policy would be a major exception to the untrammelled rights of individual property owners to use their land as they wished. The increased destruction of state forests after 1760 and 1789 and concern about the practices of private owners led the Napoleonic regime to reassert the national interest over private exploitation of timber resources. The state of the forests was particularly serious, since inhabitants of many highland areas had used Napoleon's seizure of power as an opportunity for a renewal of illegal tree-felling. By 1800, the forested area of France may have been as low as 10–12 per cent, the smallest extent in history. The reinforcement of state controls under the Consulate permitted the forest administration to have a series of laws promulgated reorganizing its personnel and re-establishing a centralized forests policy. Napoleon's restructuring of the forest administration in 1801 was the first effective post-revolutionary reassertion of a centralized forests policy along similar lines to that of Colbert in 1669. In March 1802, forests belonging to communes were placed under the same control as state forests.[4]

Officials of the French forests administration reconstituted in the early-nineteenth century lent their weight to the perpetuation of a *légende noire* of the Revolution: that the revolutionary period was an unmitigated disaster for the natural environment until the re-imposition of effective authority under Napoleon.[5] During the Empire, prefects were several times required to report on the condition of their department: its resources, production, character and public opinion. Not surprisingly, the prefects assured the Emperor that everything was improving, and they used the 'excesses' of the Revolution as the backdrop to Napoleon's achievements in ending forest depredation and illegal land clearances. From the department of Loire-Inférieure in the west, Jean-Baptiste Huet de Coetlizan claimed that tree-felling during the Revolution had reduced rainfall and increased silt in rivers, both of which were ruinous for the Loire. The only animals which had increased in numbers were wolves; there were fewer deer. The Prefect of Bas-Rhin in the east complained that, along the river, the killing of birds (especially magpies and pigeons) had had the effect of allowing the increase of weeds, caterpillars, bugs and bats. The population of rats had multiplied with the killing of foxes, wild-cats and other hunting animals. Here as elsewhere, there had been a proliferation of goats, 'the resource of the poor'.[6]

No doubt the revolutionary decade had been a period of acute pressure on wildlife and the landscape it inhabited. In other ways, however, the revolutionary changes to the legal, economic and social framework were to have a more durable impact on the environment. The abolition of seigneurial dues and tithes, the creation of uniform, national economic and legal systems and radical changes to transport would combine to accentuate the attractions of market-oriented agriculture. In the 1830s, provincial cities continued to source most of their foodstuffs from intensively farmed land within a 15-kilometre radius. Paris drew on a wider network, reaching as far as 120 kilometres.[7] But all this was starting to change. Beginning with regions close to major cities or transport routes, increasing numbers of landowners were able to abandon polyculture for monoculture. More than ever before, regions became known for particular produce. In the words of David Nicolas, a farmer from near Béziers (Hérault), in May 1799, his fellow farmers had 'embraced changes and innovations which may be fruitful for them. They have abandoned the routine practices of our grandfathers'.[8] In his locale, this meant being more sensitive to market demand, especially for wine.

The appearance of the landscape changed rapidly in some regions. There are examples, particularly in northern France, of the ways in which revolutionary measures facilitated a monocultural agriculture, based on large-scale ownership or renting of land and the employment of labour. For example, in 1786, the Thomassin family of Puiseux-Pontoise north of Paris owned about four hectares and rented 180 more from the seigneur. During the Revolution, they bought up large amounts of nationalized property from the abbey of Saint-Martin-de-Pontoise, the Sisters of Charity and other ecclesiastical landowners; by 1822, they owned more than one-quarter of the land in the commune. This land was now used for commercial grain-growing and, finally, for sugar beet and in 1856 a sugar distillery.[9] In the Norman countryside around Bayeux, the Church had insisted on wheat, maize and rye being grown on land it rented out because grain crops were liable to pay the tithe. After the abolition of tithes in 1791, the heavy, damp soils were quickly converted to orchards and cattle-raising, and pasture replaced sown crops across the landscape.[10] South of Poitiers, similarly, the end of restrictions with the abolition of the tithe meant that wealthier landowners were able to plant large fields in fodder crops such as sainfoin, lucerne and clover, marking a key point in the development of the livestock industry and leading to the clearing of large areas of small, hedged fields.[11]

Change was especially dramatic in the south. Today, much of Mediterranean Languedoc depends on wine and tourism, but 250 years ago, it had an extremely diverse economy. At the base of this was subsistence grain production (wheat, rye, barley, oats) and commercial stock-raising of sheep. For example, in the impoverished region of the Corbières, southeast of Carcassonne, nearly one million sheep, the largest flocks in France, supplied one of the major industrial centres of the kingdom, the Carcassonne textile industry, which had employed 18,000 full-time and 30,000 part-time workers making woollen cloth mostly exported to the Middle East. The evidence of this vast pastoral industry is still visible today on the landscape of the Corbières and other parts of Languedoc in the presence of the walls of abandoned drystone walled sheep enclosures and shepherd's stone huts (*cabanes*) (see Plate 4).

Three-quarters of the Corbières were covered by rough hill pastures known as *garrigues*; these were managed by the seigneurs, who extracted a small levy from the local community. After 1789, this land became the property of the communes – hence common land – unless the former lords could produce titles of their private ownership, whence came a half-century of legal action and illegal land occupation. As common land, and in some sense the 'people's', the *garrigues* were particularly vulnerable to demands from the poorest section of the community to be given land to clear and cultivate in opposition to the larger landowners who dominated local political power and who also possessed the largest flocks of sheep.[12] Centuries of tree-felling and of grazing by goats and sheep on the thin soil of the hillsides had denuded many of them, exacerbated by unchecked seizure and clearing of plots after the Revolution of 1789 (see Figure 2.2). The bare hillsides and erosion in parts of the Corbières today are witness to that history, the slowly crumbling drystone enclosures and *cabanes* artefacts of an ancient landscape that has almost disappeared.

The tensions over the use of the *garrigues* and the depleted forest resources were profound throughout the Mediterranean backcountry. In the village of Villesèque, south of Narbonne, they had festered for decades and exploded into violence after the Revolution of July 1830. An angry stand-off between, on the one side, two noble landholders, their private forest-guards and some gendarmes, and, on the other, one hundred villagers, resulted in the collective killing of the landholders.[13] The murders were a rare extreme in the endemic conflict over resources, but its story exemplifies many of the pressures on the rural environment, which reached their pinnacle at mid-century. The landscape of modern Languedoc was born in this violent struggle over who owned the *garrigues* and for what they were to be used.

Subsistence crops were not all that the land clearers wanted to grow. The Revolution dramatically accelerated the development of market-oriented viticulture, the basis of today's wine industry. While there is evidence of winegrowing in the Corbières from the time of the Roman occupation in 120 BCE, this wine had been overwhelmingly for local consumption. One reason why the land clearers of Languedoc were desperate in their desire for an arable plot, particularly to plant grapevines, was because of the collapse of the textile trade with the Middle East after the outbreak of war in 1792 and because of competition with British mechanized production. Carcassonne, Bédarieux, Lodève and other textile towns were plunged into protracted economic recession.[14] In the Corbières, there was a sharp consequent decline in the great flocks of sheep which had roamed the stony hillsides. From an estimated 878,000 in 1789, numbers declined to about 450,000 in 1814. They were to disappear almost completely with the large-scale importation of Argentinian and Australian wool later in the century.[15] A similar story played out across the entire Mediterranean backcountry.

The ending of seigneurial and church exactions in grain, coupled with the collapse of the textile industry, further impelled peasants to turn to wine as a cash crop. For example, at Ribaute, the seigneur, the abbey of Lagrasse, had taken one *setier* (about 85 litres) of wheat for every thirteen hectares of land, cultivated or not, necessitating the growing of grain on almost all cultivable land. The community also needed the abbey's permission to clear new land. With the end of these constraints, the area under vines at Ribaute increased from 83 to 186 hectares in the forty years after 1789. The total area under grapevines in the department of Aude increased from about 29,000 hectares in 1789 to about 51,000 in 1829. Further south, in Tautavel, which finally capitulated in 1826 after a long battle with the former seigneur over ownership of the *garrigues*, the mayor forwarded a list of those who had illegally cleared plots; in all, no fewer than 324 individuals had cleared 758 tiny parcels between 1784 and 1819. Virtually all of them had been planted in vines.[16]

Elsewhere on the lowlands of Languedoc, similarly, peasants started extending their vineyards and olive groves into fields formerly used for growing grain to pay tithes and dues and onto stony hillsides formerly used for pastures. Contemporary administrators estimated that the area of cultivated land in Aude had increased by almost 64,000 hectares (20 per cent) in the period 1789–1800 because of the clearing of common land, often illegally. Where smallholding peasants felt greater security about producing for the market, the results could be dramatic, particularly in winegrowing. In the east of the department of Gard, more than 70 per cent of the formerly uncultivated land which had been seized and cultivated in villages such as Tavel, Pujaut, Orsan and Saint-Victor-la-Coste was planted in vines.[17]

Across France as a whole, winegrowers were producing one-third more wine by 1812 compared with the years before the Revolution, and the total area under vines may have increased by 10 per cent. Jean-Antoine Chaptal, a brilliant chemist, agronomist and industrialist who became minister of the interior under Napoleon, concluded in 1819 that 'the division of properties, and above all the clearance of lands which proprietors would have previously left uncultivated, and which are today planted with grapevines, has prodigiously increased viticulture since 1789.'[18] Looking back in 1828, the mayor of Lagrasse expressed a powerful image of the change:

The high and low Corbières were formerly inhabited by a nomadic people . . . the quantity of wool was very considerable, and of the best quality for the cloth industry since it was as good for warp as it was for weft, an advantage no other wool had . . . since 1789, this land has gone from being a place of a nomadic people to one of an agricultural people.[19]

The southern landscape, in particular, was taking on the appearance familiar to us today.

The final defeat of Napoleon's armies at Waterloo in 1815 and the collapse of the Empire resulted in the restoration of the Bourbon monarchy under Louis XVI's younger brother, Louis XVIII. The Revolution had left few physical monuments in the landscape, and the officials of the restored monarchy wasted little time in felling any liberty trees remaining from 1789–94. Supporters of the Restoration monarchy welcomed the chance to inscribe their own memories on the landscape, most notably in a huge expiatory chapel erected in 1829 on 'Martyrs Field' in Brech, west of Vannes (see Figure 3.1). The chapel holds the remains of more than 200 royalists executed in 1795 after the destruction by republican troops at Quiberon of a joint force of more than 5,000 royalist *émigrés* and many thousands of Breton peasant *chouans*.[20] Royalists nostalgic for imaginary idylls of pre-revolutionary

FIGURE 3.1 Royalists inscribed their memories on the landscape at Brech (Morbihan) in 1829 by erecting this expiatory chapel for the remains of some of those killed on the nearby champ des Martyrs (Martyrs Field) during an unsuccessful invasion against the French Republic in 1795. Peter McPhee.

France were to be disappointed, however, by the Restoration's acceptance of revolutionary changes to the meaning of private property and the lure of more productive uses of the landscape.

In particular, the first decades of the nineteenth century were busy for canal builders as they created engineered landscapes through hitherto unwelcoming terrain, especially where rivers shifted course and volume through the seasons. The pride of the Ancien Régime had been the Canal du Midi; now it was to the northeast that the monarchy turned its attention. Shipping along the river Somme, for example, had always been a challenge because of the shifting channels of the broad estuary and its vast tidal wetlands. In 1785, Louis XVI had agreed to a project to channel the lower Somme from the mouth at Saint-Valery-sur-Somme to Abbeville, but the project foundered because of technical difficulties in creating locks in the alluvial soils, and it was not until 1827 that Louis' youngest brother Charles X was able to open the canal. It would ultimately be linked to a network of canals through the northeast, from Calais and Lille to Saint-Quentin and Amiens. Eventually, there would be no free-flowing or 'wild' rivers in the northeast. While largely used for pleasure craft today, in the nineteenth century, these canals were the transport template on which an entire landscape was transformed.[21]

France's elaborate system of canals is often attributed to the foresight of the monarchy's engineers in the centuries before the Revolution of 1789 or the public works programme of public works minister Charles de Freycinet from 1878, but in fact 70 per cent of the network that criss-crosses the landscape today was the result of an ambitious project led under the Restoration monarchy after 1815 by Louis Becquey (1760–1849). Becquey was a fervent counter-revolutionary but equally committed to a vision of creating a unified national network of navigable waterways. France had approximately 1,000 kilometres of canals in 1800, but the project inspired by Becquey in the 1820s was to result in an extra 2,900 kilometres by 1848. The project was never as successful commercially as envisaged, in part because of a failure to secure a sufficient degree of uniformity in the engineering specifications, but it facilitated internal trade before the dramatic acceleration of railway construction after mid-century.[22]

The ambitious transport projects of the early decades of the century created a lattice of straight lines which mark the landscape to this day. The first half of the nineteenth century witnessed a great shift from water-borne transport as the most reliable to an emphasis on better roads.[23] The July Monarchy (1830–48) increased the construction of all-weather roads threefold, to 1,326 kilometres per year. For the millions of tourists who drive, ride and walk the roads of France each year, an iconic image is of straight stretches of roads bordered by plane trees. For others who hire barges along the 8,500 kilometres of canals and navigable rivers, there are similarly bucolic sights. They matter to French people, too: attempts by road safety campaigners to remove roadside trees have been thwarted by public backlash, most famously under President Pompidou in 1970. More recently, widespread dismay greeted news that more than 40,000 plane trees along the Canal du Midi, afflicted by the canker stain fungus, would probably be felled by 2040 (see Plate 3).

It is popularly believed that these millions of trees are part of France's Napoleonic heritage, planted to provide shelter for his troops marching along dusty southern roads in summer heat and for the labourers who worked the barges and locks along the canals. The story has an important grain of truth in it, even though it is to the *Ancien Régime* monarchy that we need to look for its origins in 1720. Certainly, Napoleon intensified the policy, instructing his prefects in the 110 departments of the Empire to establish tree nurseries for the purpose and, in 1806, encouraging property owners by allowing them to use public land along the roadsides if they planted trees at regular intervals. There were some notable successes in particular areas, but the Emperor gave impulsion to an existing policy rather than initiating or completing it. The scale of the project was simply too great to be realized easily: the main Paris-Bordeaux road needed 400,000 trees, or a forest of 1,500 hectares.[24]

Most of the trees first planted were in fact fruit trees; the plane trees that are ubiquitous today are a cross between eastern and western varieties that were developed to replace the trees killed by a microscopic mushroom, *Ceratocystis platani*, probably introduced into France in wooden weapons cases by US troops in 1944. But there are imposing examples of older, surviving plane trees: in the north of the department of Aude, for example, at Caunes-Minervois, two massive plane trees said to date from 1792 (others say the 1820s) on the Place de la République are dubbed by locals 'Robespierre' and 'Danton'.[25]

After the overthrow of the Bourbon Restoration in the Revolution of July 1830, the nature and range of economic intervention by its successor, the July Monarchy, were to be an important new departure in the direction of state-stimulated capitalism, which was to create new lines of communication across the landscape. Contemporaries such as Marx and Tocqueville mocked how the government conducted itself like a board of directors, but it was particularly bureaucrats such as Alexis Legrand (1791–1848), the director of Roads, Bridges and Mines, who trained in administration under Napoleon and now applied 'national interests' to the economy and pushed through plans for social, financial and communications infrastructure. We would today call their strategy one of private-public partnerships. So, for example, the project to build a canal to link the Meuse with the Seine basins via canals linking the Sambre and Oise rivers procured the necessary land and was then contracted out to the private firm Urbain et Piard in 1833. Works were carried out in 1834–9, together with river canalization.[26]

Most startling of all, however, were the first signs of a new form of transport, powered by coal-fired steam, which would create an entirely new network of *chemins de fer* (literally 'iron pathways') across the landscape. The new regime embraced the age of the railway, aware of the example of the steam-powered Liverpool and Manchester railways in 1830. In the words of Louis Estancelin, deputy for the Somme from the town of Eu in 1833, 'The government of the

Restoration wanted to mark its epoch by the general canalization of France, just as we want to mark ours by the railway, which in our enthusiastic imagination is today criss-crossing the kingdom'.[27] Trains introduced strange new sounds and smells into the landscape, and initially new terrors as well. In May 1842, a train returning to Paris from Versailles caught fire near Meudon. So intense was the conflagration that the exact numbers of dead passengers, locked in their carriages, could not be determined. There may have been up to two hundred, including Jules Dumont d'Urville, who had recently returned from celebrated voyages exploring the South Pacific.[28]

The railway strengthened the power of the state in its primordial claims over landscape. In the origins of railway construction of the 1840s, the state bought the land and built the lines, while private firms supplied the rolling stock and management. An important piece of legislation passed in 1833, regulating compensation for land appropriation by the state for railways, represented a significant, revealing victory of a concept of land as a commodity whose value was simply its market price against those who argued in vain for a concept of land having a 'valeur d'affection' for those who had worked it for generations.

A similar shift in the meaning of landscape and its use occurred in coal mining. Since the 1770s, the Norman entrepreneur Pierre-François Tubeuf, who had discovered a rich seam of coal at La Grand'Combe near Alès, had been dogged by the noble Castries family, recalcitrant local peasants and workers, and state indecision about below-surface mining concessions on private land. Tubeuf always hoped that the state would separate access to coal from the ownership of surface land. Only after 1830 was a régime in place with an approach which encouraged large-scale mining leases. By then, both Tubeuf and Castries had sold their mines to two local bourgeois, Jean-Jacques Puech and Pierre Goirand, who formed the La Grand'Combe company, backed by the prominent politician Odilon Barrot. In 1837, the July Monarchy granted them a loan of six million francs and opened one of the country's first railway lines, 100 kilometres from the mine via Nîmes to Beaucaire on the Rhône.[29] Today, the formerly bustling mining communities of La Grand'Combe and Decazeville, like the once proud textile centres of Lodève, Bédarieux and Clermont-de-Lodève, are deindustrialized shells. Bulk winegrowing on the lowlands of Languedoc was to become essentially an 'industrial' activity of far greater importance than coal mining. Instead, the northern extremity of winegrowing, which had reached as far as Laon, was to slowly retreat south to the Loire, while the slag heaps and pit heads of coal mines became prominent features of the landscapes of the Nord-Pas-de-Calais region in the northeast, the upper Loire region in the centre and parts of the Vosges and Jura mountains.

In some other regions, the years of the July Monarchy were a time of considerable change in output and soil use.[30] For example, well before the arrival of the railway, the lowland regions of the Ain and Jura were specializing in wine, the uplands in timber and stock-raising, as well as in silk and wooden and cow-horn combs and spindles used in textiles. In Mayenne, a proliferation of lime furnaces for fertilizer (from 88 to 200 in 1831–45) permitted a reduction in fallow from 150,000 to 100,000 hectares by 1850 and increased wheat yields from thirteen to fourteen hectolitres per hectare. In the years 1836–50, the area of sown pastures in Doubs increased from 13,000 to 30,000 hectares; the yields of wheat, barley and *méteil* rose by 25 per cent.[31]

The confidence of the middle-class improvers who dominated the July Monarchy was immortalized and satirized by Gustave Flaubert, whose *Madame Bovary* described the annual agricultural show in the town of Yonville, almost certainly based on Ry, northeast of Rouen in Normandy, in the 1830s. As Rodolphe seduced Emma, councillor Lieuvain from the prefecture extolled the virtues of agricultural improvement after the sadness of revolutions past:

> Everywhere commerce and the arts are flourishing; everywhere new means of communication, like so many new arteries in the body of the state, establish within it new relations. . . . our ports are full, confidence is born again, and France breathes once more! . . . Apply yourselves, above all, to the improvement of the soil, to good manure, to the development of the equine, bovine, ovine, and porcine races.[32]

Despite Lieuvain's panegyric and the dramatic intrusion of railways, new roads and canals, and coal mining works, the landscape of much of France remained dominated by traditional artisanal industries alongside pastoralism and subsistence agriculture. Rural France was more 'industrial' than before or since. The Provençal department of Var, for example, exported specialized crops such as olives, flowers and mulberries, as well as the products of craftwork. In the large villages (*bourgs*) around Brignoles, there were small perfumeries, soap works, tanneries (fifteen in Barjols alone) and paper manufactories. In 1845, there were over 700 corkmakers in the small communities of the Mauges; in the wooded uplands of the massif of Sainte-Baume, there were lignite mines, and *forges à la catalane* using local charcoal and iron ore from Elba.[33] The Provençal landscape, now dominated by vineyards, forests and the inexorable spread of housing, was then one of busy human and animal activity in a milieu of polyculture and manufacturing. But already the spread of large lavender fields around Valensole for the Molinard perfumerie in Grasse, founded in 1849, was prefiguring the landscape we know today. 'Eau de fleurs' had been produced in Grasse and elsewhere since the seventeenth century, but its commercial production was now to create a distinctive Provençal landscape.[34]

A key legacy of the French Revolution had been the fundamental principle that individual landowners had the right to exploit their property as they wished, but a major qualification had been the reassertion that the state had overarching power over all forest resources, not just state forests. Deep antipathy to the privileges that had once belonged to 'corporations' within the state – such as the Catholic clergy, the nobility and trade associations – had led revolutionary assemblies to abolish self-regulating or autonomous institutions. The imperatives of environmental protection now impelled the state to recognize the need for other limitations to individual rights. Post-revolutionary governments were forced to recognize the utility of the associations (*wateringues*), which controlled lowlands prone to flooding and tides, as in 1798 in western France along the deltas of the Sèvre Niortaise, Charente and Loire, and in 1806 along the delta of the Aa River from Saint-Omer to Dunkerque. This was extended in 1837 by a royal ordinance which sought to codify arrangements for the protection of lowlands prone to tidal flooding or on coastal deltas, creating a national system of proprietors' associations to which landowners contributed in proportion to their properties.[35]

The realization that the state had an essential role to play in mitigating the excesses of private enterprise and in protecting the environment did not extend to a valorization of particular landscapes as significant in themselves. In 1833, the historian and novelist Prosper Mérimée was appointed to the new position of inspector-general of historical monuments, with the mission to identify those buildings and other monuments in need of protection and restoration. Mérimée threw himself into the task, making nineteen tours to different regions of France by 1852. In 1840, he published the first official list of monuments, with 1,082 entries; by 1848, there were 2,800. But these were urban constructions threatened with decay, not landscapes. One of his most extensive tours was through the Auvergne in 1838, but his travels across the great plain of the Limagne led him only to a detailed analysis of the Battle of Gergovie, where Gallic tribes under Vercingetorix gathered to confront Julius Caesar's Roman legions in 52 BCE.[36] Had Mérimée detailed his observations on the Limagne as a landscape, he would have noted that locals were continuing to drain the ponds and swamps, and that livestock and orchard industries were giving way to the cultivation of wheat, barley, tobacco, and sugar beet.[37]

The surface calm of much of the French countryside today shrouds a history of tensions over resources which had erupted in 1789 and remained volatile across the first half of the nineteenth century. The entire period 1789–1851 was one of deep-rooted conflict over who controlled the landscape and how it was to be used. Honoré de Balzac's great rural novel *Les Paysans* (1846) – in his words, 'the most important of those I've resolved to write' – showed in an expert way the ongoing struggle of the rural poor to maintain collective rights, in this case in the department of Yonne in Burgundy during the Restoration. The 'social question' was also explored in George Sand's rural novels of 1845–7, the best of the eighty or so novels she wrote: *Le Péché de M. Antoine*, *Le Meunier d'Angibault*, *François le Champi*, and *La Mare au diable*.

It is difficult to hear the voices of French peasants articulating what they made of the great stress placed on the landscape by the revolutionary years of conflict over rural resources and the impact of the demands of war on forests in particular. We can listen to their voices primarily in courts of law when they were being prosecuted for the illegal use of forest or other resources and therefore in circumstances where they were least likely to be candid about their motivations and attitudes. Their resentments of restrictions on ancient collective rights to use forest resources and common land are nonetheless palpable. Certainly, there were influential, educated voices of concern, such as the engineer François-Antoine Rauch (1762–1837), a foundation advocate of French environmentalism. Rauch highlighted the acceleration of tree-felling and land clearing during the Revolution and the increased vulnerability of Paris and other cities to floods as a consequence of deforestation. Rauch described the 'deplorable' state of much of rural France, with an exhausted environment struggling to meet the needs of what he saw as rapacious rural inhabitants.[38]

Rauch's love of landscape found an echo in art. In France, as elsewhere in Europe, there had been a long tradition of landscape painting, although it was almost always a way of providing a physical background to a human subject or building, as in the work of Jean-Victor Bertin. It was at Bertin's instigation that the revived Académie des Beaux-Arts, dissolved during the Revolution, created a special prize in 1817 for 'historical landscapes'. The prize-winners would be artists whose huge masterpieces would privilege classical antiquity and its most famous sites, exemplified in the Italian landscapes of the initial winner, Achille-Etna Michallon.[39] The favoured style reflected the strictures of the first French treatise on landscape painting, Pierre-Henri de Valenciennes' *Practical elements of perspective for the use of artists . . . on the genre of landscape painting* (1799), in which he advocated for 'historical landscapes', a sub-set of epic historical paintings.[40] Those few artists who depicted the countryside painted tortured landscapes under stormy skies as allegories of the revolutionary tempest, notably in the work of Georges Michel (see Plate 7). Others, less commonly, turned to coastal landscapes. While the sea had been imagined popularly as a source of terror, monsters and death as well as of food in the eighteenth century, in the early decades of the nineteenth century painters such as Camille Roqueplan and Eugène Isabey increasingly painted the shore as a place of leisure and restoration.[41]

Only with Camille Corot and others of the Barbizon 'school' did the landscape per se, rather than its emotional register, become the subject. In the spring of 1829, Corot first came to Barbizon to paint in the forest of Fontainebleau. While there he met the members of the Barbizon school, among them Théodore Rousseau, Charles-François Daubigny and Jean-François Millet. Millet soon distinguished his work by a prolific output of paintings of peasants at work, in which the landscape was contextual (see Plate 9), but Corot and others found in the oak and beech forest of Fontainebleau, its rocks, streams and sand, the perfect refuge from the pollution, noise, disease and political instability of Paris. Rousseau, Corot and others campaigned against the introduction of non-native pines which the forest administration saw as the rapid solution to illegal tree-felling.[42]

Environmental pressures only increased across the first half of the century. Between 1811 and 1841, the rural population – people living in communities with fewer than 2,000 inhabitants – increased from 23.4 to 26.9 million (15 per cent). The rural population was at its historic peak. It was in the Pyrenees that population pressure on soil resources was most acute. In the first half of the century, the population of Ariège increased by 36 per cent, of Hautes-Pyrénées by 44 per cent and that of Haute-Garonne (excluding Toulouse) by 31 per cent. In the region of Couserans, the population density was fifty persons per square kilometre, whereas a century later it would be only twenty. As a consequence of population increase and more extensive cultivation (from about 16 million hectares in 1789 to 20.6 million in 1840), greater strain was placed on the environment. This was particularly the case in forests and on 'wastelands', which sustained bird and animal life. The increasing demand for charcoal for industry and heating accelerated tree-felling: in Pyrénées-Orientales, where there were many small *forges catalanes*, the forested area declined from 300,000 to 66,000 hectares in 1730–1830, and by 1850 was at its smallest ever size. In steep river valleys, this led to erosion and ruinous lowland flooding.[43]

Despite the increasing use of coal for domestic fuel and for steam-powered transport by water and rail, the pressures on France's forest resources were acute at a time of increasing population and the continuing reliance on wood and charcoal for fuel. Conscious of the pressures increased populations were placing on dwindling forests, the state sought, in 1827 and 1846, to restrict access to resources formerly available for wood-gathering, especially for heating and for stock-grazing. Even though the extent of forested land increased, perhaps to 15 per cent by mid-century, the provisions of these forest codes disadvantaged the rural poor in relation to the needs of the military and the interests of wealthy individual proprietors and entrepreneurs. They threatened the viability of thousands of highland communities in the Ardennes, Jura, Alps, Massif Central and Pyrenees. In the central Pyrenees, for example, income from private forests had trebled since 1789, largely because the number of forges had increased (from 43 to 57 in 1818–44) and the additional forges alone needed 15,000 hectares of forest per year.

Further state intervention proved necessary in order to regulate the Revolution's abolition of the hunting privileges of seigneurial lords. The wholesale destruction of wildlife finally convinced the government to pass a law in May 1844 seeking to constrain 'democratic' hunting; however, the right it accorded to large landowners to control who could hunt on their property was hotly resented by poorer hunters. Again, the recognition in November 1793 of 'the right of all to fish in all waterways' had resulted in severe overfishing and a law of April 1829 introduced limits on the taking of fish species and on fish sizes, policed by fishing inspectors.[44] A similarly revealing ambiguity existed in hunting laws, tightened in 1844 to protect wildlife endangered by the democratization of hunting after 1789 but permitted to those with the money to purchase the requisite licence.

Another of the great unresolved issues of the revolutionary period, the confrontation of ancient collective rights (*droits d'usage*) to forests, common land and gleaning with the individual property rights sanctified in the Code Rural of the Revolution and subsequent legislation, was still being played out in the 1840s.[45] Conflict over control and use of forests was endemic, especially in the Pyrenees and the east. While anger at the forest codes of 1827 and 1846 underpinned popular action, local factors often made a tense situation more complex, where large landowners had sought to limit community access to their private forests for fuel and pastures because of the value of wood as fuel for forges.

When news of the overthrow of the monarchy and the proclamation of the Second Republic in February 1848 reached the countryside, those regions where conflict over resources had been most acute erupted in violent protest. The collapse of political authority and the assumption that the new régime was somehow 'the people's' emboldened rural inhabitants to attack the local manifestations of structures of power and wealth which threatened their existence. For several months in 1848, as during the French Revolution sixty years earlier, the tensions at the heart of rural life spilt over into attempts to appropriate the landscape to different ends. This was especially the case in forested areas in the Pyrenees, Cévennes and Alps. So widespread were the illegal collective invasions of forests in the spring of 1848 that the new republic needed to mobilize nearly 50,000 soldiers in its endeavours to enforce the forest codes of previous administrations and the private property of individual owners of forests.

Elsewhere, communal land was the focus of protest. In Paimpont (Ille-et-Vilaine), rural people invaded former communal lands which had been sold to a noble for forestry, taking with them their cattle and erecting two liberty trees. In at least fifteen communities of the Pyrénées-Orientales, collective action resulted, albeit temporarily, either in alienated communal lands being returned to collective use or in the lands being subdivided equally between all inhabitants or families. Similarly, at Plomion (Aisne), popular action opposed the council's decision to lease out communal lands and instead demanded successfully that they be equally divided.[46]

The mid-nineteenth-century crisis was multifaceted. While commonly seen only as a failed attempt to establish a new republic, it was more broadly the culmination of a sixty-year period of intense conflict over control of the landscape and its resources, which had become open in 1789. The disastrous grain and potato harvests of 1846 created a durable economic depression aggravated by revolution and acute political divisions after 1848. A profound social and political crisis spilt over into civil war in Paris in June 1848 and in parts of the south after Louis-Napoléon seized power by military *coup d'État* in December 1851. About 100,000 rural people took up arms in protest against the *coup*, the largest rebellion since the Great Fear of 1789.

But it was also a crisis of demography and of pressure on the environment. By 1850, the rural population of France reached its historic peak: of the 35.8 million French people in 1851, about twenty-seven million would have been directly dependent on agriculture and pastoralism. The pressure on natural resources, especially on forests and vulnerable hillsides, had never been so acute. In the spring of 1851, the quinquennial census showed a total population of 35,783,000, a minimal increase (383,000) over that of 1846. While the national rate of population growth had been 0.68 per cent per annum in the five years before 1846, in the years of crisis thereafter it was just 0.22 per cent. In twenty-one of the eighty-six departments (and 137 of the 363 districts), the impact of emigration more than cancelled out any natural increase in population.

This was a critical turning point in the demographic history of France, one which would have major repercussions for rural landscapes and their uses. While the urban population continued to increase, the rural population declined in absolute terms for the first time in a century. It never recovered. Migration from the most impoverished areas of the countryside began to quicken its pace and incidence as families found it more difficult to balance their desire to keep the family together against the survival of the household. In some mountainous southern departments in the Pyrenees, southern Massif Central and Alps the population fell by 2 to 3 per cent between 1846 and 1851. Years of political uncertainty aggravated the sharp economic rationale for this emigration and also led people to delay marriage and conception.[47]

For many members of the most embattled rural communities, the hopes invested in the new republic were too distant in the face of the economic crisis, which broke in 1846 and deepened after 1848. The response of the rural poor was often to postpone having children or simply to leave the countryside for good. The mid-century economic crisis had made life impossible for huge numbers of people. The countryside they left behind was to become steadily less populated but more productive, and its landscapes more highly valued.

4 'MANY CONQUESTS TO MAKE', 1850–80

Never had the landscape been so crowded with people and their livestock as in 1850; never before had resources been so stretched and woodlands so exploited. By the mid-nineteenth century, the population of rural France had reached its historic peak (about twenty-seven million) and the cultivated land surface had reached its maximum area. Then a gradual rural exodus, already apparent in the poorest highland regions in the 1840s, was accelerated by the protracted economic and political crisis of mid-century. The economic crisis of 1846–51 had had a ruinous impact on many small rural industries dependent on a buoyant agricultural climate. A combination of the decline in work opportunities and the perceived attractions of the city quickened the exodus of the poorest sections of rural society.

In the fifteen years after 1851, the years of the most rapid urban population growth in the nineteenth century, sixty-five rural departments experienced an excess of emigration over natural increase.[1] Many of the people who left were young labourers wholly or partly dependent on wage work, a declining birth rate in consequence aggravating the effects of their departure. There were fewer wage-labouring poor in the countryside compared with small farmers. In the northern coastal department of Manche, for example, the proportion of labourers in the male agricultural workforce declined from 34 per cent in 1851 to 12 per cent in 1882, while that of landowners increased from 49 to more than 62 per cent.[2]

Paradoxical as it may seem, the countryside was becoming more 'rural' in appearance. Much of the manufacturing in pre-industrial France had been rural handicrafts (or 'proto-industries') in textiles and metallurgy, activities which after 1850 gradually became concentrated in urban centres. Subsequently, the more frequent purchase of urban manufactures, many of them previously produced within rural communities themselves, made much of the countryside more agricultural. This was a rural landscape dominated more than ever before by farms smaller than 10 hectares, some 68 per cent of all properties in 1852 and steadily increasing.[3] Many of the tiny plots of the very poor who had left for the cities were added to larger peasant holdings. Intensively farmed small holdings remained a singular feature of the French landscape, the durable consequence of the successful peasant revolution after 1789. In good times, for example, a holding of 2 hectares in wine country could support 20,000 vines and a family.

Across the decades after 1850, the countryside slowly became less crowded and more prosperous for small farmers. But the relative prosperity of the countryside was not universal. The exodus of the rural poor towards cities and towns was accelerated after 1850 by a series of biological crises, which particularly hit plants which had thrived on poorer, terraced hills in the south. In 1860 and 1865, the Ink disease, a plant pathogen, killed many chestnut trees in the Massif Central, and then silkworms were killed by the pebrine epidemic. Louis Pasteur's discovery of a solution to the epidemic came too late for most producers. Finally, from 1862 until the late 1870s, the phylloxera aphid devastated at least 40 per cent of France's vineyards.

The experience of the department of Ardèche exemplifies the impact of these diseases. Here, as in other departments ringing Lyon, the first half of the century had been boom years for the supply of the raw materials for the silk industry concentrated in the city. Mulberry trees – dubbed 'the trees of gold' – had spread across the stony plateaux and hillsides, competing with a staple food of the poor, the chestnut. In the words of Jules Michelet in 1844, 'this rough countryside, where all is rock, or mulberry trees and chestnut trees, seems to do without soil, living from air and stone'. By the late 1840s, there were as many as four million mulberry trees in Ardèche, with the well-fed silkworms producing 3.5 million kilograms of cocoons. The pebrine disease which killed young worms was catastrophic: by 1857, only 550,000 kilograms were produced. By the 1880s, silk-throwing factories were using raw silk from Piedmont and Japan, and, by the 1950s, local production had fallen to 90,000 kilograms. At around the same time, the Ink disease began attacking the extensive chestnut groves, and most trees were felled, never to be replanted. Instead, visitors to the Ardèche are today far more likely to see fruit trees, particularly peach trees.[4]

A third crisis coincided with the mulberry and chestnut tree diseases when the phylloxera lice began attacking grapevines. The parasite appeared in Gard in 1862, reached Beaujolais in 1871 and Burgundy in 1878. By 1876, one-third of the vineyards in Ardèche had been destroyed. In the southern Ardèche village of Balazuc, only one hundred hectares of vines, one-sixth of the total, produced any wine in 1876. The silkworm industry had already collapsed. Locals quipped that the long-awaited railway had arrived just in time, in 1876, for people to catch it as they left the area for good. Five years later, the population had fallen from 802 to 694. The winegrowing industry slowly recovered in Balazuc, but the 90 hectares of mulberry trees were gradually abandoned altogether, and today they survive only among the bushes which have reclaimed the stony fields (*gras*) around the village.[5]

The time and costs involved in the reconstruction of vineyards resulted in northern regions ill-suited to winegrowing abandoning it almost entirely: Bresse, the Paris basin, the areas of heavier soils in the Limagne in the Auvergne, the north of Burgundy and elsewhere. Only in areas capable of producing high-quality wine were terraces replanted, their closely defined lines one of the most distinctive and valued features of the southern landscape today, for example, on the Côte Vermeille near Banyuls-sur-Mer, the Côtes de Millau in Aveyron, the *restanques* of Cassis and Bandol in Provence, the scattered terraces between Thann and Ribeauvillé in Alsace and the vineyard of Saint-Joseph Hospice in Tournon (Ardèche). In Alsace, where the total area of vineyards had reached 30,000 hectares by 1828, only about 9,500 would be reconstituted after the phylloxera and *mildiou* crises, a size that persisted into the 1960s. Unlike most of France's other wine areas, however, such was the quality of wine that subsequent producers were able to achieve with pinot gris, muscat, riesling and other white wines that today the Alsacien *vignoble* covers about 15,500 hectares.[6]

The disappearance of many small industries like raising silkworms combined with the fundamental economic change in rural France in the nineteenth century: the transition from essentially subsistence polyculture or mixed farming to market-oriented specialization. While in some regions this transition resembled the English model, characterized by extensive grain production on large-scale tenant farm holdings, elsewhere a more common pattern involved peasants becoming small entrepreneurs or specialized farmers. In certain regions – the Paris basin, the northeast, the environs of cities – this transformation had long predated the nineteenth century; in other areas – parts of Brittany and the Massif Central – it did not occur until the early decades of the twentieth century. In most regions, however, there were clear signs of change across the early decades of the nineteenth century. Then the rapid expansion of the railway network under the Second Empire further enabled this agricultural specialization, changing the landscape in the process.

The combined impact of these changes – rural emigration, falling birth rates, plant diseases, the collapse of many rural industries and an acceleration of specialized agriculture – was to render much of rural France a different world from that of the 1840s. Much of the occupational complexity of rural communities began to disappear. In turn, regional landscapes themselves became less varied as farmers concentrated on the most productive use of the soil. Though this process varied in timing across the face of the countryside, it proved to be inexorable.[7] Agricultural specialization and the 'deindustrialization' of rural life hastened the breakdown of ancient agrarian routines and, with them, the celebrations and festivals associated with the seasonal routines of agricultural and religious life. By 1880, rural France was more 'agrarian' than ever before, with whole regions now becoming monocultural and dependent on the urban suppliers of manufactured goods formerly produced within the community. In countless villages, the grocer and baker replaced the charcoal burner and weaver.

Physical remnants of this great shift in the use of landed resources are to be found across the landscape today, especially in the southern half of the country.

As the first harvesting and threshing machines increased agricultural productivity dramatically on the plains and valleys, many thousands of kilometres of ancient terracing were abandoned, their ruins still visible today on hillsides south of a line running from Biarritz to Strasbourg. The mountainsides of the Massif Central, Languedoc and Provence are today studded with drystone huts varying in size from tiny shelters to substantial dwellings, but all of them are remnants of pastoral economies that have either disappeared or have been relocated in towns. In Provence, these *bories* or *cabanes* were used as animal shelters or temporary dwellings by farmers on plots distant from home; in the Massif Central, the *burons* in the high pastures of the Cézallier and the Aubrac were where men spent summer producing cows-milk cheeses such as Cantal or Salers; on hillsides in Languedoc and Roussillon, the *cabanes*, *capitelles* and *baraques* are evidence of a pastoral economy of sheep and goats which has almost disappeared.

The most famous example of the *bories* is the village of the same name, a collection of twenty dwellings outside the town of Gordes (Vaucluse), but equally important are the forty or so *capitelles* spread over three hundred hectares of the commune of Conques-sur-Orbiel north of Carcassonne (see Figure 4.1). These are not to be confused with the more recent small drystone shelters which dot vineyards, usually called *cabanes* in the south and *cadoles* in Champagne,

FIGURE 4.1 Across the stony hillsides of Conques-sur-Orbiel (Aude), there are about forty drystone *capitelles*, used as dwellings by shepherds of the vast flocks of sheep which rapidly declined across the nineteenth century. Peter McPhee.

Beaujolais and Burgundy.[8] Most remarkable of all, however, is one of the least known landscapes of France, the Plateau de Leucate, a vast, craggy limestone bluff which separates the Mediterranean from the Étang de Leucate between Narbonne and Perpignan. Here there are more than two hundred drystone enclosures and *cabanes* on about ten square kilometres, now slowly disappearing under regenerating scrub and trees (see Plate 5). Many of the drystone walls run in parallel lines, built to shelter narrow fields from the powerful north wind (*tramontane* in Catalan, *cers* in Occitan), icy in winter and searing in summer. The walls of the fields could be used as shelters for almond trees and vines in particular, but above all for the hundreds of thousands of sheep which wintered there from the Pyrenees.[9]

The plateau dominates the autoroute and railway lines which carry millions of tourists annually between France and Spain but, apart from local enthusiasts, it is known mainly to the windsurfers on the *étang* who have used the sheltered areas between the walls for rough camping. There are hundreds of other examples of these enclosures on the arid limestone hills in the surrounding area, at Fitou, Opoul, Estagel and elsewhere, testimony both to the harshness of the environment and a pastoral economy which has disappeared. The surrounding hillsides of the eastern Corbières have never recovered from many centuries of deforestation and grazing. They are also evidence of the long struggle dating back to the French Revolution when the poorest peasants in the *garrigue* areas of Languedoc seized sections of rough hillside pastures formerly controlled by local lords in the hope of planting vines or grazing animals.

Rural landscapes were changing in another, more direct way. While railway lines had commenced under the July Monarchy, the great boom of construction began after 1848: by 1871, there were 15,632 kilometres of lines and 40,838 kilometres by 1911. Demand for coal, iron and steel trebled accordingly in these decades. From the 1840s, the landscape of the northeast was abruptly altered by the impact of coal mining in a crescent 120 kilometres by 30 kilometres from Aire-sur-la-Lys to Valenciennes and by the intricate system of railways to support its extraction and metallurgy. Here, the dominant built features on the landscape would now be the pitheads and slag heaps of the mines rather than the church steeples of the villages.[10] The great shift from timber and charcoal to coal as the primary source of combustion was by now definitive, although France would never be self-sufficient in coal.

Rural landscapes, which were studded with stone farmhouses, villages and towns, were now being criss-crossed by the new *chemins de fer*. In places, the demands of topography resulted in towering works of engineering brilliance that rivalled the medieval cathedrals. Along the gorges of the Sioule river in the Auvergne, for example, are two astonishing viaducts, the first of the type for which a young engineer named Gustave Eiffel (born 1832) would become famous. The 130-metre Viaduc de Rouzat and the Viaduc de Neuvial (both in Bègues, Allier)

FIGURE 4.2 The Rouzat Viaduct, at Bègues (Allier), was one of several dramatic intrusions into the landscape on the Commentry-Gannat railway line in 1869, constructed by the company formed by Gustave Eiffel (b. 1823). Peter McPhee.

were constructed in 1869 to carry a railway high above the gorge between Gannat and Commentry, west of Vichy, as part of the Lyon-Bordeaux line (see Figure 4.2).

The public works agenda of the Second Empire also completed or added nearly 630 kilometres of canals, including the canal of the Houillières de la Sarre built to carry coal from the mines around Saarbrücken in Germany and others oriented around the coal mining and industrial centres of the east and northeast. Others linked the mining areas of the upper Loire with Paris via the canals of Bourgogne and the Nivernais. The planting of trees along the banks of the canals – today such an iconic feature of France's canal system – was undertaken to prevent evaporation and to protect workers and animals who laboured along the banks. The Canal du Berry alone already had 188,000 trees by 1847.

Increasing ease of rapid movement of goods by rail, canal and macadam roads accelerated the transition to regional specialization according to soil types. Much of Languedoc abandoned its traditional triple production of wheat, olives and grapes to concentrate solely on the last. Fruit, vegetables and flowers for major urban centres could be cultivated along the lower Loire, the Garonne and the Rhône, where this was a time of mass plantings of cypress pines, and later poplars, as windbreaks. Only more isolated regions perpetuated the subsistence polyculture typical of France for centuries. Instead, much of Normandy became a massive dairy produce region, with the emergence of 'specialties' like Camembert or petits-suisses at Gournay-en-Bray.[11] The opening of a railway line linking Bayonne to Bordeaux and Paris in 1856 enabled regions such as the undulating Chalosse around Dax in the distant southwest to develop its fame as a land of high-quality beef cattle and wine rather than subsistence polyculture. The celebrated Corsican citron (*alimea* in Corsican or *cedrat* in French) was now exported in huge quantities as *confit* for confectionery and cooking.[12]

Black truffles, the fruiting body of a subterranean fungus, had been prized in gastronomy for many centuries but now would become more readily available. In the first half of the nineteenth century, enterprising cultivators around Carpentras in Provence had begun to see the possibilities of commercial cultivation of the tuber around plantations of oaks which favoured its growth. But it was particularly the impact of phylloxera in the 1860s which drove small farmers in the Périgord Noir in southwestern France to shift from winegrowing to truffle cultivation, aided by the new network of railway lines which enabled truffles to arrive fresh in Paris. The invention and utilization of sterile conservation, following the discoveries by Nicolas Appert earlier in the century, facilitated their export worldwide. By 1890, *truffières* (truffle plantations) covered 750 square kilometres of land in France, and 2,000 tonnes of truffles were produced in that year.[13]

Driving the infrastructure projects across the landscape was the zeal of Louis-Napoleon himself. The revaluation of 'wasteland' was for him a national mission in which he would set a personal example. After seizing power by military *coup* in December 1851, in April 1852 he took one of his first trips as prince-president into the Sologne, where, at Lamotte-Beuvron in the heart of the region, he later bought an estate of 3,382 hectares around the Château de Saint-Maurice. He gave new impetus to the complex drainage systems oriented around the relaunched Canal de la Sauldre. The canal, constructed to drain marshes and transport marl (a mix of clay and limestone used to improve acidic soils), would have a short working life, but today it is celebrated by tourists on bicycles and barges. Under Louis-Napoleon more than 100,000 hectares were replanted in pines. Forests now cover three-quarters of the region between the moors and peat bogs, although the pines have been at the expense of the indigenous oak and birch. Similarly, in the Champagne region east of Reims, Napoleon III established new forests on 100,000 hectares of *savarts*, dry grasslands on limestone, on which flocks of sheep had grazed.[14]

On 9 October 1852, the prince-president made a crucial speech at a banquet organized by the Bordeaux chamber of commerce, with repeated allusions to the transition to a new Empire, like his uncle's:

I must admit that, like the Emperor, I have many conquests to make. . . . We have huge uncultivated territories to clear, roads to open, ports to dig, rivers to render navigable, canals to finish and our network of railways to complete . . . That is what I shall understand the Empire to mean, if indeed the Empire is to be re-established.[15]

The speech was doubly significant: first, because of his explicit references to his uncle and to 'Empire', foreshadowing the plebiscite of November which made him emperor; and second, because of the clear agenda outlined for an economic expansion based on state infrastructure initiatives through the private sector.

By 'uncultivated territories to clear', Louis-Napoleon was thinking of the vast *landes* which stretched hundreds of kilometres south and west of Bordeaux to the foothills of the Pyrenees. His uncle had hoped to see them drained and cultivated. The Landes de Gascogne covered about 600,000 hectares, including the department of Landes but also parts of Gironde and Lot-et-Garonne. The law of 19 June 1857 authorized and required the draining of nearly 300,000 hectares of the moors, mostly on the vast commons on which sheep had grazed. Communes were required to plant and sell off their common lands at auction. The most ambitious public works project since the construction of the Canal du Midi in the seventeenth century was to transform the region and create the landscape of the southwest as we know it today.[16]

To agricultural 'improvers' since the eighteenth century, the *landes* had been visualized as a barren wilderness, even a 'desert', because of the aridity of the thin sandy soil in the parched summers. In fact, the *landes* were neither barren nor a desert. They were peopled by thousands of pastoral families in which those entrusted with shepherding the sheep famously did so at times on *escaça* or stilts, both to gain a vantage point over the flat pastures and to avoid the winter bogs.[17] The region was covered with patches of indigenous tree cover across its moorlands. In winter, however, the clay-based subsoil known locally as *aliòs* prevented rainwater from permeating, creating vast marshes and replenishing the lakes (see Figure 4.3).

Napoleon III's vision was to use a combination of drainage and forestation works to create plantations of maritime pine trees, the basis of an economy of timber and resin. The Emperor took a close personal interest in the project and purchased more than 7,600 hectares in the area, creating a new commune in 1863 by consolidating several neighbouring communes and naming it after his victorious battle at Solferino against the Austrian army in June 1859. There had already been about 184,000 hectares of forests on the moorlands by mid-century, but in the twenty years after 1853 this increased to 604,000. There was a consequent sharp decline in the numbers of livestock, from 540,000 sheep and 34,000 goats in 1852 to 300,000 sheep forty years later. Not only did the decline in livestock numbers deplete the manure for the soil, but a remarkable pastoral culture was eroded and finally destroyed.

Along the coastline was a distinct zone of the *landes*, a shifting shoreline of sand dunes, some of them immense, like the Dune du Pilat, one hundred metres high. Even before the Revolution, officials had begun to plant pines and marram grass around fishing communities such as La Teste in the hope of preventing them from being engulfed by sand. The railway and property entrepreneurs Émile and Isaac Pereire, who had grown up in the region, were pivotal to a radical transformation of the Atlantic coastline. Until the 1850s, Arcachon had been a community of a few hundred fishers and peasants; by 1859, the Pereires had linked it by rail to Bordeaux to facilitate visitors to their new casino and resort, and Napoleon had proclaimed it a separate commune. Its population grew from 736 in 1861 to 3,696 within a decade. The Pereires themselves created the immensely profitable Pereire Company for the Development of the Landes and bought 10,000 hectares, which were cleared and planted in pines for the sleepers for the rails which would transport produce.[18]

The adventures with maritime pine were not unchecked successes. In the Sologne, the hard winter of 1879–80 was too much for them, and they were replaced with Baltic pine and chestnuts. In the department of Landes, the ease with which the displaced shepherds could reconquer grazing lands by arson has been compounded ever since by the vulnerability of the pine forests to summer bushfires. Some 30,000 hectares of young forest were burned in Landes in 1868–9.

With the incorporation in 1859 of Savoie and Nice during the Second Empire, metropolitan France reached much the same dimensions as today, about 550,000 square kilometres. Perhaps 17 per cent was wooded, but at a time when France was overwhelmingly powered by wood and the railway boom was commencing, this was critically low. The territorial expansion brought hundreds of thousands of hectares of Alpine forest into France, adding to the Second Empire's ambitious reforestation project, which ultimately covered 1,182,000 hectares. This was one of the most dramatic transformations in the history of the French landscape, not only in the *landes*, the Sologne and parts of Champagne but also in the Corbières, Larzac and on Mont Ventoux in Provence. Mont Ventoux, described in the 1850s as 'the sole realm of thyme and lavender, almost devoid of trees', is today mostly covered in dense forest. At its foot, the village of Bédoin, today famous for its forested entry onto the most challenging stage of the Tour de France, was then similarly bare.[19]

Napoleon III was further impelled to act by an ecological disaster, in large part caused by the denuding of forest cover on uplands such as Mont Ventoux. Agronomists and scientists were well aware of the connections between deforestation and the floods which had been frequent in France, especially since the mid-eighteenth century. By the mid-nineteenth century, however, the consequences had become ruinous. In 1836, 1840, 1846 and especially 1856, huge areas were devastated. The flood of 1856 impacted fifty of France's eighty-four departments: parts of the east and southwest received up to 300 millilitres of rain in May, causing the Loire to rise to a height of 7.5 metres in places. Thirty people drowned in regions along the river. Floodwaters in the Saône swept through Lyon before joining the Rhône and flooding Avignon and Arles, then killing livestock in the Camargue, which was under more than two metres of water. The great plain from Toulouse to Bordeaux was inundated, and crops were lost across 46,000 hectares. Ultimately, the pressure from scientists like Alexandre Surell and the administration of both Ponts et Chaussées and Eaux et Forêts, which had suffered huge losses of infrastructure, impelled the government to introduce legislation in 1860 and 1864.[20]

A combination of reforestation following these laws and the decline in the population of beleaguered upland communities permitted the slow, chequered recovery of mountain ecologies. Some hillsides had been so denuded by overuse over the centuries that they were never to recover. There were other areas, however, where forests had been saved from the devastations of fire by the presence of highlanders clearing undergrowth and smothering spot fires.

The zeal of the forests administration to rehabilitate 'devastated' forests took little account of the farming practices of highlanders in regions such as the Pyrenees and Savoie.[21] Just as in the Alps, however, attempts by the regime to tame and 'civilize' the landscape were contested and sidestepped by local populations. The same applied in Corsica, where the practice of *vaine pâture* – whereby local communities could take their flocks onto untilled pastures, particularly on hillsides – was integral to the pastoral industry. Government concern over the degradation of forests by goats led it to ban the practice altogether in June 1854. The inspector of forests at Ajaccio had calculated that such pasturage was worth 1.5 million francs annually but that damage to forests cost nine million, including that from fires lit by shepherds to encourage new growth. But such was the dependence of the mass of the peasantry on this extra resource that the law was ignored altogether and abrogated in 1891.[22]

Land deemed to be 'wasteland' was not only to be used for reforestation. The government of the Second Empire was determined to diminish the attraction of socialism for the rural poor and saw land sales as one solution. An 1860 report claimed that there was abundant common land that could be privatized: 2.7 million hectares of uncultivated commons (often known as *landes, garrigues* or *terres vaines et vagues*); 322,000 hectares of cultivated land in the public domain; and 58,000 hectares of swamps that could be drained. The new law on commons lands of 4 August 1860 in effect completed the law of 1857 on the Landes de Gascogne.[23] The lawmakers claimed that remaining common land would be better managed and protected if sold off to private owners, anticipating a famously controversial argument by the American ecologist Garrett Hardin in 1968 that 'the tragedy of the commons' was that common ownership led to individual misuse. In pastoral areas especially, however, rural communities had long shown themselves to be capable of sustainable collective management on common land and, as in 1793, resisted pressures to divide commons that were more valuable as a community resource for pastures than as tiny individual plots. Hardin himself later regretted his simplification.[24]

The impulse to *revaloriser* so-called wastelands was just as powerful in the French colonies. So in Algeria, the colonial administration facilitated the private ownership and use of land forested with Aleppo pines and cork oaks and set aside forests for trees rather than shepherds and peasant farmers. As in the Alps and the Pyrenees, determined administrators perceived nomadic pastoralists to be responsible for the exposed hillsides.[25] In 1838, the forest code of 1827 was applied to Algeria, and after 1850, forest administrators proceeded on the basis that the problems and policies were the same, despite stark differences in the nature of the forests and the culture and economy of their inhabitants.

The forest code was never as successfully applied in Algeria as in France itself. As in the *landes*, local populations of shepherds resorted to arson to protect pastures from the encroachment of private property and new uses of resources. The project in Algeria had parallels with the 'improvement' schemes for agriculture in the *landes*, not only because it involved a radical replacement of an existing biosystem but also because, like the shepherds of the southwest, colonial indigenes had been described as 'savage'. Certainly, administrators were determined that their presence was not to be an impediment to progress. The same was generally true later in the century in French colonies in southeast Asia, where the application of French forest policy and techniques seemed deaf to local knowledge and prioritized commercial exploitation over sustainability.[26]

*   *   *

The slight easing of pressure on soil resources is one reason why the decades between 1852 and 1880 have been described as 'the peak of rural civilization'. While forest resources were at their lowest extent, on cultivated land peasant polyculture was conservative of soil resources.[27] A growing population in town and country was fed without recourse to artificial fertilizers and pesticides; virtually all human and animal wastes were returned to the soil; and a rich variety of plant sub-species and local farming practices flourished. Never before had so many countryfolk lived in relative security and even prosperity for many, nor had such easy access to education, travel and outside ideas. And never again afterwards would rural France be such a diverse human and natural environment in its languages, cultures, fauna and flora, and patterns of production.

At the same time, the signs were evident of the future decay of this agrarian civilization, which was ultimately to prove incompatible with market-oriented agriculture. Specialized agriculture and the collapse of part-time industrial work narrowed the range of occupations and skills within the community and the household. The dramatic expansion of the road and canal network, and the first signs of the possibilities of the new railways represented a transport revolution which would further change the landscape. Changes in resource use, land clearance and reclamation, and monoculture would place greater strain on the environment and reduce the variety of plants and animals. The depopulation of mountain areas permitted the first steps towards reforestation, but elsewhere, the transition away from peasant polyculture was to be deleterious to the regional cultures and natural ecologies of the countryside.

The cumulative effects of these slow and uneven changes – rural exodus and agricultural specialization, greater prosperity for most of those who remained – were to be felt in urban attitudes towards the countryside. The multifaceted transformation of rural life after 1851 meant that, already by the late 1860s, the countryside appeared to urban élites as a rustic haven from the congestion and pollution of sprawling cities and the menace of urban working-class communities. This was reflected in the transformation in the depiction of rural life between the Second Republic and the 1860s in, for example, the work of Jean-François Millet, who had followed Rousseau to Barbizon in 1849. Millet, whose controversial paintings of 1848 (*The Winnower*) and 1850 (*The Sower*) had seemed redolent with the threat of peasant revolt, thereafter produced before his death in 1875 scores of studies of peasants at work, capturing the dignity and diversity of rural toil in a world where the ideal of the self-sufficient subsistence family was slowly disappearing in the face of change.[28]

While the reforestation projects after 1860 were motivated essentially by a desire to develop denuded hillsides and perceived 'wastelands' into productive resources, the evidence of landscape degradation impelled others to act in the interests of threatened national heritage. Théodore Rousseau had joined Camille Corot and others at the artists' colony at Barbizon in the forest of Fontainebleau in 1848. In his words, 'I listened to the voice of the trees; the surprises in their movements, the variety of their forms and their singular attractions towards the light revealed completely to me the language of forests'. In 1861, an imperial decree responded to Rousseau's advocacy by declaring a *réserve artistique* of 1,097 hectares, France's first nature reserve, about 6.6 per cent of the forest of Fontainebleau, and the planting of pines was ended. The local oaks became a symbol of an untouched landscape.[29]

During the late 1860s, the Barbizon painters attracted the attention of Claude Monet and a younger generation of French artists studying in Paris. Several of those artists visited Fontainebleau to paint the landscape, including Monet, Pierre-Auguste Renoir, Paul Huet, Alfred Sisley, and Frédéric Bazille. As a younger man, Monet had also been profoundly influenced by the coastal landscapes of Eugène Boudin (1824–98), 'the king of the skies' in Corot's words.[30] In the 1870s, these artists, among others, developed the movement called 'Impressionism' and practiced *plein air* painting using the innovation of oil paints in tubes. Unlike the Barbizon school, however, their evocations of landscape abandoned traditional techniques of lighting (*chiaroscuro*) and perspective in favour of using light strokes and sharp contrasts of colour to capture not only light and movement but even warmth and odour.

Underpinning these cultural shifts was a profound cultural nostalgia for a vanishing rural society made accessible by the expansion of the rail network after 1850 and the rapidly expanding tourist demand for the countryside as a haven from urban tumult. This cultural movement coincided with the development of geography as a major discipline in France, as reflected in the school syllabus. There was a profound belief in the status of human geography as the study of the relationship between people and their landscapes. Under the Third Republic, far more attention was paid to a deliberate endeavour to inculcate values of patriotism and republican unity, with regional diversity used as a way of celebrating France's natural richness. In *Le Tour de la France par deux enfants* by G. Bruno (Augustine Fouillée), which went through 209 printings in 1877–91 and sold eight million copies by 1914, children all over France were presented with an image of their nation as a land of natural beauty and social harmony, a society of peasants and artisans in a cultivated landscape. The success of Bruno's bucolic vision drew on deep emotional wells of regret for the loss of Alsace-Lorraine in 1870.[31]

The loss was also reflected in the proliferation of memorials to the war of 1870 erected in rural communities, emulating an older practice in cities. The memorials, typically drawing on the symbol of Marianne from the French Revolution to celebrate the birth of the new republic in September 1870, were the most prolific political intrusions into the village topography.[32] In many areas, they brought the angry republican-royalist divide of the 1870s and 1880s into the landscape. In deliberate contrast were the hundreds of mission crosses erected at prominent crossroads as well as in village centres by evangelizing priests and their local followers who were determined to rechristianize rural areas at risk of being seduced into scepticism by urban influences. Often two metres high and made of wrought iron, the mission crosses are not to be confused with the far older 'croix de chemin' which had the purpose of indicating directions as well as serving as a place of spiritual reflection (see Figure 4.4).

It was in the decades after 1850 that, according to the historical geographer Robert Specklin, the rural landscape was 'completed'. Specklin distinguished three broad types of landscape: the irregular plots of land of southern communities; the *bocage* fields of the west bordered by hedges and trees; and the open field strip-farming of the north and east.[33] Each of these types had many local variants, of course, and were a product of the interaction of topography, climate and soil. Distinctive settlement and field patterns became fixed as the population stabilized and the extension of cultivated land reached its limits. This landscape is still visible today. By the 1860s, the area under *bocage* probably reached its greatest extent, as the existing areas of the northwest and centre were joined by the Avesnois in Nord (for fruit trees) and Burgundy (for Charolais cattle farming). The dense hedgerows filled the core functions of enclosing cattle and acting as windbreaks, while also providing cover for birds and reptiles which controlled pests. Estimates have suggested that there were up to two million kilometres of hedgerows, of which 70 per cent would later be destroyed in little more than a century in Brittany, Normandy and Poitou to enable broad-acre crop farming.[34]

The regional variations in the physical relationship of countryside and human habitat remained distinctive and intact. The contrasts between clustered villages, dispersed hamlets and isolated farmhouses were a function of both geography (the interaction of soil types and climate) and history (state legislation and the spread of transport infrastructure). In much of the south, communities were clustered in stone houses, from which peasants left for their fields of vines, fruit trees and vegetable plots. In the upland pastoral areas of the south, the design of isolated farmhouses varied from the stone *mas* of Languedoc, Roussillon and Provence to the timbered *oustau* and *baserri* of the Basque country. In other regions, such as the Auvergne, the more substantial houses were often isolated farmhouses, with animals at close quarters for warmth and safety. The imposing *censes* or manor houses of the north, often at a distance from their villages, were designed around courtyards for physical safety, with wings reserved for families, horses, livestock

FIGURE 4.4 The mission cross at Boistrudan (Ille-et-Vilaine), erected in 1884, one of thousands which recall the efforts to reinforce faith at a time of sharp church-state conflict. Boistrudan is 30 kilometres southeast of Rennes in Brittany. Licensed under the Creative Commons Attribution-Share Alike 4.0 International license.

and implements. Through much of the west and Brittany, the distinctive landscape survived of small *bourgs* or village centres surrounded by scattered hamlets and farms through the *bocage*. Despite the inexorable spread of new, often uniform housing developments across much of France since the 1960s, many of these historical features survive today.

Like the particular local types of agriculture and fields, housing was a reflection of the exigencies of climate, the needs of farming and the availability of building materials. It was at this time that the regional distinctiveness of housing in the rural landscape reached its zenith, with the disappearance of much of the poorest, flimsiest housing and before the intrusion of 'exotic' housing styles from other regions. Houses became larger and more often made of stone or brick.[35] Increasingly, mass-produced tiles started to replace the last of the thatched rooves, except in parts of Normandy. The use of thatching – cool in summer, warm in winter, but a constant source of house fire – is no longer evident today. But the slope and nature of rooves remain sharply differentiated, from the varied styles of slate or wooden tiles of the northern half of France – at angles of up to 60 degrees in Alsace – to the rounded tiles and shale tiles of the south. Indeed, in very general terms, it is even possible to visualize a north-south divide along a line roughly from Bordeaux to Geneva which differentiates the north of sloping slate rooves and open field farming from the south of scattered plots and flat tile roofs, coinciding also with ancient distinctions between the northern *langue d'oil* or French and the southern *langue d'oc* or Occitan, and with pre-revolutionary law (customary in the north, written in the south). The line between rounded and slate tiles cuts through the great plain of the Limagne in the Auvergne, where railway transport after 1850 enabled slate tiles to be imported from around Angers to replace thatch, and in particular for small, hooked tiles (*à crochet*) as the *dernier chic* for the most prosperous families.[36]

By the end of the century, virtually all houses were made of stone. In the decades before 1880, the cattle farmers of the high hamlets of the Auvergne marked their new prosperity and social position by placing lintels with the date, often with the owner's name, above the doors of their solid basalt dwellings. In the 1850s, 20 per cent of houses had thatched roofs, especially in the northwest; by the 1880s, most were tiled. Nevertheless, house design and tiling patterns remained as regionally varied as habitat and field patterns, reflecting topography, soil use, custom and climate.

The ecology of the countryside was also changing within an ongoing diversity. Peasant polyculture had generally been conservative in terms of resources and reliant on human and animal manure. While forest cover was only beginning to recover, hedgerows were extensive and the skies were dark. After 1850, coastal and inland swamp-draining and the bringing into cultivation of 'wasteland' would be detrimental to the rich fauna and flora of delicate ecologies now 'reclaimed' for human use. The changes in rural society after 1850 thus also had negative effects on the environment, symbolized by the steady march of the phylloxera beetle through unbroken vineyards. Their reconstitution in the 1880s by grafting French vines onto American stock would not only destroy the hopes of small winegrowers, for costs were very high, but would prioritize the use of artificial pesticides in the prevention of future catastrophes.[37]

Nor had the wild animal population ever been so depleted, not only because of human competition but because the 'democratization' of hunting since 1789 had made the killing of animals and birds for food a common dimension of rural life. The law of 1844 on the right to hunt 'dangerous or verminous' animals exacerbated this because of the vagueness of its definitions. Wolves were particularly vulnerable because their natural prey in mountainous areas (deer in particular) had declined in number, and their need to feed on livestock made them the object of hatred and fear. The decline of upland human populations after mid-century and reforestation after 1860 did not enable them to flourish because traps became more effective and the artificial forest plantations did not encourage wildlife. By the 1880s, wolves had largely disappeared from France.[38]

The most important transformation in the nineteenth-century landscape was the impact of the transition in most regions from peasant polyculture to specialized small farms. Cash-cropping for the market, evident only in the hinterland of large cities in the eighteenth century, had been facilitated by the Revolution, which removed the controls of seigneurs and church, put up church and *émigré* property for sale, and created the institutional environment for a national market. This transition was accelerated in the decades after 1850. The dramatic expansion of road, canal and rail networks created the transport infrastructure for the national market and transformed the physical appearance of lowland areas in particular. By 1880, too, the *paysage* was being appreciated in new ways. The deep attachment of rural populations to their *pays* was now being joined by interventionist administrations determined to maximize the productivity of the nation's resources and by the sensibilities of painters, for whom the landscape was an invitation to sharpen the senses dulled by the clamour of urban life.

5 'A LANDSCAPE WORTHY OF BEING PRESERVED', 1880–1914

Charles de Freycinet (1828–1923) was the consummate product of the French Revolution and nineteenth-century France. A Protestant from the southern department of Ariège, he was the nephew of the explorer who had produced the first complete map of the Australian coastline in 1811. Charles was intelligent and ambitious, an engineer whose writings ranged across urban sanitation, agriculture and foreign affairs. The consolidation of the Third Republic in the late 1870s offered him a way to implement his vision of internal and external glory for the nation, despite the loss of Alsace-Lorraine to Prussia in 1870. Four times prime minister between 1879 and 1892, he was also at various times minister for war, foreign affairs and public works.[1]

Freycinet's greatest impact was on the French landscape. In January 1878 he presented his 'plan Freycinet', which would become law in July 1879. He recalled that

> at least 15,000 kilometres would be added to the railway network built or conceded. This would thus be increased to nearly 40,000 kilometres, a figure roughly equal to that of our national roads. . . . The supporting report highlighted the true role of inland waterways and showed that their purpose was not to compete with railways, but to rid them of heavy, low-value materials that clog them and prevent the regularity of traffic.[2]

It has been estimated that railways carried three billion tonne/kilometres of freight in the decade 1865–74 and seven times as much by 1905–14. But this was nation-building for the new republic. The lines were also designed to ensure that every one of the 86 prefectures and 383 sub-prefectures in metropolitan France were linked by rail, and where possible, the more than 3,000 cantonal centres as well.[3]

The Freycinet plan of canals and navigable rivers covered a network of 14,600 kilometres linking the North Sea and the Seine, Loire and Rhône rivers. Only one canal among the 1,900 kilometres of new projects – that linking the Adour and the Garonne rivers in the department of Landes – would be south of the Loire.

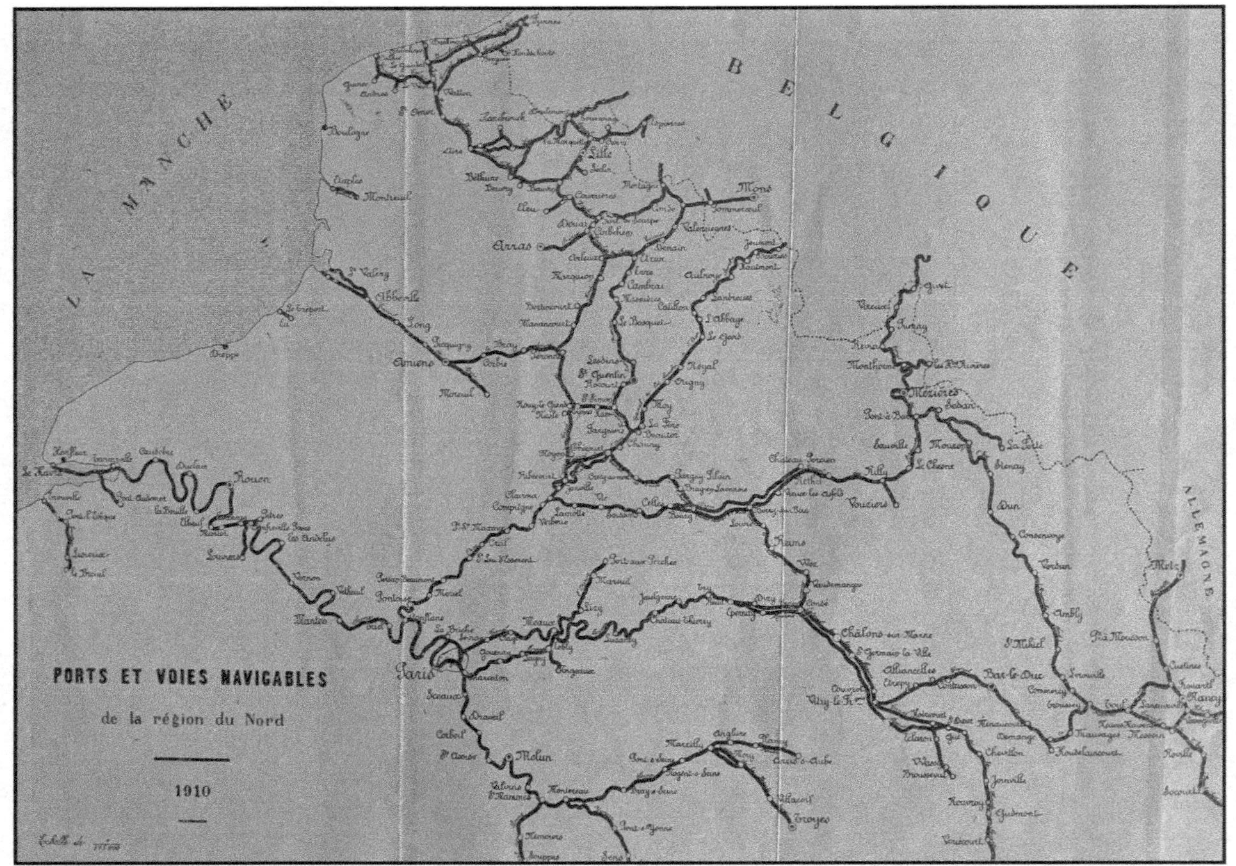

FIGURE 5.1 By 1910, canals marked all the industrial areas of northeastern France, linked to rivers made navigable. There were no longer any 'wild' rivers. G. Garry, *La Baie de Somme et le canal de la Somme* (Abbeville: Imprimerie F. Paillart, 1920), annexe G.

PLATE 1 The rich upland plateau of the Limagne, looking towards the volcanic mound of Usson (Puy-de-Dôme), 45 kilometres south of Clermont-Ferrand. Earlier a region of polyculture, the arrival of the railway in 1858 enabled the region to specialize in cereal crops. Licensed under the Creative Commons Attribution-Share Alike 4.0 International license.

PLATE 2 The ancient and carefully maintained vineyards of Collioure (Pyrénées-Orientales) look north over the fertile plain of the Roussillon, today increasingly under the 'peri-urban' spread of housing, retail outlets and tourist infrastructure. Peter McPhee.

PLATE 3 The seventeenth-century Canal Royal du Languedoc, renamed the Canal du Midi in 1789, was a major transport artery until the railway age. Today it is a tourist attraction, its towpaths used for cycling, while its disease-ridden plane trees are gradually being replaced with mixed plantings, as here at Quarante (Hérault). Peter McPhee.

PLATE 4 The drystone walls and vineyards of the hillsides of the Corbières (Aude) recall the great shift from a pastoral to a viticultural economy from 1780–1830. The small green oaks in the foreground were vital for charcoal in the tanning industry. Peter McPhee.

PLATE 5 The great limestone plateau of Leucate (Aude), between Mediterranean and lagoon, is covered by lines of drystone walls formerly used to enclose and protect sheep, remnants of a vast pastoral industry which had denuded the Corbières mountains in the distance. Peter McPhee.

PLATE 6 Jean-Baptiste Lallemand, *Pastoral Landscape with Figures, c.* 1750. One of the few eighteenth-century painters to focus on landscape, Lallemand preferred imaginary settings for imposing built structures. Public domain via Creative Commons.

PLATE 7 Georges Michel, *Stormy Landscape with Ruins*, *c*. 1830. Michel's romanticism was reinforced by his use of the power of nature to evoke revolutionary ruin and upheaval. Public domain via Creative Commons.

PLATE 8 Gustave Courbet, *The Source of the Lison*, *c*. 1864. Courbet's painting of a river near his home in eastern France was to become a significant symbol in the creation of strengthened laws of landscape protection. Public domain via Creative Commons.

PLATE 9 Jean-François Millet, *Haystacks, c.* 1873. The landscape was the centre of the labour of humans and animals in the 'realism' of Millet. Public domain via Creative Commons.

PLATE 10 Claude Monet, *Haystacks at Giverny, c.* 1885. In an urban world of industrial movement and noise, the rural landscape offered Monet and others the challenge of capturing an alternative sensory experience. Public domain via Creative Commons.

PLATE 11 Chaïm Soutine, *The Big Blue Tree*, *c*. 1920. The shattered post-war world reinforced Soutine's experience of landscape battered by southern winds. Public domain via Creative Commons.

PLATE 12 Successful businessmen in late-nineteenth century Languedoc-Roussillon marked their wealth on the landscape by erecting mansions, often mocked for their ostentation, as here at the Château de Valmy at Argelès-sur-Mer (Pyrénées-Orientales). Peter McPhee.

PLATE 13 War in the landscape: the battered Pointe du Hoc between Utah and Omaha beaches northwest of Bayeux, captured by the US Army in June 1944, and now a memorial site. Licensed under the Creative Commons Attribution-Share Alike 4.0 International license.

PLATE 14 The Millau Viaduct, at 330 metres the highest bridge in the world, was opened in 2004, its lines dominating but complimenting the mountainous landscape of the surrounding *causses* of the southern Massif Central. Licensed under the Creative Commons Attribution-Share Alike 4.0 International license.

PLATE 15 An innovative attempt to bring the countryside into an urban environment has been made in a social housing initiative at Saint-Nolff (Morbihan), while abandoning the goal of emulating surrounding Breton housing. Peter McPhee.

PLATE 16 For centuries, the expansion of Paris had resulted in the small Bièvre river south of the city being paved over and used as a drain. Since 2003, sections have been uncovered and rehabilitated, as here at Arcueil in 2020. Peter McPhee.

The canals were, above all, to facilitate activity in the industrial north (see Figure 5.1). Despite a number of financial setbacks, by 1900 more than 2,100 kilometres of rivers and 2,600 kilometres of canal works had been added to the network. The canals altered the landscape in other ways, through the necessity of constructing reservoirs where water was scarce or where locks were in hilly country: 178 locks were needed along the 314 kilometres of the canal from the Marne to the Rhine; 189 along the 242 kilometres of the canal de Bourgogne. Fifteen canal bridges were constructed above ground, most spectacularly the aqueduct linking the canals of the Loire and Briare in 1894. At Briare, a canal linking the Seine and Rhône rivers had been commenced in 1604; then, in 1827–30, that canal was linked to the Loire, and in the 1890s completed by the Eiffel company with an imposing and ornate iron aqueduct of 660 metres, until 2003 the longest in the world.[4]

In 1882–4, Gustave Eiffel constructed what some consider his masterpiece, the Viaduc de Garabit, a railway arch bridge spanning the Truyère River, near Ruynes-en-Margeride in Cantal. The viaduct is 565 metres long and weighs 3,587 tonnes. At 124 metres above the river, the bridge was the world's highest arch bridge when it was built. The overall project cost was 3,100,000 francs, staggering for a single line used for one train each way daily. But the modernity of iron was already being challenged by the early use of reinforced concrete (*béton armé*), as, for example, in the 45-metres-long bridge erected across the Tech River at Amélie-les-Bains in the eastern Pyrenees in 1909. In the same year, the Fades railway viaduct was put into operation near Les Ancizes-Comps, in the department of Puy-de-Dôme, crossing the Sioule river like Eiffel's viaducts at Rouzat and Neuvial forty years earlier. It was then the tallest railway bridge in the world and remains the tenth tallest today. Its 92-metres-high quarried granite pillars have bases the size of tennis courts.

The international exposition of 1889 in Paris attracted as many as 175,000 people per day to marvel at the exhibits of the modern world. The highlight was Eiffel's soaring tower, celebrating the centenary of 1789 and the triumph of the Republic over the forces of reaction. In its use of iron instead of stone, it was a *chef-d'oeuvre* by a railway engineer of the new age. But opposition forces found ways to contest the triumph of the Republic by ostentatious constructions in the countryside. Just outside the village of Sainte-Anne-d'Auray, northwest of Vannes, a massive statue was unveiled in 1891 to the Comte de Chambord (1820–83).[5] The count is depicted kneeling in readiness to receive the golden crown at his feet (see Figure 5.2). It was Chambord who, as the royalist pretender Henri V, had refused the pleas of constitutional monarchists in the early 1870s to abandon his rejection of concessions to constitutional and democratic government. His rebuff was the last gasp of popular monarchism in France. At the pretender's feet stood Joan of Arc, the two of them gazing 700 metres into the distance towards the basilica dedicated to Saint Anne in 1872, as if to symbolize the unity of militant royalism, Catholicism and the glorious French past. With the mausoleum devoted to royalist martyrs in

FIGURE 5.2 Inscribing politics in the landscape: in 1891 royalists erected this imposing statue of the royal pretender Henri V (the Comte de Chambord, d. 1883) near the basilica of Sainte-Anne-d'Auray, west of Vannes in Brittany. Peter McPhee.

1795 just a few kilometres away at Brech (see Figure 3.1), these imposing structures inscribed upon the landscape a historical identity etched deep into local culture.

Economic change eroded such continuities. The population of France increased by 9.7 per cent from 36.1 million in 1871 to 39.6 million in 1911. Despite the decline in the percentage of households designated as 'rural' (that is, living in communes with fewer than 2,000 people) from 73 per cent in 1856 to 56 per cent in 1911, France was still primarily a rural society. At the turn of the century, only one person in six lived in a city of more than 100,000 people. In the 1880s, there were still almost 13.7 million rural properties under 20 hectares, covering almost half the country, compared with one-third before the Revolution of 1789. Although less than 1 per cent of properties, farms larger than 50 hectares covered more than 35 per cent of the area of France. But even in the flat, open-field regions such as in Artois-Picardie, small farms still dominated the landscape.[6]

The continuity in the size of the rural population and the survival of small farms hides the long-term changes in the relationship between rural people and the landscape they laboured. Across France, distinctive settlement and field patterns became fixed as the expansion of cultivated land reached its limits. Advances in specialization facilitated the retreat of fallow land. On the eve of the French Revolution, it has been estimated that about one-third of cultivated land needed to be left in fallow every year to enable pasturing and manuring. By the 1890s this had declined to 13 per cent with the introduction of root crops which also replenished the soil, such as potatoes, beans, sugar beet and turnips.[7] A German chemist had first demonstrated how to extract sugar from *betteraves* (sugar beets) in the eighteenth century, but it was the British trading blockade around France during the Napoleonic wars which cut it off from its Caribbean colonies and impelled the Emperor to push production onto a commercial scale. By 1875 vast fields of sugar beet dominated the northeast of France and it had become the largest producer in the world. The industry is still important today even though the 400,000 hectares are less than half the area cultivated in 1950.[8]

The exigencies of soil and climate had always meant that there was a distinct regional specialization in the use of land, but after 1880 a series of changes enabled a greater commercialization than ever before. The marketing of agricultural produce was facilitated by the extension of canals, all-weather roads and railways. Improvements in productivity and, above all, the completion of the vast railway network linking production and markets created greater certainty for farmers. The most marginal country was abandoned to *friches* (uncultivated land), and farmers concentrated on regional strengths.

In the two decades after 1892, the area under wheat increased by almost 12 per cent in Poitou-Limousin and fell by nearly 19 per cent in the damper soils of Normandy. In contrast, the area under grapevines in 1912, compared with pre-phylloxera levels, had tumbled by one-half or even three-quarters across the northern half of the country and highland areas. Brittany, Normandy and Poitou became more than ever devoted to animal husbandry and dairying. In parts of the southwest, tobacco became more attractive than wine: in the department of Lot, 2,100 hectares in 150 communes were now planted with tobacco compared with 500 hectares a century earlier.[9] Railway transport also facilitated the expansion of specialized cropping to meet national and international demand, as in the spreading of walnut groves around Grenoble where, by the end of the century, 80 per cent of the annual crop of 8,500 tonnes was being exported to the United States. The lure of easy profit from adding poor-quality walnuts to bulk overseas shipments was to be a key reason for major anti-fraud legislation in 1905, which is still the basis of such law today.[10]

The Mediterranean lowlands had become increasingly monocultural across the century, creating a remarkable 'golden age' of wine until the phylloxera louse began its destruction after 1862. Over the next twenty years, the area of vineyards shrank from 2.5 to 1.0 million hectares, and production fell from 54 to 29 million hectolitres. The phylloxera crisis not only meant the end of almost all the French root stock, since grafting onto American vines proved the best solution; it also had significant social effects. Even though the price of agricultural land would fall by one-third between 1880 and 1912, the costs of reconstitution were too great for many smallholders. Some of those who could no longer hope for economic independence as small winegrowers joined the flood of migrants to Algeria: there were 272,000 French Algerians in 1872 but 800,000 by 1914. Their exportation of cheap wine to France after 1900 was to be one reason for the wine glut that resulted in massive protest in 1906–7 by those they left behind in Languedoc.[11]

By now, farmers were starting to use chemical fertilizers for the first time, above all, by adding potassium through the use of potash and superphosphate and doubling the total from 800,000 tonnes in 1890 to 1.6 million tonnes a decade later.[12] In the future, more specialized agriculture, increasingly using chemical fertilizers and pesticides, was to create long-term problems of soil and water degradation.

In highland areas, too, the ecology of the countryside continued to evolve. The certainty of the French forests administration was that uplands belonged to trees. Foresters had subjected ancient pastoral communities to increasing constraints since the laws of 1827 and 1860, which had facilitated state alienation of common lands and forbidden pasturing animals and the gathering of firewood. Transhumance of livestock, particularly goats, was assumed to be inimical to healthy forests. However, many highland communities insisted on their rights to continue to have access to pastures. A new law on 'restoration and conservation of Alpine lands' in April 1882 sought to balance national forests policy with rights of local access.[13] A combination of reforestation following the new laws and the continuing exodus of people from upland communities permitted the slow expansion of wooded areas. For example, between the government surveys of 1878 and 1904–8, the forested area of the five departments of Languedoc-Roussillon increased by about one-seventh, to 475,000 hectares, half its present extent. This increase was largely due to reforestation in state forests. This was enabled by the gradual but fundamental shift from timber to iron and steel in construction and from wood and charcoal to coal, oil and hydroelectricity for energy. Cheaper imported wool and skins from Australia and New Zealand undercut demand for local supply, and the size of French flocks of sheep continued to decline.

Ultimately the ministry of Eaux et Forêts (Water and Forests) won control of the mountains. The law of 1882 strengthened those of 1860 and 1864 to enable the restoration of state forests degraded by erosion in mountainous areas by 'covering the surface as quickly as possible with a protective vegetal layer capable of preventing erosion and regularizing water courses'. It was an ambitious project. In the archives at Digne, the capital of the department of Alpes-de-Haute-Provence, thousands of silver gelatin bromide photographs on glass plates preserve a startling

FIGURE 5.3 Before the ministry of Eaux et Forêts (Water and Forests) began large-scale reforestation in the Alps in the late-nineteenth century, its agents took thousands of photographs of the state of mountainsides, as here at Saint-André-les-Alpes (Alpes-de-Haute-Provence), a major pastoral and woollen textile centre. AD Alpes-de-Haute-Provence 29 Fi 0066.

FIGURE 5.4 Largely devoid of forest cover in 1900, the mountain slopes dominating Saint-André-les-Alpes today are a tourist magnet for walking and paragliding. There are very few farms. Peter McPhee.

record of the state of many of the Alpine mountainsides late in the nineteenth century (see Figures 5.3 and 5.4).[14]

The reforestation of the Alps was a massive undertaking, less extensive than that in the Landes region of the southwest after 1860 but far more successful in terms of landscape regeneration. In all, some 100,000 hectares were affected

FIGURE 5.5 Early postcards of Villard-de-Lans (Isère) towards 1910 showed the surrounds of the village and the towering Pic Cornafion under intense cultivation and pastures as well as forest. Mairie de Villard-de-Lans: https://www.annuaire-mairie.fr/photo -villard-de-lans.html.

by a combination of planting and natural seeding. It marked the decisive act in a centuries-long struggle between rural communities and the national administration of forest and water resources. The final act of many peasants was to take on work replanting the slopes before they left their *pays* for good. Today, one-third of the entire region is forested, compared with 19 per cent in 1878, and the landscape of the Alps has its iconic status as a region of thick forests along dramatic escarpments.[15]

The transformation of the meaning of 'Alpine landscape' was rapid and profound. As forests replaced people in many Alpine areas, so regions previously seen as remote, wild 'enclaves' were made accessible by road and rail. Intrepid mountaineers and lovers of snow sports became seasonal visitors. The first photographs in the 1860s of the small town of Villard-de-Lans in the heart of the Vercors Massif show the lower slopes of the Roc Cornafion covered with pastures and cultivated terraces. There had been no all-weather road into the town until the nineteenth century, then a tramway connected it to Grenoble in 1911. Villard is now a booming vacation town and ski resort. The Roc Cornafion is now covered with pine trees, rock climbers, paragliders and ski runs (see Figures 5.5 and 5.6).

The forests administration, now responsible also for water resources as it had been before the Revolution, continued to acquire private and communal land for reforestation, and the Audiffred Law of 1913 gave it the right to acquire whatever land it deemed necessary and to supervise the management of private forested

FIGURE 5.6 Today Villard-de-Lans (Isère) is a bustling tourist town, and the forested Pic Cornafion is a magnet for walking, ballooning and winter sports; there are only a few substantial dairy farms. Peter McPhee.

land. However, the victory of the most uncompromising policymakers in the forests administration was never complete. While shepherds were often blamed for forest fires as they sought to encourage new growth for their herds, the dwindling populations actively using the forests increased the likelihood of fires spreading through thick undergrowth. So, while the landscape of highland France has not been as thickly wooded since 1770, it has also never been more prone to wildfires. At the same time, others were concerned about what such a purist forests policy would mean for cultural heritage and the sustainability of rural communities. In France's overseas empire, especially northern Algeria, the clash of such ideas was also experienced, and the forest code of 1903 sought (with limited success) to combine reforestation with the safeguarding of the pastoral economy.[16]

Elsewhere, too, there were sharp contrasts between the rural landscape then and now. The earliest photographs of most rural communities, taken to meet the huge demand for postcards at the turn of the twentieth century, show remarkably denuded landscapes. In the Limousin region, today dominated by cattle production and forests, the landscape was still being denuded through the pressure of the timber and porcelain industries.[17] In most regions, however, the late-nineteenth century represents a turning point in tree cover, and the postcards show much of the countryside on the cusp of reforestation.

Some uses of the landscape did not change despite the best efforts of government. In July 1889, the National Assembly effectively abolished the ancient practice of 'droit de parcours', whereby farmers could use ancient collective rights to move livestock across private land, and reaffirmed the rights of landowners to refuse 'vaine pâture', the ancient practice of allowing the poor to graze their animals on recently harvested land. Such practices were centuries old, and even the lawmakers of the French Revolution had been powerless to abolish them in the name of private property rights. Coming just a few days before the celebration of the centenary of the Revolution of 1789, the new law smacked of regression.

The Assembly gave communes a year to respond. Regions where the practice of grazing a few animals was a vital resource for the poor – particularly where phylloxera had destroyed vineyards – were quick to object. Ultimately, the Assembly decided it would be prudent to leave the matter in the hands of the 41,000 municipal councils. By 1898, 8,370 communes had decided to maintain their collective practices, while 27,777 communes no longer – or had never had – them. In the northeast and east, they were common, but in the department of Somme, only 35 of 836 councils agreed to end the practice, and many of these councils were urban. In Corsica, as in 1854, local authorities simply ignored the law. Everywhere, however, the compromise in the law meant that issues of grazing, gleaning and *grappage* (the right to pick grapes left on the vines) had to be negotiated and resolved in the complex arrangements of individual rural communities.[18]

Political and economic change combined to generate a cultural shift in appreciation of the countryside and its landscapes. The term 'rural' had had a sharp pejorative edge around 1870: the conservative National Assembly elected in February 1871 had confirmed urban radicals in their conviction that the countryside was 'primitive' and reactionary. Now, after the republican electoral triumphs in 1877 and 1878, 'peasants' were increasingly seen as the sturdy personification of republican virtues. At the same time, as Alain Corbin has shown, there was even a shift in urban perceptions of agreeable smells: a more prosperous countryside, which was seen as the stable base of republican régimes and which was now easily accessible by train, seemed less the home of the offensive smells of manure-heap and sweat and more a flowered, authentic haven of nature.[19] Rural landscapes became a favoured subject of artists across the country.

The sentimental rural scenes of Jules Breton, Jules Bastien-Lepage and Julien Dupré found a ready urban market with their images of honest labour by well-fed, clean peasants in bucolic surroundings. In contrast, the evocation of the interplay of the natural world, light and movement through bold brush strokes, contrasting planes of colour, even dots, by Claude Monet (see Plate 10), Georges Seurat, Paul Signac, Paul Cézanne, Vincent van Gogh, Camille Pissarro and other 'post-Impressionists' would take longer to appeal. Cézanne's masterpieces painted near Aix-en-Provence, such as *The Red Rock*, seemed to make the canvas shimmer in the southern heat. 'Fauves' such as Georges Braque, Henri Matisse, André Derain, Raoul Dufy and others would take this boldness further in response to the colour and heat of the south and of Collioure in particular. By early in the twentieth century, landscape painting had become a major dimension of the art world, in sharp contrast to its marginal status in the eighteenth century.

The new appreciation of landscape as a desirable focus for painters of all levels of expertise and fame was interconnected with a wider sensitivity to the vulnerability and worth of the landscape itself. While modern legislation focussing on the protection of 'monuments historiques' goes back to 1790, when revolutionary assemblies became concerned at the destruction of edifices now in the public domain, legislation extended to the landscape was more recent. In 1861, the artists known as the Barbizon school had successfully sought the protection of about 1,000 hectares of the forest of Fontainebleau from the same commercial pine plantations proceeding apace in the Landes region of Gascony. This was the first 'nature reserve' in the world, preceding the vast Yellowstone National Park in the United States in 1872.

In the 1890s, the owner of a mill on the Lison River in eastern France sought a permit to use the river's source to power machinery. Locals, worried about the impact on water supply as well as affronted by the damage to a grotto made famous in a painting by Gustave Courbet in 1864 (see Plate 8), petitioned their deputy Charles Beauquier, who famously exhorted the Chamber of Deputies: 'Let us save the Lison, but save all the Lisons in France as well!'. He was instrumental in the foundation of the Société pour la Protection des Paysages de France (SPPF) in 1901 and the law of 21 April 1906, on the protection of natural sites and monuments. This was a key turning point in the historical juridical paradigm, since it gave authorities the power to block damaging works on particular sites or even to purchase the site in question.

The Society was co-founded by the poet Jean Lahor (pseudonym of Dr Henri Cazalis) and from the outset could call on prominent supporters: its first president was the 1901 Nobel Prizewinner for Literature, Sully Prudhomme. The first issue of its *Bulletin* in January 1902 had as its patrons the ministers of education, fine arts and agriculture and prominent members included the authors Ludovic Halévy and Frédéric Mistral and the artists William Bouguereau and Jules Breton. The Society promised that

> we will fight energetically against the extraordinary lack of consideration with which our natural resources, trees, cliffs, waterfalls and waterways are being wasted. The felling of trees, the blasting of rocks, the damming of rivers is today happening across France with an unimaginable lack of foresight.

It blamed 'vandals' and 'barbarians'.[20]

The Beauquier Law of April 1906 was a major outcome of the activities of the SPPF, establishing a commission for natural sites and monuments in every department, presided over by the prefect, and including senior local representatives from the ministries of Ponts et Chaussées (Bridges and Roads) and Eaux et Forêts, local government and associations, and the Club Alpin, the Touring Club and the SPPF. Beauquier was also president of the first international congress on the protection of landscapes, held in Paris in October 1909, and brought together delegates ranging from Frédéric Mistral to the Club Alpin and the Saint-Hubert Club, the latter a hunters' association. The congress affirmed the worth of 'natural beauty in the context of problems posed by industrialization, hydroelectricity and tourism' and stressed the interconnections between nature and 'hygiene, sport, schooling, literature, even the protection of fauna and flora'.[21]

One of Beauquier's key members at the SPPF was the young lawyer Fernand Cros-Mayrevieille (born 1882), who defined landscape as

A group of elements resulting from nature, like rocks, trees, sudden and accidental changes in the appearance of terrain and other transformations which, separately or together, form an impressive aspect, a landscape worthy of being preserved. A landscape is a part of nature presenting an aesthetic character through the disposition of its contours, forms and colors.[22]

Cros-Mayrevieille's grandfather had been a prominent promoter in Carcassonne of the necessity for the restoration and recognition of its ancient *cité*. Fernand himself was to play a major role in the protection and celebration of Occitan culture and the landscapes of Languedoc. He would be gratified that, in the decades since his death in 1939, his fellow citizens in Aude have founded more than four hundred local cultural, historical and environmental associations in their 432 communities.[23]

The revaluation of rural life was paralleled by the proliferation in the early 1880s of 'colonies de vacances' organized by churches and municipalities to take urban working-class children for extended summer holidays in the fresh country air.[24] The network of railway lines which had spread across the country since 1840 did more than create a national market for produce and a more mobile population; it was also the network on which a tourism industry could be created. Distant places which for most people had existed purely in the imagination could be contemplated as places to visit. By the 1880s, the Gorges du Verdon, for example, started to attract attention as a tourist destination.[25] Until the introduction of paid holidays in the twentieth century, however, trips to places as remote as the Gorges were the preserve of the well-to-do, such as Colette, who travelled 400 kilometres by train through Brittany in 1910 to Cancale and her lover Mathilde ('Missy') de Morny's mansion 'Rozven':

I am dazzled as I enter this yellow kingdom of broom and gorse. Gold, copper, bronze too – for pale rapeseed is part of the mix – make these barren headlands glow with an unbearable light. . . . We are passing through fire, mile after mile of gorse in bloom, a desolate richness that discourages even the goats.[26]

This more intent concern for the natural world came, in the words of the historian Caroline Ford, from motives that were 'at once patriotic and aesthetic'. New associations driven by particular interests but united by a love of natural beauty included the Club Alpin (founded in 1875), the Touring Club de France (1890), the Société des Amis des Arbres (1894), and above all, the SPPF (1901). Their elite membership and networks were to prove crucial in initiating a long series of laws seeking to protect the landscape from the worst effects of unchecked exploitation. At the same time, patriotic impulses were strengthening popular appreciation of the variation and majesty of particular landscapes, evident in the surging popularity of the Tour de France after its inauguration in 1903. Unlike its highly variable route today, the early tours were deliberately staged around the periphery of France. In 1910, the first tour to include the Pyrenees, the fifteen stages covered 4,734 kilometres, from Paris to Roubaix then clockwise around the frontiers. Cycling enthusiasts relished the changing landscapes that challenged their heroes: the circulation of the sponsoring newspaper *l'Auto* boomed from 25,000 in 1903 to 250,000 in 1908 and 850,000 in 1933.[27]

In the 1890s, Armand Peugeot, Albert de Dion, Georges Bouton and the Renault brothers had started producing automobiles and by 1903, France was producing more than 30,000 cars (almost half the world's total). One of the reasons why the prestigious Touring Club de France became a major player in landscape protection in France was that its members were thrilled by access to natural beauty and horrified at evidence that it could be destroyed. Their efforts were linked to those of the SPPF and a new sensibility to the beauty of the natural world, now readily accessible by car as well as train, and seen as threatened by thoughtless development. In 1892, a 'Festival of Trees' was held in Nice. Then, in 1901, a successful campaign was waged to protect the pink granite rocks of Ploumanac'h, near Perros-Guirec on the north coast of Brittany (in 2015, it was voted 'the village most preferred by the French'). This was followed by others to protect the source of the Lison in Jura, the oak forests in Normandy, the ancient towers of the village of La Garde in Var and the fountain of Vaucluse. This was above all a definition of landscape beauty which privileged exotic or unusual forms: rocky outcrops, waterfalls, picturesque ruins, rather than fauna and flora. The first classified site under the new protection in 1906 was the Island of Bréhat off the northern coast of Brittany, in July 1907. Between 1916 and 1929, 458 other sites were classified, and a supplementary law of May 1930 extended the protection to the surrounds of sites. Inspired by examples in the United States and Switzerland, the first national park of Bérarde on the highlands of Pelvoux in the Alps was proclaimed in 1913.[28]

The proliferation of new organizations dedicated to protecting the environment early in the twentieth century demonstrates a heightened awareness among many of the most educated and well-travelled elites of the impact of unchecked despoliation of the natural world. It would be incorrect, however, to see this as a new ecological awareness, which these elites would then slowly struggle to communicate downwards to the masses. Rural people were often well aware of the environmental and aesthetic consequences of intensified or changed use of natural resources, just as their ancestors had been in 1789.

The decades after 1880 were characterized by a revaluation of the cultural weight of terms such as 'paysan' and 'paysage' and rural folk themselves articulated a stronger sense of their standing as the backbone of the country and guardians of precious regional cultural and agricultural identities. Local learned societies, particularly those interested in geography, had already begun advocating for the writing of community histories, notably in Lozère in 1862 and Loiret in 1874. By 1874, there had been 421 completed in the former, mostly very brief. In 1877, the senior educational administrator Louis Maggiolo had used village teachers to provide him with information about the level of knowledge of French and had received 16,000 responses.[29] But greater momentum came from the Ministry of Public Education in the context of celebrations for the great international exhibitions of 1889 and 1900, with a view to encouraging both village pride in education and a greater knowledge of geography and history. Village schoolteachers were pushed to compile brief histories of their communes, drawing on village records and oral accounts. In virtually every case, this was the first attempt to do so. Tens of thousands were completed.

Today, these village histories are kept in departmental archives. Some departments have no records at all; others have hundreds. Those completed for the exhibition of 1889 are the most detailed. In Meuse, for example, there are ninety-seven surviving monographs. That of Beaulieu-en-Argonne, in meticulous handwriting, enthused that, as its name indicated, Beaulieu 'enjoys one of the most beautiful points of view in the department and this is why a large number of tourists come to visit during the warm months'. In Haute-Garonne, 530 of the 589 communes produced one in the years 1885–6. In Montréjeau, a new boulevard 'offers a particularly remarkable point of view. In springtime, nothing equals the beauty of the panorama which unfolds before the eyes of the viewer, from the banks of the Garonne to the highest peaks of the Pyrenees'. In contrast, in Mayenne, where 268 monographs from 1899 have survived, the teacher in Carelles had consulted the village archives dating back to 1616 and the oldest inhabitants, but no one knew the origin of the village name. He confessed that he had found nothing remarkable about his 'rustic' village, neither buildings nor individuals.[30]

The popular revaluation of rural France and its landscapes was the result of a series of shifts: the political weight of the peasantry in a proud republican regime, the implementation of free and compulsory primary school education, profound patriotism fed by the loss of Alsace-Lorraine and by colonial conquests, and the committed activism of conservation bodies. All of these created a political and cultural environment favourable to reform which would extend landscape protection beyond reforestation. It was a major shift in the meaning and value of *paysage* itself.

Others created images of the countryside which were far less attractive, recalling their own experiences. Eugène Le Roy was born in 1836 in Hautefort, in the department of Dordogne, where his parents were farm servants on the estate of the Baron de Damas, a former government minister. While Le Roy received an education and became a public servant and author, the angry memory of his family's poverty never left him, as captured profoundly in *Le Moulin de Frau* (1891) and *Jacquou le Croquant* (1899). In turn, Le Roy's writing inspired the Bourbonnais sharecropper Émile Guillaumin (1873–1951) to write *La Vie d'un simple* (1904) before devoting himself to trade union activities among his fellows. Others felt equally strongly that the price to pay for economic progress and national identity had been too high for the distinctive cultures and agrarian systems of linguistic minorities. It is no coincidence that in 1854 the Félibrige was founded to safeguard Provençal language and culture, nor that in 1859 the poet Frédéric Mistral (1830–1914) wrote *Miréio*, a nostalgic homage to the cultural traditions of the Provençal countryside. When Mistral wrote his memoirs at the beginning of the twentieth century, he felt traumatized by the 'gigantic crabs' which now mechanically harvested crops 'in American style, cheerlessly, in haste, without any joy or singing . . . That's progress, that's the terrible, inevitable harrow against which nothing can be done or said'.[31]

Despite Mistral's gloom, small farming continued to co-exist with large-scale, capitalist farming in most areas, but it became more specialized by region across the century. Of course, socio-economic transformations of such magnitude were infinitely varied in their specific nature, timing and intensity across the face of a large, diverse country. Some regions, notably the upland areas of Brittany, the Massif Central and the Pyrenees, remained polycultural, peasant lands into the twentieth century, while the collapse of local industries slowly drained people and wealth away. Long-sawyers who trudged from the Massif Central in the 1890s to spend the winter cutting wood in the Morvan before returning to their farms for the summer harvests were following ancient practices of seasonal migration.[32] But no community lived through the nineteenth century without a major change to its population, social structure, economic base and the landscape itself.

This transition from polyculture to monoculture was abrupt in particular regions, for example, the Mediterranean coastline of Languedoc and Roussillon. In the Catalan village of Canet in the 1820s, the arable land along the River Têt was used for wheat, rye, oats and vegetables. A little wine was grown for local consumption. Huts made of reeds between the large *étang* or lagoon and the Mediterranean provided shelter for fishers. The low, stony hillsides were pastures for large flocks of sheep, joined in winter by others which wound their way down from the Pyrenees. Seventy years later, there were far fewer sheep; most of their dry, stony pastures were now vineyards, a transition that had begun in the 1830s. There were many more people in the fields: more than 900 in the 1890s compared with 370 in the 1820s. However, since the 1890s, the population of Canet has exploded with a spectacular new migration of tourist entrepreneurs, land speculators, vacationers and pensioners from the north. The sandy, windswept coastal strip of common land between sea and lagoon known as la Marenda, which was divided among households in 1869 – for many of them the only land they owned – is now prime-value real estate. But impoverished Canetois had had to sell their plots long before the village became a *station balnéaire*.[33]

This increased accessibility to the outside world was one reason why the rural population continued its long decline, accelerated by the phylloxera crisis in viticulture after 1862 and the depression of prices in the 1880s.[34] Two other crises – the 1890s depression and the wine-market crisis of 1900–7 – further advantaged large landholders with the capital to reconstitute and rationalize their vineyards. The spread of vineyards was marked by a distinctive architectural appearance in their midst. The vineyards of Languedoc-Roussillon were the first to recover from the phylloxera crisis, and the great surge in wine production on the plains after 1880 created massive wealth for some producers, merchants and industrialists, and they sought to inscribe this prosperity on the landscape by building ornate mansions in the middle of their rural properties. These mansions are sometimes mockingly called 'châteaux pinardiers', from the 'pinard' word for soldiers' cheap wine rations during the First World War. They stud the southern countryside today, such as the château de l'Esparrou (1891) in Canet and the château de Valmy (1900) at Argelès in the Pyrénées-Orientales, both designed by the Danish architect Viggo Dorph-Petersen. Valmy was one of three pseudo-châteaux the Perpignan cigarette-paper maker Jean Bardou had built for his children (see Plate 12). These follies are particularly common in the Béziers-Narbonne area, where the late impact of the phylloxera disease in the vineyards compared with other winegrowing regions led to extraordinary fortunes before the glut of production after 1900. There are scores of such mansions still visible in the region today, in eclectic styles ranging from neo-Gothic to Louis XIV.[35]

Together, all these changes slowly transformed popular perceptions of time and space. Most people in the 1780s were born into a world where the most common way of moving about, even over long distances, was on foot. The rhythms of the day were marked by the sound of distinctive church bells from churches in the neighbourhood and nearby villages. By 1910, city dwellers in particular were becoming used to motorized transport: 64,000 motor vehicles were registered, and the Paris 'Métropolitain' transported hundreds of thousands of people daily. However, rural people had also come to understand and value time and distance in new ways. The remembered appearance of the first bicycle in the western village of Mazières-en-Gâtine in 1890, as in countless other villages, touched a deep chord among people for whom walking great distances had been part of daily life.[36]

In one of the most isolated communities of the Massif Central, Le Pont-de-Montvert, improved road transport had enabled a shift from polyculture (chestnuts, rye, wheat, sheep and cattle) to predominantly cattle production. Access to the village had changed dramatically since the famous arrival of Robert Louis Stevenson and his donkey in 1878. Such was the use made of the newly paved road that in 1906 the mayor decided to change the location of the market because 'velocipedes and automobiles are all using the new road, and this could start a panic among the animals'.[37]

By 1914, the French railway system had reached its greatest ever extent, 60,000 kilometres, but the demands of combustion engines for private automobiles would soon start to eclipse the railways from another direction. In the Languedoc village of Gabian, where the arrival of the railway in 1879 had caused great excitement, people soon began complaining of the time it took to travel to Béziers, 30 kilometres away. In 1916, the village council petitioned for a subsidy for a local bus that could cut the distance and time in half.[38]

The decades after 1880 were a time of rapid acceleration in the use of hydroelectricity and coal as the core of France's energy generation for manufacturing, transport and domestic use. The thousands of medieval mills dotted along France's rivers and tidal flats bear witness to the long history of water-driven energy, but now it was to be used in a revolutionary way. In 1869, Aristide Bergès, like Freycinet a native of the southern department of Ariège, had used hydrological energy at Lancey (Isère) to power defibering machines to make paper pulp, then in 1882 to power a paper-making machine. He had begun referring to hydroelectricity as 'houille blanche' (white coal).[39] In 1879, Thomas Edison's incandescent light bulb created a new way of producing light. In the same year, the first hydroelectric power station began operation in Switzerland. Then, in 1889, a 14-kilometre wire connected the Cascade des Jarrauds waterfall to the small town of Bourganeuf (population 4,000) in the department of Creuse. Two other towns had already begun to use hydraulic power for electricity, but Bourganeuf was the first to use a distant source. The power was used for 106 lamps along the streets and in the town hall, church, and cafés. The first telephone in the region linked the power station with the town.[40] So began a new industrial revolution based on electricity, the telephone and telegraph which was not only to transform domestic amenities, social relationships and the economy but was to mark the landscape profoundly as well. It was the small-scale beginning of a lighting revolution which would slowly illuminate the night sky to the detriment of nocturnal animal, bird and insect life.

The extensive river systems of the Alps, Pyrenees and Massif Central were to be irresistible for hydrological engineers and few significant rivers would not be dammed after 1900. Far more intrusive in the landscape were the coal mines of the north and centre. In 1885, Émile Zola published the best-selling of his novels, *Germinal*, drawing on research he had done down the pit in Denain, near

Valenciennes, in the department of Nord. Zola described the sight that confronted his hero, Étienne, as he approached the Voreux mine through flat fields of sugar beet:

> He only perceived, very far off, the blast furnaces and the coke ovens. The latter, with their hundreds of chimneys, planted obliquely, made lines of red flame; while the two towers, more to the left, burnt blue against the blank sky, like giant torches. It resembled a melancholy conflagration. No other stars rose on the threatening horizon except these nocturnal fires in a land of coal and iron.[41]

The expansion of mining had a dramatic impact on the rural landscape, not only across the fertile plains of Artois and Picardy in the northeast but in the other great coal-mining basins of the Massif Central, around Saint-Étienne and Alès and around the Schneider iron mines and forges near Le Creusot. The slag heaps and pitheads of the mines are the visual expression on the landscape of the wicked equation of the Anthropocene: the dramatic expansion of the use of fossil fuels as the price paid for an unprecedented range of human comforts.

Towering above the small town of Wallers, just 6 kilometres north of Zola's Denain, are the restored coal-mining buildings of a mine which from 1899, extracted 32 million tonnes of coal from the Arenberg mine until its closure in 1985. Today, the buildings are part of the Arenberg Creative Mine, a centre dedicated to visual and digital media. The entire mining basin has been on the UNESCO World Heritage List since 2012. The landscape of Wallers-Arenberg is far better known, however, for a remarkable 2.3 kilometres straight stretch of cobblestones between towering trees, familiar to those passionate about cycling, and one of its most famous races, the annual Paris-Roubaix (see Figure 5.7). Every April, the hazardous crossing of the trench by scores of cyclists is the highlight of the race, one of world cycling's 'classics'. The straight line of the four-metre-wide cobbled road, known officially as the Drève des Boules d'Hérin ('the Hérin bowling alley') but to everyone else as the 'Trouée d'Arenberg' ('the Arenberg trench'), takes its popular name from the straight trenches that later crisscrossed the area during the First World War. Like many of the mines in the basin, that at Wallers had attracted many Polish immigrants; one of them was Jean Stablinski, who used to mine the coal under the road and ride along the cobbles for leisure. Today, a statue of Stablinski commemorates this national cycling champion who secured the place of the Arenberg Trench in the Paris-Roubaix race.[42] The cobblestone road, often assumed to be connected to the mining industry, was in fact one of many constructed under Napoleon to provide sure footing for his cavalry and supply trains through the sodden forest of Raismes-Saint-Amand-Wallers towards the front.

Coal mining in the decades after 1880 would thoroughly transform parts of the northeastern region from a rich agricultural area of stone villages to a land of

FIGURE 5.7 The cobbled 'Arenberg trench' slicing through the forest in Wallers (Nord) was made for troop movements under Napoleon and later made famous by the Paris-Roubaix cycling classic. The bridge over the road was used to carry shale from the Arenberg coal mine to its slag heap. Licensed under the Creative Commons Attribution-Share Alike 4.0 International license.

slag heaps, pitheads and new brick houses, but the consequences of mining have not all been negative for the landscape. The 'Arenberg trench' borders a treasure of biodiversity created by subsidence in 1930 due to the coal mining, a nature reserve known as the 'Mare à Goriaux' (the 'pigs' pond' in the local Picard slang), a 90-hectare lake home to two hundred bird species.

6 'CORPSES OF TREES COVERING THE CORPSES OF MEN', 1914–50

In May 1906, the American writer Edith Wharton (1862–1937), accompanied by her husband and brother, travelled by car from Boulogne to Bourges. 'The motor car has restored the romance of travel', she averred, away from the 'ugliness and desolation' of railways. Edith described the first stretch from Boulogne to Arras as a land 'where agriculture has mated with poetry instead of banishing it', describing the 'beauty of detail' in the old villages and towns. She delighted in the 'agricultural landscape, disciplined and cultivated to the last point of finish . . . In France everything speaks of long familiar intercourse between the earth and its inhabitants, every field has a name, a history, a distinct place of its own in the village polity'.[1]

When war broke out in August 1914, Wharton resolved to stay in France and devoted herself to the war effort. She was relieved to find, when she revisited the area around Arras in 1915, that 'the disfigurement of war has not touched the fields of Artois. . . . On all sides wheat-fields skirted with woodland went billowing away under the breezy light that seemed to carry a breath of the Atlantic on its beams.' Further north, however, she drove through a forest where 'half the poor spindling trees were down, and patches of blackened undergrowth and ragged hollows marked the path of the shells. . . . there was something humanly pitiful in the frail trunks . . . lying there like slaughtered rows of immature troops'. In Lorraine, too, she noted that Sermaize had been 'a pretty watering-place along wooded slopes, the others large villages fringed with farms, and all now mere scrofulous blotches on the soft spring scene'.[2]

Earlier, Wharton had made another trip north from Paris, this time with her husband and Henry James, and delighted in comparing the southern city of Carcassonne with the 'concentrated power' of the massive château de Coucy, near Arras, and 'the lovely country enfolding it in woods and streams . . . the distinct and exquisite physiognomy of the tiny old town which these ramparts enclose'.[3] Coucy, constructed in the 1220s, was indeed as dominant a feature of the landscape as was the *cité* at Carcassonne, but in March 1917, the German army, which had occupied Coucy in 1914, destroyed the keep and the four towers. The ruins were later declared a 'memorial to barbarity' and today they are a haunting, shattered remnant above a village that was obliterated during the war.

Much of the region of Artois which Wharton was relieved to see untouched in 1915 would soon be devastated. Over the years 1914–18, a swathe of land 700 kilometres long from the Channel to the Swiss border became a tortured landscape of death, of mud and craters, often filled with human and animal bodies and stagnant water, of obliterated villages and churned fields. From Dunkerque to Verdun via Arras and Reims, the northeast was ravaged: hundreds of villages were damaged, many completely destroyed and hundreds of thousands of hectares of forests were levelled. In Arras itself, three-quarters of the city had to be rebuilt after the German bombardments of May–July 1915. The elegant Flemish-style houses which line its famous squares today are faithful copies of the eighteenth-century edifices, funded by reparations paid after the war. In Verdun, similarly, three-quarters of the old town had been damaged or destroyed, and the rest was mostly uninhabitable. By 1929, it too had been rebuilt.[4]

There are many places where the extremes of wartime horror have been seared into the landscape. One is the Chemin des Dames, which runs for 30 kilometres along a ridge between the Aisne and Ailette rivers near Laon. Named after Louis XV's sisters Adélaide and Victoire and completed in 1789, the road became the focus of protracted shelling and combat in 1917, leaving 271,000 French and 163,000 Germans dead and wounded. The scale of the fighting, poor supplies and delays in extracting the wounded led to numerous mutinies among the French troops. There are scores of memorials and cemeteries, German, French and British, all along the Chemin. Among the most harrowing scars on the landscape, however, is the site of the former village of Craonne, one of a number of villages obliterated by the shelling, and today a silent space of hollows and stones amid the trees.[5]

Nowhere is the scarring of the landscape more evident than at Douaumont, northeast of Verdun. Here a small village of fewer than two hundred inhabitants had lined a single road along a hilly spur until, following defeat in the Franco-Prussian war of 1870–1, a massive fort was constructed nearby, along with others at Vaux, Souville and Froideterre. By 1885, there were almost six hundred construction workers and members of the garrison. Although the Douaumont fort was abandoned as outdated by 1915, it became a key symbolic target in German advances and French defences in 1916 (during which a young artillery captain, Charles de Gaulle, was taken prisoner and sent to Germany). One explosion killed 800 German soldiers, most of whose remains are interred in a walled necropolis near the site of the former village.[6]

The village was never rebuilt, one of nine in the department of Meuse to be obliterated. Instead, in 1929 the French government opened the massive war memorial to the Battle of Verdun, which had cost the lives of 300,000 French and German soldiers. The vast cemetery, covering 145,000 square metres, has the graves of 16,142 known French soldiers, including nearly 600 Muslims from the colonies; the ossuary contains the bones of 130,000 unknown French and German soldiers. The bodies of another 160,000 men were never found.[7] In the canton of Lassigny (Oise), where the front line was embedded for most of the war, all of the twenty-three villages were either damaged or destroyed. The landscape was lunar in appearance by 1918. In the department of Oise as a whole, about 163,000 hectares had to be recreated as fields, about one-third of the total, and more than 2,400 kilometres of roads.

Through this desolation ran corridors of timber-lined trenches: in 1916–18, annual timber consumption was about twenty times pre-war levels, and almost half of France's forests (182,000 hectares) were felled. The government later estimated that 3.3 million hectares of land had been affected by the war, including more than 4,700 communes across ten departments. Almost half of that land needed radical rectification. Barbed wire covered 375 million square metres, and there were 333 million cubic metres of trenches to be levelled. Much of the post-war reconstruction further transformed the landscape: around Verdun, the forests would now cover almost 16,000 hectares rather than the pre-war figure of 5,700. Forests had always played a central role in warfare, whether as sources of timber and food or places of refuge and recuperation. But never before had they been subject to the industrial-scale assault unleashed in 1914. Apart from the 182,000 hectares of forests which had been destroyed, another 150,000 had been damaged by premature felling. The scale of destruction of France's forests would take decades to be matched by replanting.[8]

The affected area covered about one-fourteenth of the area of France but was among the most valuable land, responsible for one-fifth of tax revenues. Senator Paul Doumer, a local politician from Laon who had lost four children and his family home during the war, described in 1919 'a desert, a zone of death, assassination and devastation . . . There are corpses of horses, corpses of trees covering the corpses of men'. Over 1,200 villages had been destroyed or damaged. Almost 300,000 buildings and farmhouses had been destroyed, and a further half million had been damaged. While 1.7 million hectares of land needed clearing of war debris, a further 1.5 million needed far more considerable work. In all, only 423 of the 4,726 communes in the region had not suffered damage; 620 had been completely destroyed and 1,334 were more than half destroyed. At least 830,000 cattle, 290,000 horses, 800,000 sheep and 330,000 pigs had been killed.[9]

In all, approximately 30,000 square kilometres of land – about one-quarter the size of England – were affected by the war, especially the line of most intense bloodshed that snaked from the Vosges mountains to Lens. Quite apart from the hundreds of villages and towns that needed to be rebuilt after the war, the affected rural areas needed to be resurveyed and forests replanted, all in the context of a shattered local population.[10] The physical devastation had been matched by the nationwide trauma of protracted warfare associated with the loss of swathes of young men, resulting in all between 1.7 and 1.75 million deaths in a population of 41.6 million. Another 200,000 died of pneumonia; a similar number was simply never found. The national population did not recover to a similar level until 1950.

The department of Marne in the Champagne region had been particularly hard hit. The creation of the 12,000-hectare Châlons military camp near Châlons-sur-Marne in 1857 had been the first permanent military camp on the French landscape, like later training camps located on what the government and military deemed poor-quality soil, a designation always contested by local communities.[11] It was at the heart of the fighting after 1914. In the entire department, less than 20,000 hectares of farmland were unaffected, from a total of 185,000 hectares. North of the town of Suippes, combat had obliterated seven villages and reduced the landscape to an open cemetery. In 1918, the Bishop of Châlons described it as 'an absolute desert, without water, people or vegetation . . . the land is colourless, and is like the corpse of a *pays*'. Today, Suippes is both an army camp and a museum of the Great War, with the ruins of the villages preserved within its boundaries.[12]

The major French and allied war memorials – Verdun, Thiepval, Villers-Bretonneux, Delville Wood and others – tower over the landscape, but physical reminders of mass killing are also located in thousands of small village cemeteries and memorials. Despite the intense efforts to erase physical reminders of trench warfare from the landscape, there are startling reminders, none more so than the Grande Mine or Lochnagar mine crater at La Boiselle, northeast of the town of Albert in the department of Somme. The crater – 21 metres deep and 100 metres wide – was the result of mines laid by the British Army's Tunnelling Company Royal Engineers underneath a German strongpoint on the morning of 1 July 1916. Despite the scale of the explosion and the deaths of German soldiers, others of them managed to defend the strongpoint, killing hundreds of British soldiers in the process.[13]

The scale of reconstruction was staggering. The 333 million cubic metres of trenches were filled in, and the 375 million square metres of barbed wire were collected. Nearly two million hectares of farmland were cleared and levelled, and volumes of production were back to pre-war levels by the 1930s. There are few obvious traces of the war, such as the Grande Mine crater, in the agricultural landscape today, apart from thousands of cemeteries and war memorials (see Figure 6.1). But the landscape was irrevocably altered: the style of housing created after the war was radically different from what it had been. The typical Picard village beloved of Edith Wharton, of a street of closely spaced houses in wood or stone, with thatched rooves, and large farms around courtyards (*courts*), had been replaced by uniform village housing in mass-produced brick or concrete blocks with tile rooves, deliberately spaced to provide small gardens, interior light and footpaths. Locals complained that the houses were too white and the roofs too red, even though they were more spacious and the villages more regular in appearance. This is the village landscape today.[14]

FIGURE 6.1 War in the landscape: one of thousands of monuments and cemeteries in the northeast, this Australian First World War monument at Sailly-le-Sec overlooks the river Somme 30 kilometres east of Amiens. Peter McPhee.

Another dominant feature of the landscape had disappeared from the reconstructed countryside. A study of 500 *châteaux* and manor houses which had been destroyed or badly damaged in Picardy found that only thirty-nine were completely restored and that, of those, twenty-eight were rebuilt in radically different, eclectic and more modest styles. State funding was not available in any case. A central feature of the northeastern landscape – the prominence of the massive, enclosed farmhouse or *court* which gave its name to so many villages – had disappeared from hundreds of communities (see Figure 1.1).[15]

Towns and villages were now linked by the long, straight roads through the region that we know today, such as those radiating from Amiens to Arras, Saint-Quentin, Noyon and Cambrai. Nor were the reconstituted fields the same as before 1914. There had been local initiatives showing how land redistribution between proprietors at the local level could achieve the benefits of larger and contiguous plots, but the process was accelerated by the terrible damage to land in the northeast during the war. Why not take advantage of the need to reconstruct the fabric of entire villages to also reorganize the scattered plots into larger farms? On 27 November 1918, a new law on *remembrement* sought to accelerate the process.[16]

Such were the continued horrors awaiting France with the depression of 1929, the rise of fascism and deep political divides in the 1930s, and renewed invasion after 1940 that the interwar period has had a durable image of political stalemate and ineptitude under the darkening shadows of looming catastrophe. In fact, these twenty years were a time of significance for a changing relationship between French people and their landscapes, indeed for the cultural meanings of landscapes themselves.[17]

Far away from the front, on the high plain of the Limagne near Clermont-Ferrand, the war had had a very different impact. Upwards of one thousand German prisoners of war were deployed in heavy manual work digging drainage ditches across the vast plain, whose richness of soil had always been vulnerable to stagnant floodwaters held by the impermeable volcanic subsoil. For hundreds of years, farmers and governments had sought to divert water into the River Allier, which runs through the plain, but now a far more concerted effort was made. By mid-century, some 20,000 hectares of the most affected areas were drained, mills were closed, and 150,000 trees felled. At the same time, efforts were redoubled to convince farmers of the virtues of *remembrement*: in La Sauvetat, for example, the surface area of 750 hectares had been formerly divided into 3,841 separate parcels among 641 landowners. The great plain was taking on its present appearance of a great swathe of undulating cropland, among the most productive in Europe, while today maize has come to be the most lucrative crop of all (see Plate 1).[18]

The rural landscape remained dominated by small family farms, except for broad-acre farming in the Paris basin and small vineyards along the Mediterranean coastline: there were 764,000 farms between 10 and 50 hectares in 1892 and 973,000 in 1929, covering half of all farmland. Increasingly, however, these were farms which specialized in local produce while seeking to produce their own vegetables and meat as well. The appearance of the landscape was continuing to evolve, even though the diversity of agricultural practices has been described as 'a museum of agrarian structures', with extremes of mechanized, industrial-scale production of wheat near Paris and subsistence polyculture in parts of the Limousin and elsewhere. While there were still artisan industries in substantial villages (*bourgs*) – farriers, barrel-makers, carpenters, stonemasons and shoemakers – the landscape had a more rural appearance than ever as mechanical work concentrated in towns.[19]

The large-scale rebuilding necessitated in the northeast after 1918 was not replicated elsewhere. By the end of the 1930s, eight rural families in ten lived in houses built before 1871, and six in ten were much older. The place of the village in the rural landscape had scarcely changed in appearance for a century, in part because in most regions there was no shortage of housing with the exodus of the very poor. There were twice as many new farm buildings as there were farmhouses built in 1929–39. What changed, however, was the disappearance of thatch except in Normandy and Brittany and of earthen floors and houses without windows, all changes which had begun well before 1914. Automobiles and motorcycles were becoming a common sight across the countryside: there were more than 630,000 kilometres of roads in 1933, compared with 476,000 in 1914. While major railway lines had basically reached their limit, there had been a dramatic expansion of local branch lines, seen as the mode of transport of necessity: local lines covered 30,200 kilometres in 1936 compared with 11,600 in 1910.[20]

The interwar years witnessed a dramatic acceleration in the construction of a new lattice of infrastructure that would be even more obvious than the canal, road and rail networks and which would continue to be a prominent – and often contested – feature of the landscape today. By the close of the nineteenth century, the industrial production of electricity through coal and hydroelectricity became possible, and communities could begin to contemplate domestic as well as public and industrial uses. In 1919, only about 7,000 of the 41,000 communes had electricity; by 1938, there were 36,528 which did so. The length of power lines increased accordingly, from 900 kilometres in 1923 to 12,400 kilometres in 1946, not counting the millions of lines connecting power lines to houses.[21] The first pylons or *poteaux* along rural roads were simple affairs in timber and wrought iron, often quite delicate, even graceful. They were superseded by the ubiquitous pylons of reinforced concrete and steel still used today, often seen as ugly and prone to corrosion (see Figure 6.2). Since then, the technical demands of linking nuclear power plants to large cities have created great chains of massive pylons. Most are 55 metres high and weigh 40 tonnes, but there are some more than 110 metres high near Bordeaux and Nantes.

The extension of electrical infrastructure across the landscape was matched by the increased use of mechanical equipment on large farms everywhere. One example comes from Saint-Aignan, a village in the very heart of Brittany, on the border between the departments of Morbihan and Côtes-d'Armor. Its verdant, hilly landscape winds along the Blavet River, paralleled along the eastern border by the great canal from Brest to Nantes, completed in the first half of the nineteenth century. Its mayor for more than forty years (1904–47) was a remarkable agronomist, Paul Lotz (1877–1967), a First World War veteran who later also became a deputy for Morbihan (1932–6) and a leading figure in agricultural circles in his district. For forty years, from around 1890, Lotz took photographs of his family and travels, but especially of the manor house and estate of Bot-Pléven, of which he was the proprietor. Lotz was also an enthusiast for electricity, and it is no coincidence that a large hydroelectric dam, the Barrage de Guerlédan, was completed on the Blavet along the northern boundary of his commune in 1930. A small museum of electricity in the village marks the achievement. Many of Lotz's photographs are of the dam; even more are of his other great love: agricultural improvement. But while the photographs were designed to record mechanical innovation – such as the proud use of a reaper-binder

FIGURE 6.2 The electrification of rural France from the late-nineteenth century radically altered the conditions of rural life, but often at the expense of landscapes, as here in Brittany. Mobile phone towers have compounded the clutter. Peter McPhee.

for cereal harvesting – they also document the continued dominance of animals in the rural landscape. In this Breton Village, two horses and two bulls were commonly harnessed together for ploughing and sowing in particular (see Figure 6.3).[22]

The experience of almost all villages in the decades after the First World War was a steep decline in the number of families directly involved in agriculture. The landscape had fewer people at work within it, as, for example, in truffle-farming areas in the Périgord, where there was large-scale emigration of small farmers, compounding the loss of life of troops in the war. From the nineteenth century to the present, truffle production fell by 97–99 per cent, from 2,000 tonnes in 1890 to 20–50 tonnes annually. The use of pesticides and fungicides after the Second World War was to further restrict truffle production, and today it is the preserve of highly skilled artisan producers competing with Italian and overseas suppliers.[23]

In most areas, there were also fewer animals to be seen. A typical example is the Picard village of Rainneville, just north of Amiens, where in 1900 there had been

FIGURE 6.3 The introduction of agricultural machinery initially relied on animal power, as here at Saint-Aignan (Morbihan). This photograph of a reaper-binder, invented in 1872, was probably taken around 1920. Bullocks and horses have now largely disappeared from the landscape. AD Morbihan 8 Fi 193.

113 horses, 3 mules, 15 donkeys, 340 cattle (including 205 cows), 300 sheep, 75 pigs and 25 goats on the 700 hectares, much of which were planted in sugar beet. Today, Rainneville is surrounded by broad-acre farming of wheat, maize and sugar beet, and only a few cows have survived. Where the village differs from most is that, despite the sharp decline of numbers of farmers, the total population has doubled from 563 in 1901 to more than 1,000 today, as Rainneville becomes a popular dormitory suburb for Amiens. Until the Second World War, all but the very wealthy travelled by bus when they visited Amiens and by horse or on foot around the village.[24]

Far away to the south, in the Mediterranean backcountry village of Gabian (Hérault), there was a similar accentuation of monoculture: in 1913 there were 730 hectares of vineyards, and by 1935 there were 857 hectares, covering two-thirds of the commune. Postcards from the 1930s record a landscape almost devoid of trees (see Figure 6.4). As in Rainneville, an older pastoral economy was continuing to decline: there were still 394 sheep and 60 goats in 1913, but by 1932, there were just 150 sheep. Cereal crops had disappeared altogether, except for stock feed. In 1903, there had been seventy-four horses and fifty-four mules, they were still useful for ploughing between the rows of vines in the 1940s, even if their owners now got about more frequently by bicycle, motorbike and even by car.[25] Elsewhere, particular animals came to dominate as the use of the landscape became more selective. So, in the Vivarais region, essentially the department of Ardèche, the number of cattle had increased 40 per cent in the century after 1852, from 48,000 to 68,000, especially in upland areas. But the numbers of sheep had tumbled, from 315,000 to about 75,000.[26]

FIGURE 6.4 Postcards of southern communities such as Gabian (Hérault) early in the twentieth century document a denuded landscape dominated by vineyards. The collapse of an older pastoral industry and restrictions on winegrowing have since enabled extensive revegetation. Licensed under the Creative Commons Attribution-Share Alike 4.0 International license.

The obliteration of extensive tracts of the landscape during the war impelled governments to take more decisive measures to protect landscape heritage. The law of 31 December 1913 protecting historical monuments was expanded on 2 May 1930, into the protection of 'natural monuments and artistic, historic, scientific, legendary and picturesque sites' (*sites classés*). This sought to protect such places from inappropriate development and included both natural and constructed landscape. Landscape was now understood to be a central element of the nation's patrimony.

The Société pour la Protection des Paysages de France (SPPF), founded in 1901, carried on its advocacy through the First World War with a network of about 1,000 prominent members across the country. Its primary aim was 'to develop and spread the idea that all-natural beauty, separately or collectively, can be an object of public utility as necessary to mankind and the riches of a land as to its beauty'. It could boast that its advocacy had largely been responsible for the laws of April 1906, under which 500 natural sites had been classified, and that of May 1930, which had led to 400 others being protected. It had achieved high-level access to power, holding its meetings at the Ministry of Agriculture and having representation from the ministries of Eaux et Forêts and Beaux-Arts, the Préfecture de la Seine, the Office National du Tourisme, the Club Alpin, the Touring Club and the Société Nationale d'Acclimatation. But it insisted in the final issue of its bulletin in 1939:

what remains to be done is immense. The harmonious landscapes of France are the most menaced and yet, in the moral order as in material world, beauty is the most precious of goods. The Society protects from the malevolence of individuals, collectivities and crowds that which is the property of all: flowers, plants, trees, sites, monuments, villages with their regional character, towns and memories of the past.[27]

The Society had worried about the menaces of 'malevolence' towards the landscapes it valued, but a new democratic basis had been created for the appreciation of landscapes. Until the introduction of paid annual leave, wage-earners could travel for pleasure only on Sundays and on the 7–10 days of public and religious holidays. The Matignon Agreements signed on 7 June 1936, between the Léon Blum Popular Front government, employers and the CGT trade union, guaranteed two weeks of paid annual leave for workers and limited the working week to forty hours. This leave increased to three weeks in 1956, four weeks in 1969, and five weeks in 1981. For the first time, wage-earners could contemplate leisure travel to places from which they did not need to return on the same day. Rural people had always had an appreciation of the aesthetic value of their immediate environs; now they could contemplate travel to different, distant landscapes of which they had only learnt in school. The introduction of paid annual leave in 1936 marked the beginning of a mass tourism industry and the direct experience of huge numbers of urban people with contrasting rural landscapes.

After the First World War, the *avant garde* in painting focused its creativity on capturing the pain of a world fractured by the unprecedented killing of the war, the nature of the urban industrialization which underpinned it, and the raw clash of polarized ideologies. Fewer prominent painters focused their creative talents on the countryside compared with the pre-war post-Impressionists. There were some important exceptions. The Belorussian Chaïm Soutine used his time after 1919 in the foothills of the Pyrenees at Céret, beloved of Picasso, to capture a tortured, sinuous landscape buffeted by the Tramontane winds (see Plate 11). Pierre Bonnard moved definitively to the Côte-d'Azur in 1925 and sought to capture its sharp contrasts of colour and line. Never before, however, had there been so many amateur and part-time painters with the greater accessibility of paint in tubes, and it was in this world of democratized art that landscape painting became the dominant genre and remains so to this day. The choice of subject matter reflected the new values of the SPPF: the spectacular, the verdant and the coastal.

The heightened sense of national identity created by the horrific experiences of war underpinned a surge in initiatives to strengthen national and regional identities through the protection of product names or *appellations*. This was not entirely new: as long ago as July 1824, the Chaptal law on *marques régionales* had sought to protect regional wines and their names against misleading claims by competitors from elsewhere and from downright fraud. The law had been used for the first time in 1844 in a famous judgement to protect champagne.[28] In December 1908, another decree defined the precise region with the right to use the appellation. The champagne producers of the department of Marne were extraordinarily successful, not only in marketing their product as denoting 'luxury' and *savoir vivre* but also in convincing national governments and even their fellow citizens that champagne was quintessentially 'French'. In turn, they won the right to limit the region that could claim to produce it, thereby guaranteeing themselves a privileged place in the market against all those other regions which might argue that their sparkling wine was of similar quality.[29]

After the First World War, the practice of associations of regional producers seeking protection and commercial advantage became widespread. The wine crisis of 1906–7 had highlighted the problem of fraud in marketing and its potential health consequences. On 6 May 1919, the Assembly voted a law on *appellations d'origine contrôlée* (AOC), recognizing those with legitimate claims to constitute an association to control an *appellation*, but avoided setting standards, referring only to 'durable and faithful local usage'.[30]

While Léon Bel had registered his cheese brand 'La Vache qui rit' with authorities in Lons-le-Saunier (Jura) in April 1921, the first AOC for a cheese was secured in July 1925 by the Société Roquefort. Only those cheeses ripened in the natural caves of Mont Combalou in the village of Roquefort-sur-Soulzon were now authorized to carry the name Roquefort. Today, the sheep milk for the cheese comes from a closely defined and protected area of about 2,000 farms across the Larzac Plain in upper Languedoc. While Roquefort had succeeded in 1925, Camembert was thwarted the next year: it was simply too widely produced to be able to be confined to a particular region of Normandy where it had allegedly been invented in 1791. Only in 1983 did it succeed in achieving AOC status if producers used local milk.[31] The semi-soft blue cheese Haut-Jura, or Gex-Septmoncel, won its appellation in April 1935. So interested were producers elsewhere becoming in the commercial advantages of the AOC label that the government passed a new law defining the process in July 1935. It was soon taken up successfully by products ranging from Martinique rum (April 1936) to Gevrey-Chambertin wine from Burgundy (July 1937) and Grenoble walnuts (June 1938).[32]

The interwar proliferation of AOC product protection may have been generated primarily by the impulse to seek marketing advantages over other regions and against fraud. However, it also contributed to a distinctive characteristic of the resonance of *paysage* in public life. Even as the spread of uniformity was inexorable through the accessibility of nationwide communications, marketing and culture, French people were valuing the appeal of regional diversity that came with the identification of particular landscapes with specialized products. That remains the case today and drew on the drive for a national reconstruction after the First World War, a nationalism in which regional identity and diversity were central.

National regeneration was expressed in other ways. Germany had occupied almost all of Alsace and part of Lorraine from 1870 until 1918. The last great canal in the national project was fittingly in Alsace, along the Rhine immediately across the border with Germany. Almost 150 canals had been constructed in France, ranging from the disused Canal de Beuvry (0.6 kilometres) near Dunkerque to several over 200 kilometres in length: the Canal de la Marne à la Saône, the Canal de la Meuse, the Canal du Midi, the Canal du Rhône au Rhin and the Canal de la Basse Seine. The last great canal project, the Grand Canal d'Alsace (constructed 1932–59) was to be the most dramatic in its impact on the landscape. The canal, just 50 kilometres in length, runs beside the Rhine between Kembs and Vogelgrun, a stretch on which the fast-flowing Rhine is not navigable. The canal allows the passage of about 30,000 vessels annually between Basel and Strasbourg, and four major hydroelectric installations power one of the major industrial regions of Europe. It also provided water for the nuclear reactor at Fessenheim from 1977 until its closure in 2020.[33]

The determination to deter the neighbouring German state from again invading France – as it now had four times since 1792 – was expressed in major works of fortification, in particular the Maginot Line running 200 kilometres along the border with Germany from Luxembourg to Switzerland. There were interconnected bunker complexes for thousands of soldiers. There were 45 main forts (*grands ouvrages*) at intervals of 15 kilometres, 97 smaller forts (*petits ouvrages*) and 352 fortified gun emplacements or casemates between them, with over 100 kilometres of tunnels. The specifications of the line were extraordinary and ultimately may have engendered a false sense of security within the French military command, as the eventual invasion further north through the Ardennes mountains from Belgium in 1940 was to demonstrate.[34]

One of the most imposing Maginot Line intrusions into the landscape is near the village of Schoenenbourg, today famous for its *grand cru* white wine: riesling, muscat and pinot gris. Voltaire once owned vines there. Just outside the village is the 'Ouvrage de Schoenenbourg', a colossal fortification which received saturation bombing in 1940 as part of the Maginot Line but survived and was operable until decommissioned in the 1970s. Three kilometres of railways connected the eight blocks. While these were underground, the massive entry above ground is an extraordinarily imposing fortification. Today, the Schoenenbourg fortress is visited by walkers and tourists rather than soldiers. Other forts along the line have similarly found peaceful vocations as mushroom farms, residences, wine cellars and even as discothèques.[35]

Schoenenbourg speaks to us today about the tragic trust of the French military leadership in the construction of a line of fortresses which would make France finally safe from invasion from the East. Other physical reminders in the landscape recall the horrific consequences of the failure of that confidence. The original village of Oradour-sur-Glane (Haute-Vienne) was destroyed on 10 June 1944, when 642 of its inhabitants were massacred by a company of troops belonging to a Waffen-SS unit of the military forces of Nazi Germany in reprisal for resistance activities. As at Craonne in the 1920s, a new village was built after the war on a nearby site, but, on the orders of President de Gaulle, the original village has been maintained as a permanent memorial.[36]

Normandy's beaches and coastline, the 200 kilometres from Barfleur to Honfleur, are marked with physical reminders of the Allied landings in June 1944: the remains of German fortifications erected in 1942–4, some of the craters made by bombing, and the memorials erected after the war. Perhaps the most dramatic example of the physical impact of the war is at the Pointe du Hoc, overlooking Omaha Beach in Normandy. There on 6 June, US soldiers overwhelmed the gun emplacement on high cliffs. The 14-hectare reserve is studded with deep bomb craters (see Plate 13). More recently, three massive batteries, known collectively as the Maisy Battery, with tunnels 3 kilometres in length, have been uncovered near the village of Grandcamp-Maisy, suggesting that the emplacement at the Pointe du Hoc may have been something of a diversionary target.[37]

Inland from Utah Beach, in the channel department of Manche, 617 of 648 communes experienced some form of damage, including to about 100,000 buildings, after the Allied landings. While most of these were rebuilt, more permanent change was written on the landscape, especially with the rupturing of hedgerows. In 1944, American and British troops had to hack and blast their paths through the hedgerows of the *bocage*, heavily mined and laced with barbed wire. In all, some 200,000 hectares of farmland through the departments of Calvados and Manche were affected by landmines, craters and military occupation. Many of the hedges would never be replaced.[38] Final victory in the protracted 'battle of the hedgerows' (*Bataille des Haies*) resulted in US forces constructing a dozen military airports, demolishing hedgerows and levelling ground in the process. In more than one hundred communes where extensive damage had been done to the countryside, authorities took the opportunity to push through new measures of *remembrement*.[39]

The battles of the Second World War left few permanent marks on the landscape elsewhere, unlike in urban areas which were bombed (such as Orléans and Saint-Nazaire), but the proliferation of memorials to the *maquis* (meaning both the guerrilla-type resistance and the dense scrub in which it hid and lived) remains testimony to the close links between topography, landscape and war. Unlike the First World War, whose built memorials are in tens of thousands of village and town squares, the great war memorials on the battlefields, and the hundreds of small cemeteries along the front, those commemorating the Second World War are often dotted through the landscape in areas of major resistance to the German occupation.

The Vercors plateau south of Grenoble in particular is studded with monuments to the memory of extraordinary heroism.[40] On the eastern border near Annecy, a

FIGURE 6.5 In October 1941, German authorities retaliated for the killing of an army commander by executing twenty-seven hostages in a sand quarry outside Châteaubriant, between Rennes and Vannes. The monument there dates from 1950. Peter McPhee.

towering monument on the plateau commemorates the battle of Les Glières. Here, up to 450 *maquisards* sustained by airdrops from British aircraft fought a series of battles with Vichy French militia and German troops before being overwhelmed in March 1944. The bodies of eighty-eight of the resisters are interred in the national cemetery at nearby Morette. In a quarry outside Châteaubriant, a Breton town between Nantes and Rennes, is a powerful memorial to twenty-seven hostages, mostly communists, executed on 22 October 1941, as a reprisal for the murder of the German Feldkommandant of Nantes (see Figure 6.5).

The Second World War left many other sites etched onto the landscape, some of which are now major tourist attractions – including the Maginot fortifications, the Compiègne forest clearing and railway car, the 'martyred village' of Oradour-sur-Glane, Normandy beaches, and Allied cemeteries.[41] Others are less known but no less redolent of suffering, such as the concentration camp at Rivesaltes, north of Perpignan. The camp was first used to house Catalan refugees at the end of the Spanish Civil War in 1939, but most tragically, as a transit camp in 1942 for 2,251 Jews from the Drancy internment camp in Paris to the extermination prison at Auschwitz. After the war, it was used for German prisoners of war and then for 12,000 *harkis* who had fled their native Algeria in fear for their lives and who were housed there in 1962. Most recently, it was used as a processing centre for asylum seekers from North Africa before, in 2015, becoming a museum to commemorate those who had suffered there, from the Spanish Civil War to the retreat from Algeria. It is a haunting site just metres away from the autoroute and railways, today carrying streams of humans seeking the southern sun rather than being forced there for punishment or refuge.[42]

The Vichy regime had preached a 'back to the soil' message, but, apart from some marsh-drainage works, the pressures of war actually saw a decline in the total area being cultivated. The war intensified pressures on France's forest reserves because other fuel sources were restricted and necessitated extensive reforestation works after 1945. Between 1942 and 1947, 380,000 hectares of pine forests were destroyed in the *landes*, much by deliberate acts of arson designed to impede supplies to the occupying German army.

The extraordinary depletion of forest resources reversed most of the gains made since the 1860s and would take decades to recoup. In 1946, a national forestry fund (Fonds Forestier National) was given sweeping powers and resources to acquire suitable land and reforest depleted areas. By 1971, it had reforested almost 1.5 million hectares. Another immediate challenge was met very promptly, albeit tragically: in occupied areas along the coasts and in Picardy, 13 million landmines were cleared by 1950, but at the cost of the lives of 471 French landmine clearers and 738 German prisoners of war.[43]

Another 800 German prisoners of war were also deployed in finally completing the hydroelectric dam on the River Verdon at Saint-André-les-Alpes. The project, which had begun in 1929, had taken twenty years because of political and military upheaval and repeated acts of sabotage. The project drowned the village of Castillon, which gave its name to a lake, which today has further transformed the region around Saint-André into a green tourist mecca in contrast to the stony and impoverished landscape of 1900 (see Figure 5.4).[44]

The defeat of the French military in 1940, and subsequently in Vietnam in 1954 and Algeria in 1962, stiffened the resolve of later governments that such reverses would be the last. The publication of Jean Gravier's searing analysis in 1947 of the socio-economic gap between the Paris region and much of the south, *Paris et le désert français*, provided the government with the pretext to create a massive army base in the southeast. The spectacular gorges of the Verdon River in Provence flank the largest military base in Europe, the 350 square kilometres of the Camp de Canjuers, on a great semi-arid plateau at 800 metres altitude. Canjuers was announced in 1962 and created in 1970 against local objections.[45]

Today, the French military remains a major presence in the landscape of France, occupying nearly 260,000 hectares or 0.5 per cent of the total territory. While the military had originally occupied vast tracts of what it controversially deemed 'wastelands', in recent decades it has been keen to defend its occupancy as creating precious reserves for biodiversity, ignoring those occasions when it deliberately destroys the landscape and its animals.[46]

The visual impact of the First World War on the landscape was obvious: the impact of artillery fire was the equivalent of 40,000 years of 'natural' erosion. Less visible but even more fundamental was that the war highlighted the need for aviation and fuel: global oil production more than doubled in the decade after 1910. This use of fossil fuels was accelerated far more quickly by the Second World War and the subsequent Cold War, together causing a dramatic increase in production of chemical weapons, steel, plastic, aluminium and chlorofluorocarbons, and the further development of nuclear energy and weapons.[47]

In 1914–45, France had lived through what is sometimes called the Second Thirty Years' War (referring back to that in 1618–48) or the Age of Catastrophe. Two invasions and occupations had bookended decades of civil strife; millions of people had had their lives ended prematurely or wrecked in other ways. The unprecedented loss of life in warfare was matched by the environmental devastation of wartime landscapes. Now the dramatic increase in the capacity of humans to alter the landscape and its climate by the use of nuclear weaponry and mass extraction of fossil fuels was to confront everyone – from European and national governments to local community associations – with new vulnerabilities of the landscapes for which they were responsible.

7 MAKING THE CONTEMPORARY LANDSCAPE, 1950–2000

Reflecting back on the decades of economic growth after the Second World War, the economist Jean Fourastié famously labelled the years 1945–75 as *les trente glorieuses* ('the thirty glorious years').[1] Fourastié's label, evoking the memory of the three days of the Revolution of 1830 as *les trois glorieuses*, has become the byword for an extraordinary period of transition. France's gross national product grew at 4 per cent per annum, and real incomes increased by around 175 per cent across the period. While these were decades when most of France's Asian and African colonies achieved their independence, the new opportunities opened up by the European Union and its common market, bolstered by the US post-war Marshall Plan, created boom times until the oil price spikes of the 1970s.

The economic growth of the 'thirty glorious years' was underpinned by dramatic changes in farming, energy and transport, so much so that the American historian Gordon Wright concluded that the years after 1950 amounted to a 'rural revolution'.[2] Fernand Braudel, with whom this book began, would have agreed: after 1945, he concluded, 'an ancient peasant France . . . fell victim to the "Thirty Glorious Years", that period of unprecedented expansion.'[3] In the process, much of the landscape of France was radically transformed in the directions with which we are most familiar today.

Braudel, born in Lorraine in 1902, was personally aware of the previous transformations that this book has described: changes to areas under cultivation and what was produced, the introduction of fertilizers, more effective ploughs and threshers and easier transport. But it was above all the introduction of the tractor, and its capacity to plough huge areas, to pull combine harvesters and haymakers, which was transforming:

Animal teams, whether of horses or oxen, have almost completely disappeared since the war. The last time I visited my native village in the Meuse in 1980, there was only one horse left, and that was out to grass, on the farm belonging to my elderly cousin.[4]

Braudel spent the final years of his life at the other end of the country, in the small town of Céret, in the foothills of the eastern Pyrenees. He finished his last book by commenting on another consequence of the post-Second World War years: the expansion of uncultivated or 'waste' land (*friches*). The rough hillsides known in this area as *aspres* 'have reverted to nature: today only brambles, shrubs and broom flourish on the poor and untended soil. . . . (After 1950) the population gave up, leaving everything just as it stood'. Others have regretted the intrusion into this empty countryside of 'seminomadic hunters, gatherers, and fishermen, denizens of a modern Palaeolithic age: city dwellers, tourists, part-time residents'.[5]

In 1946, farming still employed 36 per cent of the active adult population, compared to 5.5 per cent in Britain and 16 per cent in the United States. There were still 2.5 million farms, of which 58 per cent were smaller than 10 hectares and 37 per cent smaller than 5. That was about to change. After the Second World War, the rural exodus continued, this time pushed by the sharply increased productivity of mechanized agriculture on easily arable land. In the decade after 1949, an average of 150,000 people per year left the countryside. Small household farms in less accessible areas became unattractive, especially as the search by city dwellers for holiday houses made it appealing to sell up. By 1970, there were only 1.8 million farms, and the numbers have continued to decline ever since.

In 1939, there had been only 30,000 tractors in France. By 1950, that had jumped to 140,000, then to 1,239,000 twenty years later. By then, more than half of all farmers owned one. There were 11,200 mechanical harvesters in 1953 and 154,000 in 1995. The advantages of mechanization for market production would shift the balance more firmly towards large-scale farming and radically alter the landscape of lowland France.[6]

The rapid mechanization of farming after 1945 was only one reason why the rural landscape was abruptly transformed in some regions. It was linked to other changes: the consolidation of small farms and scattered plots (*remembrement*); the removal of many of the hedgerows of the west (*bocage*); and the expansion of uncultivated land (*friches*).

Fundamental reforms were made as early as the law of 7 July 1945 to facilitate the practice of *remembrement*, leading to a thoroughgoing revision of the cadastral survey to recognize the widespread changes in landownership.[7] *Remembrement* was particularly attractive in areas where larger fields were accessible for mechanized cropping or where there were agricultural cooperatives, such as in lowland winegrowing areas. By 1960, the renewal and reform of the cadastral survey had covered 27,000 of the 41,000 communes, and the number of individual parcels listed had fallen from eighty-one to sixty million.

At the same time as the number of farms was decreasing and agriculture was 'modernizing' within an emerging European market, smallholders were establishing cooperatives to counter large-scale competition, mirrored by the creation of *foyers ruraux* to provide centres for practical information for small farmers and leisure activities in rural communities. But mechanization and a new rural code in 1955 further encouraging *remembrement* would dramatically reduce the number of farming families, from 7.4 million people working in agriculture in 1946 to only 2 million in 1975 and 0.73 million today.[8] The disappearance of horses and oxen has been paralleled by the declining presence of human figures in most rural landscapes.

With the dramatic mechanization of agriculture after the Second World War, the reality in regions of the most productive land was of far larger, broad-acre farms, often owned by agro-businesses such as Danone, Limagrain, Lactalis, Unibel and LU. This reality has been in sharp contrast with – but has profited from – the prized image of France as the land of small farms, regional specialties and high-quality products.[9] Some of the large-scale agriculture has been startling in its size and presence in the landscape. For example, after 1950, a massive programme of land clearance began on the impoverished, chalky soils of the Champagne-Ardenne region to enable broad-acre farming using motorized equipment such as tractors and the application of mineral fertilizers to cultivate rapeseed, cereals and sugar beet. The huge Bazancourt-Pomacle site of 260 hectares near Reims continues to convert different types of biomass (mainly sugar beet, wheat, and alfalfa) into food and stockfeed ingredients, fuel and chemicals.[10] The same is true in the Limagne, near Clermont-Ferrand. In 1965, the village of Saint-Beauzire became home to the farmers' cooperative Limagrain, now the third-largest producer of seed in the world and whose silos and plants tower over the landscape (see Figure 7.1).

FIGURE 7.1 The headquarters of the cereal and seed company Limagrain, founded at Saint-Beauzire (Puy-de-Dôme) in 1965, dominate the landscape of the Limagne plateau. While the region was once often water-logged, today water supply is a pressing problem. Peter McPhee.

The same innovations were to have a dramatic impact on the *bocage* or hedgerow landscape of huge tracts of land, especially in regions of the north and west such as Brittany, Anjou and Poitou. The increased use of mechanical harvesters, oil-based fuels and the availability of cheap fencing wire were reasons why, in the post-war period, the 'battle of the hedgerows' changed from a military conflict between Allied and German troops in 1944 into a war on the hedgerows themselves. The renewed pressure for *remembrement* from 1960–90 was the final blow in many areas. As scattered fields were made contiguous, farmers were attracted to the idea of broad-acre farming across large fields, separated only by barbed-wire fences. It is estimated that, in Brittany alone, the total length of hedgerows plunged from 74,000 kilometres in 1971 to 24,000 in 1980.[11]

Removing hedgerows permitted easier and more productive use of machines and spreading of artificial fertilizers. Barbed wire and electric fencing were simple to use and maximized the land area. The modernizing rhetoric of the PAC, the European Union's Common Agricultural Policy, effectively encouraged farmers to get big or get out. The impact on the landscape is everywhere apparent today in the northern half of the country, where remnant *bocage* areas subsist side by side with large open fields devoted to cereal and maize production or to pastures defined by wire or electric fencing. In the process, a vicious cycle was created whereby in open field farming areas, the removal of tree and hedge cover for birds made crops more vulnerable to insects, necessitating the use of chemical pesticides, which could be poisonous as well for pollinating insects and the remaining bird life.

In 1918, the Polish chemist Fritz Haber received the Nobel Prize in Chemistry for his invention of the Haber-Bosch process to synthesize ammonia from nitrogen and hydrogen. This invention was of great importance for the production of explosives but equally as significant for making fertilizers. Since 1960, the global use of chemical fertilizers has increased ninefold, even though half the nitrogen is not absorbed by plants and enters the soil and waterways. There had been 473,000 tonnes of fertilizer used in France in 1913; 822,000 in 1938; and 5,683,000 in 1995. The balance of risks in the use of chemical fertilizers and insecticides to increase productivity was to become the most fraught issue in debates over the management of the French landscape. The systemic insecticide imidacloprid, for example, from a class of chemicals called neonicotinoids, was blamed for a steep decline in bees and birdlife in agricultural areas in France in the 1990s and finally banned by the European Union in 2018.[12]

There were particular regions which had their own reasons for resisting the pressures both for *remembrement* and for removing their hedgerows, none more so than the distinctive area of the *bocage charolais* or Charolais-Brionnais. This region of 129 communes in southwest Burgundy has been characterized since the seventeenth century by intensive cattle farming, at the heart of which is the movement of livestock between specific hedge-lined small pastures during their life-cycles. Not surprisingly, the farmers of the Charolais rejected attempts to alter field systems. The result has been a remarkable and intensely beautiful landscape of *bocage* and well-maintained farm buildings from the last three centuries, now being considered for inclusion on the UNESCO World Heritage Register.[13] Even here, however, the use of pesticides has had an impact.

Elsewhere, the expansion of abandoned land (*friches*) was one of the most abrupt changes to the landscape since the Middle Ages. The dramatic increases in productivity on the lowlands, often intensified by chemical fertilizers and insecticides, were paralleled by the abandonment of hillsides. While the expanding forests have been a beneficiary, very often these abandoned lands have been invaded by wild herbs, broom, small oaks, ferns and invasive species such as succulents and ragwort. This is particularly marked between Rodez and Carcassonne in Languedoc and between Sisteron and Nice in Provence. The agricultural policy of the European Union has facilitated this to the point where even productive land is at times more valuable if withdrawn from creating an oversupply, of wine in particular. Across the second half of the century, annual wine consumption per capita in France declined sharply, from 124 litres in 1950 to just 58 in 2000 (today the figure is close to 40 litres).[14] Vast hilly areas of the south, while attractive as holiday retreats from expanding lowland and coastal settlements, have changed as scrub smothers remnants of ancient intensive cultivation, as Fernand Braudel regretted.

Across highland areas in particular, the terraces mostly constructed in the centuries before 1600 were largely abandoned with the trend towards larger-scale monoculture after 1850, but from the 1990s some localities saw the opportunity for refurbishing them to meet the market for boutique agricultural produce on 'terroirs'. In the Cévennes village of Saint-André-de-Majencoules in the department of Gard, for example, a cooperative of thirty farmers cultivating sweet onions on terraces received an AOC in 2003.[15] The most spectacular examples of terraces in the landscape, however, are in winegrowing areas which never abandoned terraces and where some of the finest wines are still produced today, such as along the Côte Vermeille on the Spanish border (Banyuls crus) and the Rhone Valley (Cornas, Hermitage, Côte Rôtie). There are especially remarkable terrace works in Collioure and Banyuls on the coast (see Plate 2) and in Tournon on the Rhône.[16]

After 1945, governments were profoundly imbued with the ethos of post-war reconstruction, accentuated by the collective will to obliterate memories of wartime humiliation and suffering. The mantra was 'modernization', but with a French rather than an American accent. In the long tradition of government intervention and planning going back to Louis XIV and Colbert in the seventeenth century, Charles de Gaulle impelled his governments to plan, build and improve. In the process, the face of the landscape would in many areas become one of wider, less treed agricultural and pastoral fields, contrasted with reforested hillsides. The *trente glorieuses* had a profound aesthetic impact on the landscape in other ways. This extraordinary period of economic growth and profound improvements to household amenities for most people – electricity, television, the telephone, running water – left dramatic scars across the land.

In 1945, only about 30 per cent of communities had a supply of running water; by the late 1980s, virtually all did. This was a radical change to daily life. When asked which was the most important of the changes to her domestic amenities during *les trente glorieuses*, one elderly inhabitant of the hamlet of Le Lac, north of Saint-Flour in Cantal, simply pointed to the small tap outside her front door. This was the last of the changes, only made in the mid-1960s, and ended her twice-daily trudge with full buckets from the creek running outside the village.[17] The impact on the landscape was equally dramatic. To ensure a supply of water into multi-story dwellings or in difficult locations, as many as 24,000 *châteaux d'eau* (water towers for gravity-fed distribution of water) were constructed by the 1990s as giant concrete mushrooms, which were often criticized for their bulk and profile. Twenty-five of them were over 75 metres high (see Figure 7.2). There are still 16,000 today as more are moved underground, with the associated costs of pumping.

The long post-war boom coincided with the dramatic expansion of sources of power. Electricity, first powered by coal, then hydroelectricity from around 1900 and finally nuclear power in the 1950s, was rivalled by fossil fuels: oil and gas, almost all imported. A vast network of power lines criss-crossed the nation into every village and hamlet, only a few of them underground (see Figure 6.2).

The first tidal power plant in the world opened in 1966 on the Rance River estuary in Brittany, between Dinard and Saint-Malo. It remains the second-largest in the world. The plant uses two sources of energy: tidal energy from the English Channel and river current energy from the Rance. Despite its imposing status as an early, large-scale renewable source of energy, the massive dam has had some negative environmental impacts through the increased level of silt in the habitat. Native aquatic plants suffocate in silt, and the flatfish plaice is now extinct in the area. Other organisms, such as cuttlefish, a relative of squids, which prefer cloudy, silty ecosystems, now thrive in the Rance estuary.[18]

The first nuclear power plants in France were three reactors at Marcoule, north of Avignon (1956–60), and the Chinon reactors on the Loire from 1962.[19] The oil price shocks after 1973 further convinced successive governments of the attractions of a source of energy that would be independent of global politics. By 2020, there would be fifty-six operating plants, with another fourteen shut down for maintenance. The intrusion into the landscape of the giant cooling towers of the nuclear plants came to be accepted as the price the countryside had to pay for the peaceful use of nuclear energy, which today provides almost three-quarters of France's energy needs (see Figure 7.3).

In France's colonies, however, the assumption that there were uninhabited spaces for the testing of nuclear weapons would leave a durable and negative impact on the landscape, the environment, and international relations. Between

FIGURE 7.2 The water tower (*château d'eau*) dominates the skyline of Amponville (Seine-et-Marne), 20 kilometres southwest of Fontainebleau. About 24,000 towers were erected in 1945–80; now many are being replaced by less intrusive water supply systems. Licensed under the Creative Commons Attribution-Share Alike 4.0 International license.

1960 and 1966, France conducted twenty-two nuclear tests in the Sahara Desert in southern Algeria but was ultimately forced to look further afield once Algeria became independent in 1962. Nowhere was the impact of nuclear testing on the landscape more destructive than on the other side of the globe, at France's atoll of Moruroa in the South Pacific. Here, 195 nuclear tests were detonated in the thirty years after 1966. The atoll remains closed to visitors, and the levels of damage to health and the environment are contested by Pacific neighbours.[20]

The great transition in France in the decades after 1960 to nuclear energy and renewables and away from coal is inscribed on the landscape, as at Loos-en-Gohelle, just north of Lens. Loos had been one of the northern towns completely destroyed in the First World War. Nearby Hill 70, captured by the Canadian Expeditionary Force in August 1917, is the dominant natural feature in this flat landscape, but equally dramatic are the two highest slag heaps (184 and 182 metres) in Europe, a

FIGURE 7.3 The nuclear energy site at Tricastin was put into service in 1980. Nuclear energy continues to provide more than 70 per cent of France's needs; wind energy provides only about 4 per cent. Peter McPhee.

FIGURE 7.4 The coal mine at Loos-en-Gohelle (Pas-de-Calais) was decommissioned in 1986 and its towering slag heaps, more than 180 metres high, slowly vegetated and converted into walking trails. It is now part of a UNESCO World Heritage region. Licensed under the Creative Commons Attribution-Share Alike 4.0 International license.

remnant of the coal mining which had begun in 1855. After mining ceased in 1986, these slag heaps were both rehabilitated as climbing attractions and inscribed on the historic places register as Monuments Historiques (see Figure 7.4).

Whereas reinforced concrete had been dominant in infrastructure construction before the Second World War, thereafter pre-stressed concrete would revolutionize

the construction of the shopping centres, bridges, tunnels, reservoirs and airport runways that now studded the countryside in the immediate hinterland of towns. The results could be functional and blunt (such as the 300-metre bridge over the Rhône at La Voulte, Ardèche, completed in 1955) or more graceful (the 2.8-kilometres-long viaduct connecting the Île d'Oléron to the Atlantic coast south of La Rochelle, constructed in 1966).[21]

The rush to construct infrastructure was sometimes catastrophic in its consequences. North of Fréjus (department of Var), remains may be seen of the horrific collapse of the Malpasset Dam on the Reyran River on 2 December 1959, (see Figure 7.5). The breach was most likely caused by a fault in the rock base of the reservoir, although heavy rain and explosive works for a nearby autoroute may have contributed to the disaster. A huge wave travelling at 70 kilometres per hour down the valley killed 423 people in the resulting flood.[22]

Nowhere was the post-war imperative of conquering energy and space more evident in the landscape than in the creation of a network of autoroutes. The long winter of November 1962–March 1963 in northern Europe was the harshest since modern records began, when average temperatures were more than 4° below average. An estimated 50,000 French people lost their lives, in part because of the impossibility of moving fuel and food supplies on blocked roads in rural areas. The disaster prompted radical action to emulate the autoroute system of Germany through attracting private capital. Across the half-century after 1960, the most physically imposing change of all occurred to the landscape of France, as an extraordinary system of autoroutes was overlaid on the centuries of patchwork of roads and lanes. There had been earlier autoroutes: Caen-Paris in 1940, Lyon-Marseille in 1951 and Paris-Lille in 1954, but the network expanded rapidly with all major routes opened in 1960: Paris-Lyon, Bordeaux-Paris, and Perpignan-Paris. By 2014, France was covered by a network of 11,882 kilometres (7,383 miles) of autoroutes.

This dramatic change to road travel was later matched by innovation in railways. Following the example of the Shinkansen in Japan, the French government commissioned the development of a high-speed rail network of *trains de grande vitesse* (TGV), inaugurated with a line from Paris to Lyon in 1981. The lines, branching out in four main trunks from Paris, necessitated new, separate tracks, today totalling 2,800 kilometres. These lines enabled the then fastest trip, of almost 280 kilometres per hour, in 2007. Today, the TGV network carries 110 million passengers each year within France and across its borders.[23]

The TGV lines, like the autoroutes, facilitated the rapid movement of people across the country and across Europe. Their impact on the landscape was obvious from the scale of their hundred-metre-wide slices across the countryside and the often spectacular engineering bridging of gorges in highland areas. The autoroutes also further accentuated the attractions of agricultural specialization, now on a European rather than French scale. Even local market gardens around provincial centres were now competing with fresh fruit and vegetables from neighbouring countries.

At the same time, more French people than ever before were acquiring their own private vehicles which, combined with lengthening annual holidays to five weeks by 1981, made mass tourism a feature of the summer landscape. There were 1.3 million private cars in 1949 and 8.4 million by 1965. Nor was this the preserve of the urban middle classes: by 1972, 76 per cent of rural households had a car.[24] Since 1900, French people had moved about the landscape by horse or on foot for short distances, then by rail and bus for longer travel; now the car was the preferred choice. By the end of the century, websites proliferated, enabling motorists to avoid interminable traffic jams (*bouchons*) on the worst days: orange (10 per cent of days), red (5 per cent) and black (1 per cent, famously the cross-over of holidaymakers travelling to and departing from resorts on 31 July–1 August). At such times, the landscape can appear as sections of countryside trapped between clogged arteries of concrete, steel and rubber. The longest traffic jam recorded anywhere was one which stretched nearly 180 kilometres between Lyon and Paris on 16 February 1980.[25]

The multiple impacts of rapid road transport are evident everywhere. One example is the region around the northern city of Amiens, where large numbers of tourists today visit the largest church in France and use the city as a gateway to visit the battlefields and cemeteries of the First World War. To the east of the city, along the river Somme, is a remarkable landscape created by at least seven centuries of human labour. These are the *hortillonnages*, gardens (or *hortillons* in Picard dialect) on small islands (*aires*) surrounded by a network of man-made canals, known locally as *rieux*. Today, just 30 of the 10,000 hectares of this remarkable area of wetland remain under production, compared with 500 hectares in 1900, when today's wooded landscape was largely devoid of trees (see Figures 0.2 and 0.3). The canals were originally dug to remove peat for fuel, in the process creating canals and islands regularly replenished by silt scooped from the canals. In 1900, perhaps one thousand people (the *hortillons*) worked the gardens, but since 1950 they have been in sharp decline because of the large-scale production and transport of vegetables from across Europe. They were only just saved from a major highway construction in the 1970s, and today this haven for wildlife is essentially a tourist attraction, its fragility threatened by increasing motorized boat traffic and the pressure to allow housing developments.[26]

Of course, the summer migration of tourists and their cars privileges the coasts of the west and south. The first resort in Arcachon was established in 1823, but it was the extension of the Bordeaux-La Teste railway line to Arcachon in 1857 which really opened up the new commune. Since then, the 5,500 kilometres of French coastline have become studded with more than 750 'stations balnéaires', with their familiar beachfront promenades, hotels and small casinos. Elsewhere, 'stations thermales' were created in hill towns, with their thermal resort hotels and parks, and often more casinos. The post-war boom was central to these changes.

The impact of mass tourism on the landscape was particularly acute along the coastline. On the Mediterranean, young people from nearby towns had long frequented the beach – there were swimsuit regulations for Canet near Perpignan in the 1850s – but pressure on the sandy coastline soared in the 1950s with the proliferation of automobiles and the attractions of informal camping (*camping sauvage*). Under the presidencies of Charles de Gaulle (1958–69) and Georges Pompidou (1969–74), large areas of coastline were set aside under the 'Mission Racine' for a mix of high-rise and villa development, fortunately with extensive reserves of several kilometres between each *station balnéaire*. The Mission was an extraordinarily ambitious initiative, involving everything from the creation of whole new towns with ports, roads, and airports to environmental projects such as reforestation and mosquito eradication.[27]

The explosion of the size of Canet – from a winegrowing village of 900 people in the 1890s to a busy resort of 12,000 permanent residents today – began in the early 1960s, when the population jumped from 1,850 in 1958 to 2,650 in 1962. This was paralleled in other new popular resorts – including Argelès, Barcarès, Leucate and La Grande Motte – all along the coastline from the Pyrenees to the mouth of the Rhône. The coastal landscape familiar to tourists was born, welcomed by hundreds of thousands of holidaymakers who descend for the summer to the broad sandy beaches. Canet has as many as 90,000 residents in the summer. The new tourist vista has been decried by others for the homogeneity of small, white villas and unimaginative apartment blocks and the menace of overdevelopment for fragile ecosystems already vulnerable to climate change.

This tidal wave of stand-alone housing accelerated in the decade after 1975, when an annual average of 235,000 houses were built each year. In regions most attractive to retirees and tourists – the Mediterranean and Atlantic coasts – what were once highly productive horticultural and viticultural areas, such as the Roussillon plain around Perpignan, are now residential as much as agricultural (see Plate 2). Nowhere is this more evident than in Provence. In 1763, Tobias Smollett travelled down the valley of the Rhone on his way to Italy. The view from the ramparts in Nice had entranced him:

> the plain presents nothing but gardens, full of green trees, loaded with oranges, lemons, citrons, and bergamots, which make a delightful appearance. If you examine them more nearly, you will find plantations of green pease [*sic*] ready to gather; all sorts of sallading, and pot-herbs, in perfection; and plats of roses, carnations, ranunculas, anemonies, and daffodils, blowing in full glory, with such beauty, vigour, and perfume, as no flower in England ever exhibited. . . . presents of carnations are sent from hence, in the winter, to Turin and Paris; nay, sometimes as far as London, by the post.

The lowlands of Provence remain suitable for an extraordinary profusion of plants, but the spreading suburbs and villas of the towns and villages have pushed most of the region's famed production of flowers, fruit and vegetables into the backcountry.[28]

The mass exodus of the 1950s and 1960s left many rural areas with empty farmhouses and villages, which survived essentially as retirement homes. Some 'countercultural' young people took the opportunity in the late 1960s to seek to create alternative lifestyles in the hilly Mediterranean backcountry. Villages in areas close to Paris or along the Alps, Breton coast or Mediterranean came to be dominated by holiday homes for urban family members or those with the money to buy and renovate. English holidaymakers and retirees, in particular, were attracted to Dordogne and Provence. There were 498,000 holiday homes in 1954 and 1.8 million by 1978. But most regions of France now contain areas of landscape which are characterized by fewer, larger farms, quieter villages and a relative absence of people.[29]

In the Alps and Pyrenees in particular, this continuing exodus of agricultural populations was replaced during the second half of the twentieth century by new seasonal arrivals and winter waves of enthusiasts for snow sports. Before the Second World War, these were the preserve of passionate amateurs and the very wealthy, but interest in snow tourism accelerated after the first Winter Olympics at Chamonix in 1924 and the installation of cable cars and lifts at Megève and Alpe d'Huez in the 1930s. After the war, resorts and the accompanying infrastructure were to stud mountain landscapes: cable cars and chairlifts, accommodation (often ubiquitous 'Alpine' chalets and apartment blocks) and commercial buildings. Subsequent Winter Olympics, at Grenoble in 1968 and Albertville in 1992, further spurred popular demand. As levels of snowfall slowly declined with climate change, landscapes were further marked by the artificial lakes necessary to fuel snowmaking machines.[30]

Some ancient features of the landscape have disappeared altogether. The landscape of former pastoral regions – such as the Corbières and parts of Provence and the Auvergne – is very occasionally still blocked today by herds of cattle and flocks of sheep making their annual transhumant cycles. Car drivers are uncharacteristically tolerant of the blocked roads, content to witness living traditions and secure in the promise of better meat. Even in the Alps, however, where as many as 500,000 sheep still make the annual migration from the lowlands of the Crau and Camargue to the high Alps, such as the Ubaye valley, the great majority now travel by road transport. Vast flocks of sheep on the move are only rarely part of the rural landscape today. In 1955, there were still 45,000 sheep which made the summer climb north along ancient *drailles* (pathways) from around Saint-Martin-de-Londres up to the summer pastures of the Aubrac in the Massif Central. In September 1965, the last descent occurred, with one thousand sheep taking one week to travel the 130 kilometres southwards. This great tradition has now ceased entirely, the result of lack of winter pastures because of spreading vineyards, the difficulty of moving flocks near or along roads and, above all, the cheaper solution of motor transport. Besides, cattle that could be kept in huge barns in winter made more economic sense.[31]

The dramatic pace of change to agriculture, infrastructure, transport networks and sources of energy after the Second World War finally impelled governments to intervene to ensure that there were levels of oversight over the impact of change on the landscape. In 1963, a new National Agency for Territorial Rationalization and Regional Planning (DATAR), reporting directly to the prime minister, was given a wide planning brief for major road infrastructure, hydroelectricity and nuclear power stations along major rivers and 200 kilometres of Mediterranean coastline in Languedoc and Roussillon. In 1963, a national park, the Parc de la Vanoise, was created in Savoie, the first of many. Then, in 1971, the first Ministry for the Protection of Nature and the Environment was created.[32]

Governments were also responding to public concerns. One expression of the level of this concern over the protection of landscape and the environment was the proliferation of community organizations with a focus on preservation. In the Breton department of Morbihan, for example, across the forty years after 1971, at least 115 associations were formally registered with the local administration, with names such as Union for the Aesthetic Appreciation of the Patrimony and Landscape of Morbihan, Society for the Study and Protection of Nature in Brittany, and Defense and Safeguard of the Environment in Western Ploeren. Suffusing this concern over the threat to the environment posed by pressures for urban development and industrial agriculture was a deep affection for distinctive landscapes and a sense of place linked to regional cultures and identities.[33] The 'counterculture' revolution of 1968 was only one manifestation of broader concerns about the environmental as well as social impact of industrial society. In 1977, a prominent journalist at *Le Monde*, Jean-Pierre Richardot, commented that, since 1968, ecological movements had become entwined with the renaissance of minority languages: 'clean rivers, the anti-nuclear struggle, local democracy, and the defence of the ancestral idiom appear – especially to the young – as "one and the same struggle".[34]

The surge of public interest in creating and joining associations concerned with the preservation of landscapes was matched by rapid increases in the volume of scholarly and general-interest literature. Online search engine tools that track word usage in publications make this clear. From 1770 to 1960, there was a gradual increase in the percentage of publications about or referring to *paysage* (.00020 to .00193) but from 1960 to 2004 the numbers increased sharply (.00193 to .00422). The same holds true for terms like *écologie* (which only began to be used in the 1920s) and *environnement* (the 1940s).[35]

Much of that literature was informed by a deeper public and professional concern for the preservation of landscape at a time of unprecedented change, as well as an uneasy awareness of scientific indicators of shifts in the globe's climate patterns. The publication of *The Limits to Growth* in 1972 by the Club of Rome, an informal organization of intellectuals and business leaders, highlighted what many already felt. The report examined five interconnected variables: 'population, food production, industrialization, pollution, and consumption of non-renewable natural resources'. Its warnings were clear and mostly prescient.[36]

The centrality of rural landscape and heritage to French urban identity was evident in everything ranging from election posters – notably François Mitterrand's judicious choice of the village of Sermages (Nièvre) as the backdrop for his presidential slogan of 'Steady Strength' ('La force tranquille') in 1981 – to best-selling books. Some of the best-sellers of the late-twentieth century were memoirs of rural life: Ephraïm Grenadou, *Grenadou, paysan français* (1966), Pierre-Jakez Hélias, *The Horse of Pride: Life in a Breton Village* (1975), Émilie Carles, *A Wild Herb Soup* (1977) and Antoine Sylvère, *Toinou: Le cri d'un enfant Auvergnat* (1980). Sylvère's bitter memoir of poverty sold 695,000 copies in its first year; Hélias' moving, combative memoir of Breton resilience has sold two million copies.[37]

Looking back in 1975 on the years since 1960, Hélias (1914–95) regretted the end of the peasant 'gardeners' and their 'meticulously designed landscapes':

They had necessarily to come to terms with mountainous or hilly country, leaving the heights to grow wild or bare; and to cultivate the slopes, respecting the contours; and to utilize the valleys, taking into account the rivers and streams. In short, the land and the sky were forever their masters. . . . the essential qualities of the landscapes – that is, order and harmony – were maintained.

Then the gardeners went away . . . Giant machines sliced directly into the cake of hills and let the old roads that wound slowly through the countryside revert to grass. Entire areas became wild again, while elsewhere huge factories filled the land. . . . Artifice gradually became obtrusive as man set himself up as master.

Not one to wallow in nostalgia, Hélias refused to grieve over the loss and hoped that a new beauty might one day emerge while we acknowledge 'the old farming community, the gardeners of the world'. It is doubtful whether the plethora of new holiday houses in the region would meet his standards of landscape beauty.[38]

There was also a nostalgia for an imagined past, which has suffused the popular imagery of France's eternal rural landscape even when that landscape is of comparatively recent creation. This is nowhere more marked than in the pine forests of the *landes* of the southwest. The region became celebrated for its 'untouched' wilderness of pine forests, which were in fact only a century old. In 1927, François Mauriac published his most famous novel, *Thérèse Desqueyroux*, set near Villandraut, in which the subject expresses her terror that 'one day the whole surrounding forest would crackle into flame, even the town itself would not be spared. Why was it that the heath villages never caught fire? . . . But she drove the thought from her, for the love of pine-trees was in her blood'.[39] Mauriac was the Nobel Laureate for Literature in 1952. The coastline and its hinterland were 'discovered' after the Second World War by celebrities ranging from 'Coco' Chanel to Charlie Chaplin and Winston Churchill, and in 1965, Socialist Party leader François Mitterrand purchased and renovated a farmhouse at Latche, where he retreated during his years as president in 1981–95. Visitors today can enjoy the Landes de Gascogne national park. The park was originally conceived in 1970 with a total area of 206,000 hectares but has since been increased to 315,300 hectares, more than half the department of Lande*s*.

The popular appeal of distinctive regional landscapes and their produce, already evident after the First World War, became even stronger. Even though the first AOC for cheese had been granted to Roquefort as early as 1925, it was in the post-1945 period that international competition and urbanization combined to create an incentive for major cheese industries to seek the protection that would come with exclusivity. For villages included in the approved zone to provide milk for Roquefort – one of them 50 kilometres away in the Ségala region of Aveyron – the *appellation* meant a surge in sheep farming and prosperity.[40] The other fifty or more regional cheeses which today have AOC standing were all successful after the

Second World War as they sought to exclude both French rivals from other regions and international competitors making, for example, bulk 'Roquefort' cheeses from cows' milk. One element of a new law of August 1960 facilitating agricultural innovation was the creation of 'red labels' for higher-quality produce, first awarded to poultry from the southwestern regions of the Landes and Périgord.

Increasing numbers of French people living in cities were attracted to products which combined an appeal to tradition and 'terroir' with the certainty that the product would taste the same as previously. Even if landscapes were characterized physically by fewer, larger farms, particular regions remained associated with distinctive products. When President de Gaulle famously quipped in 1962, 'how can you govern a country which has 246 varieties of cheese?', people delighted in the compliment and happily pointed out that the real figure was closer to 1,500.[41]

Some of the government's most ambitious infrastructure projects failed in the face of local protests about the inevitable damage to the landscape. Like the successful protests against proposals to build a nuclear power station at Plogoff in Brittany in 1974–81, the campaign to prevent the massive extension of the Larzac army camp by 17,000 hectares took many years. Like Plogoff, too, it was the successful linking of the campaign with environmentalism, local agricultural practices and Mitterrand's election in 1981 that was crucial. Today, the impact of the war over the Larzac plateau is engraved on the landscape only in defaced military signs, the eco-museum with its sheep sculpture outside the *bergerie* of La Jasse, near La Couvertoirade, and the large numbers of sheep still producing milk for Roquefort cheese.

In 1972, UNESCO adopted a convention on 'National Protection and International Protection of the Cultural and Natural Heritage', defining such heritage as not only buildings and monuments but 'works of man or the combined works of nature and man, and areas including archaeological sites which are of outstanding universal value from the historical, aesthetic, ethnological or anthropological point of view'. In 1979, the first five of France's World Heritage Sites were listed. As well as Chartres cathedral, the palace and park at Versailles, the prehistoric sites of the Vézère Valley, and the church and hill at Vézelay, Mont-Saint-Michel and its bay on the Norman coast were recognized. The landscape of the last had had a chequered history, with its fortified island serving as a prison for a time as well as a monastery. Despite attempts in 1856 to have the rocky island of Mont-Saint-Michel declared a protected site, local authorities lobbied to connect it to the mainland with dykes and polders constructed by the prisoners it housed, in the interests of creating more pastures and protecting the coastline from erosion. Others argued for the protection of the site, for recognition of its religious history and for the greater benefits of tourism. A society for its protection was established in 1912. The German army destroyed the polders for strategic reasons during the Second World War; after the war, the French government restored them in the interests of agricultural production. Only in the 1970s was the matter resolved, crowned in 1979 by its listing on the World Heritage Register. Today it is the most visited site in provincial France, with one million visitors annually sweeping in and out in their buses and cars like the surrounding tides.[42]

While there was an increasing willingness in France and internationally to identify and protect such significant landscapes, other pressures were far more difficult to counter. An unresolved phenomenon since 1945 has been urban sprawl, or 'peri-urbanization' and what it means for the richest agricultural land, most obviously around Paris but also in small provincial towns. Equally significant has been the connected 'hollowing out' of rural towns as 'grandes surfaces' on the outskirts replace shopping centres in old neighbourhoods, and the countryside becomes silent and villages empty, except if close to towns. The core functions of school, post office, *boulangerie* and *alimentation* disappeared from many smaller villages towards the end of the century.

The mass production of building materials enabled the proliferation of 'rurbain' developments in many villages: the intrusion of architectural uniformity through new housing estates and their homogeneous villas (*pavillons*). Mass production facilitated the construction of farm buildings to house industrial-scale agriculture (see Figure 7.6). The great boom in meat production in post-war Brittany meant that about 20 per cent of all new farm buildings in France in 1971–4 were in the region. These were typically very large steel and fibro-cement sheds suitable for winter shelter but with no architectural connection to surrounding villages – and dangerous to demolish.[43] Only with the law of 8 January 1993, on the relative responsibilities of communes, departments and the state did the 1983 zones of protection for architectural and urban heritage (ZPPAU) become zones of

FIGURE 7.6 Although part of a national park and the first UNESCO Geopark, the Valensole plateau in Provence – like everywhere else – is vulnerable to permits for amorphous buildings which compromise landscapes, in this case looking towards Montdenier. Peter McPhee.

protection for architectural, urban and also landscape heritage (ZPPAUP) and then areas for the development of architecture and heritage (AVAP) in 2010.

The second half of the twentieth century was therefore a period of unprecedented rapidity of change, in line with the increased capacity of humans to remake the landscape. At the same time, there was a greater awareness than ever before of what the costs might be to treasured landscapes and to the health of the environment itself. The uneasy balance between heightened environmental consciousness and the imperatives of productivity resulted in what the American historian Michael Bess described as a 'light green' society.[44] Governments realized increasingly that individual property rights needed to be curtailed in the interests of the environment, often under community pressure, at the same time as producers' associations and cooperatives further undermined the social model of private property. While often seen as unnecessarily destructive of wildlife, associations of hunters and fishers were among those most aware of the need to protect the environment, notable in the contribution of fishers' organizations to a key piece of legislation in December 1964 on the prevention of pollution of rivers.[45]

The preservation and rehabilitation of landscapes and their reorientation for new uses came about in different ways. Concerns about the health of rivers sometimes led authorities and environmentalists to develop the concept of 'river contracts' to pursue a holistic approach to their wellbeing. One such river is the Reyssouze, which runs 75 kilometres from the Alps into the Saône north of Mâcon and whose riverbed and surrounds had been canalized and cleared of vegetation to reduce the risk of flooding in urban areas. While there has been extensive rehabilitation in recent decades, however, it remains heavily polluted, largely through run-off from agricultural chemicals.[46]

Elsewhere, the stark population decline in particular regions of the countryside and the collapse of the pastoral and timber industries permitted some degraded environments to slowly recover. There were thousands of highland communities, such as Entrevaux and Saint-André-les-Alpes in the Alps, where battered landscapes were reforested as much by natural regeneration as by deliberate replanting (see Figures 5.3 and 5.4). The same was true of lowland communities such as Gabian on the Mediterranean plain, where land unsuitable for vineyards began to recover from centuries of overgrazing by sheep (see Figure 6.4). Elsewhere, as in Saint-Laurent-de-Cerdans, high in the eastern Pyrenees, the collapse of ancient charcoal-fired iron-making industries had a similar effect in enabling the regeneration of indigenous tree cover.

Two specific examples of rural landscapes illustrate not only the radical transformations of the second half of the twentieth century but also the challenges and opportunities for the landscape and its inhabitants. We have seen that fewer, larger farms became the norm in most rural areas. So, for example, the commune of Barre-des-Cévennes (Lozère) had fifty-eight farms in 1950 but only fourteen in 1975, of which only the eight small ones were traditional, mixed farming. These covered only 13 per cent of the commune: woodlands had been 27 per cent of the territory in 1953, but by 1988 they were more than 43 per cent. In 1856, there were 745 inhabitants scratching out a living; today, there are barely two hundred, and most are over sixty years of age.[47] A traditional world with a deep history had disappeared. While many have regretted that remaining rural populations have become 'park-keepers' dependent on state welfare, the increasingly forested landscape of Barre, like much of the Cévennes, is today valued for its biodiversity. Barre is one of 150 communes in the Parc national des Cévennes, famous for its wildlife and rivers. The European Union classification Natura 2000 for remarkable locations lists three sites there: the valleys of the Tarn, Tarnon and Mimente; the valley of the Gardon and its Cévenol hills; and seven zones of high biodiversity value.

Rather different was the story in the gently rolling Lauragais, past Toulouse and up the valley of the Garonne into the Pyrenees. While visitors here could be forgiven for enthusing about the timeless beauty of rural France, there were major environmental and social costs to the changes the American historian Peter Amann described in the 1980s. In villages such as Buzet, which had been able to sustain its population with an influx of pensioners and of commuters to nearby Toulouse, there had been a proliferation of detached villas of dubious architectural merit, and shops had been relocated to the periphery. The old village centre faced the double problem of lack of nearby shops for the elderly and increasing numbers of empty houses. While yields of crops such as maize had multiplied in Buzet, the crucial problem was the degradation – by irrigation, pesticides, fertilizers and deep ploughing – of this superb environment. Such had been the erosion in Loubens that a nearby village, once hidden by hills, was now clearly visible. Where cattle had given way to irrigated cropping, farmers found themselves trapped in a cycle of deeper ploughing and chemical fertilizing of fields devoid of animal manure. The village of Juzet d'Izaut once had a population of nearly one thousand, but in the 1980s it had a mere handful of farmers among perhaps only one hundred permanent residents. The precarious future of the school paralleled the difficulties of farming upland country, despite the use of a tonne of chemical fertilizer annually for every six hectares. Amann pondered whether the only future for this beautiful place would lie in providing services for tourists (a restaurant and a *gîte rural* were open for a few months each year) and the packs of hunters who chased the introduced boar and deer across the farmers' fields.[48] He would have been gratified to learn that since he wrote, like Barre in the Cévennes, the village has had two remarkable landscape sites classified by Natura 2000, and its population is busy with visitors.

*   *   *

The millennium ended with the most severe extratropical cyclones, or winter storms, of the twentieth century in northern Europe. On 3 December 1999, Cyclone Anatol missed France but subjected Denmark to its strongest recorded winds. On 25–26 December, Cyclone Lothar swept through France from the north of Brittany to Strasbourg, resulting in eighty-eight fatalities and billions of euros in damages. The Paris region was particularly hard hit; winds of 216 kilometres per hour were recorded at the Eiffel Tower. The park at the Palace of Versailles was severely damaged; over 10,000 trees were lost within two hours, including specimens planted by Marie-Antoinette and Napoleon. The next day, 27 December, Cyclone Martin caused further extensive damage to property and trees, moving southeast from the Île d'Oléron, where it reached 198 kilometres per hour, to Toulouse and Carcassonne. It was estimated that 140 million cubic metres of trees were felled in France. The storms left behind the wreckage of one-quarter of France's high-tension transmission lines and 300 high-voltage transmission pylons strewn across the countryside. Martin caused thirty fatalities and cost €2.5 billion in 1999 values in insured losses.[49]

The formation of such cyclones in winter is favoured by temperature differences between a warm ocean and a cold atmosphere. For many people, the shocking impact of three severe winter storms within a few weeks was simply terrible misfortune, a suitable conclusion to a century of unprecedented international warfare and upheaval. Some others thought that this cluster of wild storms suggested that something more menacing might be happening, especially when the cluster was followed more quickly by other winter storms: Jeanette in October 2002, Erwin in January 2005, Kyrill in January 2007, Emma in March 2008, and Klaus in January 2009. Scientists divided on whether climate change would make such extratropical cyclones more or less frequent or simply more severe, but agreed that their frequency was related to global warming. Some of their numbers even suggested that the globe had entered what they called a new age of the Anthropocene to emphasize the central role of humankind in the ecology of the current geological epoch: that the decades after 1950 mark the genuine commencement of the Anthropocene rather than the centuries since 1770.[50]

8 LIVING THE ANTHROPOCENE, 2000–20

In December 2004, the Viaduc de Millau opened to traffic. In beauty, cost and fame, even the previous masterpieces by Gustave Eiffel pale in comparison (see Plate 14). The 2,500-metre bridge, more than 330 metres above the River Tarn, is the tallest bridge in the world. Designed by the British architect Norman Foster, it was the last step in an ambitious project to cut an autoroute through the Massif Central from Clermont-Ferrand to Béziers, often referred to as the *désenclavement* or opening up of France's most isolated regions. The bridge has ended the summer frustrations of car travellers making the tortuous descent into and ascent from the town of Millau between two limestone plateaux or *causses*, the Causse du Larzac and the Causse Rouge. An ancient pastoral landscape, in which Millau had played a central role as a centre of tanneries and the crafting of sheepskin gloves, is now a national park across which tourists speed, if not exiting the autoroute to visit cheese-cellars in Roquefort or the craft shops of the medieval walled village of La Couvertoirade.[1]

The exhilaration travellers feel on traversing a work of soaring beauty – which complements the contrasting grandeur of the Causses – is symbolic of the long shift in public recognition of the resonance of landscape heritage. The pioneering efforts from 1901 by the Société pour la Protection des Paysages de France to extend public protection from buildings to landscapes have borne fruit. By 2015, there were almost 2,700 *sites classés*, covering more than one million hectares, and about 4,000 other listed sites covering 1,500,000 hectares. More than 4 per cent of the territory of France is covered by this protection.[2] In July 2016, a new law 'concerning creative freedom, architecture and patrimony' sought to further broaden notions of landscape heritage. It went beyond the earlier emphasis on monumental buildings and famous sites and defined a 'noteworthy heritage site' (*site patrimonial remarquable*) as including villages and neighbourhoods where there is a public interest in protecting the landscape. Among the 800 of these sites across France are scores of landscapes and 'protected areas'.

This heightened appreciation of the landscape and its ecological challenges has been interdependent with a global reconsideration of the world's treasures. As in

France, the initial concerns of UNESCO classifications of 'world heritage' sites in the 1970s concentrated on built masterpieces, such as the Salines Royales (1982), but have now been broadened to include, among other criteria, 'superlative natural phenomena or areas of exceptional natural beauty and aesthetic importance'. Among the forty-nine French sites now on the list are the Canal du Midi (1996); the Cirque de Gavarnie and the Massif du Mont-Perdu (1997); the Jurisdiction of Saint-Emilion (1999); the Loire Valley (2000); the Mediterranean agro-pastoral landscape of the Causses and the Cévennes (2011); the mining basin of the Nord-Pas-de-Calais region (2012); the Burgundy wine region (2015); and the Champagne hillsides, houses and cellars (2015). Among the thirty-seven on the 'tentative' or waiting list from France are the Montagne Sainte-Victoire; the Parc national de la Vanoise; the Massif du Mont Blanc; the Camargue; the Straits of Bonifacio; the Parc national des Écrins; the Parc national de Port-Cros; the Guérande salt marshes; the Mediterranean shore of the Pyrenees; the pastoral area of the Charolais-Brionnais region; and the Domaine de Fontainebleau. This is indeed a list of exceptional landscapes.

The strengthening of public recognition of the cultural – as well as economic – value of distinctive landscapes continues to be reflected in changing uses of the rural environment. For example, until about 1950, most seed for Dijon mustard was grown in cleared areas of forests in Burgundy where charcoal production had enriched the soil with potash. Then a decline in charcoal production and the appeal of more lucrative crops led to a collapse in seed production. By the late twentieth century about 80 per cent of mustard seed was imported from Canada, and increasingly, 'Dijon mustard' was made in North America. In 2009, however, an IGP (Protected Geographical Indication) for 'Burgundy mustard' led to increased local seed and mustard production, even though there are no restrictions on where 'Dijon mustard' can be manufactured.[3]

The concern for both healthy foodstuffs and the desire to protect regional economies has encouraged small producers in some areas to return to abandoned terraces, as in Ardèche, where in the lower valley of the River Eyrieux new crops, such as the feijoa fruit tree or the ancient potato 'échamp de l'Eyrieux' have been planted.[4] Each year, several thousand French farmers add their enterprises to the expanding list of accredited 'bio' producers, although the rapid escalation of prices as a consequence of the war in Ukraine in 2022 reduced these numbers as many consumers turned away from 'bio' products, generally 30 per cent more expensive than 'industrial' crops.[5] Slowly, too, the profound belief in the value of distinctive regional characteristics, such as diversity of produce and cuisine, has been eroded by the lure of fast food and the end of seasonal restrictions on choice.[6]

Nevertheless, there has never been such a widely shared appreciation of the value of landscapes as in contemporary France.[7] The long-term activism of professional associations has melded with deep-seated popular affection for the diversity of the countryside and a willingness of governments at all levels – from local councils to the European Union – to intervene to protect and regenerate landscapes. At the same time, however, landscapes have never been more vulnerable to the consequences of climate change and other pressures on biodiversity. The French landscape is caught in the pincers of the Anthropocene, between widespread agreement on the inestimable benefits of nurtured landscapes and the confronting evidence of irreparable damage.

The evidence of change is incontrovertible. The Euro-Climhist database, which presents evidence about weather and climate across space and time, has produced wine harvest records from Beaune in Burgundy dating back to 1354. Even allowing for changes in the nature of grape varieties and inconsistencies in the data, the results are startling. Whereas the harvest usually commenced around 28 September up until the mid-twentieth century, since 1960 the trend line has dipped sharply to an average date of 15 September today. Indeed, six of the past eighteen harvests have begun before 5 September, even in August.[8]

The evidence of the impact of a changing climate is abundant. It is threatening the health of the UNESCO-listed Camargue, the largest river delta in Europe and home to four hundred bird species. Ever since the north of the area was cultivated for cereals, then for wine and rice from the sixteenth century, the health of the Camargue has been a delicate balancing act between irrigation and the need for river flows from the Rhône to 'flush' the delta. Now rising sea levels are making the freshwater flows more difficult to manage, all the more important given the increasing toxicity of the water which has flushed through rice fields.[9]

There are parallels with the Camargue in France's second-largest wetland area, the 100,000 hectares of the *marais poitevin* (Poitou wetlands), west of Niort, especially the dampest eastern third (*le marais mouillé*) which is home to an ancient human construction of canals and islets and a remarkable richness of flora and fauna. Few areas of France have been such a focus of human reshaping, especially since the nineteenth-century projects of canal building and draining of marshes. After the Second World War, the region was especially prone to draining and clearing for cereal production. Although proclaimed a national park in 1979, it was not until 1992, under the presidency of François Mitterrand and his environment minister, Ségolène Royale, a local member of parliament, that serious attention focused on the deterioration of the wetlands, notably in annulling an earlier decision to punch an autoroute through vulnerable sections. That was not enough to save its national park status in 1996. The *marais mouillé* areas have since become the focus of local activism to the extent that national park status was regained in 2014. However, the past few decades have seen the extension of large-scale maize production across the flat landscape, with contentious extraction of groundwater to the annoyance of small farmers and fishers. Now a massive new water-storage facility covering seven hectares at Mauzé-sur-le-Mignon (Deux-Sèvres) is designed to capture winter rains before they soak into the wetlands.[10]

Along the Mediterranean, climate change is causing the decline of key elements of vegetation, such as cork oak, holm oak, beech and maritime pine.[11] Just as damaging, however, is the weight of population density multiplied by summer tourism. Half the coastline is already under macadam and concrete. For example, every summer at Argelès-sur-Mer, south of Perpignan, about 300,000 tourists flood into lodgings and camping grounds in this town of 10,000 people, placing enormous strain on a fragile Mediterranean environment. After Agde, Chamonix and Carnac, in 2023 it was the most 'over-visited' (*surfréquenté*) resort by agencies concerned with 'sustainable tourism'.[12] The impact of climate change is felt differently on the Atlantic coastline. Rising sea levels and increasing real estate values are locked in a desperate dance in the *chic* resort of Cap-Ferret, where the magnificent coastal landscape of La Pointe, the entrance to the Arcachon Bay, has had to be extensively protected by rock walls.[13]

The signs of climate change are everywhere. It has facilitated the spread northwards of the *chenilles processionnaires* (pine processionaries), caterpillars, which have been a threat to conifers since classical times and which are also a threat to human health. Once confined by temperature to southern regions, the caterpillars are now moving north at an estimated 6 kilometres annually and have reached Paris.[14] Their migration is marked by the northward extension of pheromone traps hanging hopefully in trees in parks and along France's roads. Similarly, foresters have pointed to the impact of milder winters and warmer summers on the fir and spruce forests of the Jura and Vosges mountains, where bark beetles (*scolytinae*) now flourish as in other forested areas of the northern hemisphere.[15]

The northern extremity of winegrowing, which reached as far as Paris and even Laon in the eighteenth century and then retreated south to the Loire thereafter, will once again move north as cooler climates favour white wines in particular. In contrast, while France remains the second-largest producer of wine in the world, the sight of abandoned vineyards, particularly in southern France, is direct evidence of significant economic, social and climatic change. Since 2000, France has lost at least 100,000 hectares of vineyards, and today the total winegrowing area is less than 800,000 hectares.[16] While Bordeaux winemakers, protected by the status of their *appellation*, have weathered the storm, those outside the prestige areas have been subjected to increased requirements to decrease production. In June 2023, another 10,000 hectares were identified to be uprooted, the latest manifestation of a puzzling landscape of uncultivated land (*friches*) in the midst of the world's most famous vineyards.[17]

This economic challenge has a cause-and-effect relationship with a significant change in lifestyle: wine consumption has declined by two-thirds since the Second World War. It is the regions of the *appellations* that have best survived the collapse in wine drinking, and their promoters have been alive to that shift, protecting the more prestigious regions from having vines torn out.[18] It is the vast vineyards of Languedoc that for so long produced cheap 'table wines' that have suffered, and where determined efforts to improve wine quality and local reputations have been most creative. But here, climate change is likely to make wine production impossible in areas where it has thrived since Roman times.

French people drink less but drink better than fifty years ago. This dramatic change in lifestyle is directly connected to a profound social change, the sharp decline in road deaths. When the 1972 road toll was announced as a record 16,770 deaths, the entire population of the southern town of Mazamet (then 16,610) decided to make a point by lying prostrate in the streets of the town for an hour on 17 May 1973. The road toll has since declined sharply, to 2,780 in 2020. Even since 2000, the number of deaths has halved, even though total distances travelled by motorists have increased by 80 per cent.[19]

There are other challenges beyond climate change. At the same time as there has been a renewed appreciation of the significance and vulnerability of landscapes, there have been accentuated urban pressures upon them. The modern history of the French landscape has always been in part the history of urban encroachment on the countryside, but an inexorable phenomenon since 1945 has been more rapid urban sprawl and what it means for the richest agricultural land, most obviously around Paris but also in the hinterlands of small provincial towns.

In the 2000s, an annual average of up to 55,000 hectares of agricultural land has been covered by new housing estates and all the necessary road infrastructure, including ubiquitous roundabouts (*carrefours giratoires*).[20] While the first designed roundabout in France was that on the Place de l'Étoile around the Arc de Triomphe in 1906, it was from the 1970s that their construction transformed the landscape at the entrances and exits of France's towns and villages. One recent estimate is that there are today more than 65,000 roundabouts in France, half of all those in the world. Up to 800 new ones are added annually. The roundabouts clearly facilitate the movement of traffic, but while some are attractively planted in reference to local produce, others are vast, featureless circles of concrete.[21]

French sociologists have developed a term – *périurbanisation* – to describe built spaces between urban centres and the surrounding countryside: liminal spaces, also known as 'rurban' space, outskirts or the urban hinterland. Two linked processes are at play. First is the 'peri-urbanization' of towns large and small as expanding zones of new houses and large shopping centres move to the margins between older urban areas and the countryside. Second is the 'rurbanization' of rural communities within a radius of 20 to 30 kilometres as town dwellers decide that having to commute to work by car is a small price to pay for a new home and garden in a rural community. The cultural weight placed on rural France is also belied by the creep of architectural uniformity through new housing estates and their homogeneous villas or *pavillons*.

By 2017, 93 per cent of French people lived within the 'area of attraction' of a town or 'pôle', that is, where at least 15 per cent of the working population of a community commuted to a nearby town. Paris was the principal centre, 'attracting' one French person in five, but there were 13 other towns with more than 700,000 people in their 'area of attraction', 47 with 200,000 to 700,000, 126 with 50,000 to 200,000 and 512 with fewer than 50,000. The consequences for rural landscapes are that, while 53 per cent lived within the town, 41 per cent were living in the 'couronnes' or urban ring.[22] The peri-urban zones of larger cities now encompass not only new suburbs but the expanding villages formerly in the rural hinterland, such as around Montpellier, where the population of the metropolitan area has grown from 165,000 in 1962 to 608,000 in 2017.

Typical of many thousands of villages in this regard is Saint-Nolff in Brittany, in the 'aire d'attraction' of Vannes and just 10 kilometres to its north. Since its first census in 1793, its population had always oscillated around 1,000 to 1,300 inhabitants. Suddenly, in 1975, its population increased to 1,800, and today it is over 4,000, but it is a quiet place during the day. Twice a day, the roads are busy with commuters leaving and coming home to the village by car and bus. Saint-Nolff is also a community aware of the pressures its own growth is having on a rich rural environment. Its 'green' mayor for twenty years from 1995, Joël Labbé, also a senator for the department of Morbihan, oversaw a 2005 ban on genetically modified crops in the commune, abrogated on appeal to a tribunal in the regional capital Rennes. Nevertheless, the community adopted the Agenda 21 programme on sustainable development agreed to at the Earth Summit in Rio de Janeiro in 1992 and is one of thirty-three communes in the regional park of the Golfe de Morbihan active in protecting its precious ecosystem.[23] The village has constructed an impressive new 'eco-city', the Pré Vert subdivision or 'hamlet' of 130 residences, 30 per cent of them for low-income residents, along strict lines of environmental sustainability within a pedestrian, treed precinct of rural pathways (see Plate 15). The initiative is as unobtrusive into the landscape as one could wish, if not for the unusual architectural freedom which has resulted in houses which have nothing 'Breton' about them whatsoever.[24]

In terms of landscape, many peri-urban residential areas in local government areas with strict building codes are attractive as well as comfortable, like Saint-Nolff. However, the clustering of large-scale retail chains along the major road entries into towns and cities is today the ugliest dimension of the French landscape.[25] While the demographic history of France has long been the history of urbanization, this has accelerated in recent decades as long-term residents and new arrivals have sought the pleasures of spacious and light-filled stand-alone housing with private car parking. In France – and not only in France, of course – almost all towns of more than five thousand people and increasing numbers of villages are surrounded by new developments. Chains of supermarkets, hardware stores and automobile dealers have followed to the outskirts. This is a dramatic transformation of the landscape, which also indicates a great social challenge of rural life in France as demand collapses for retail outlets at the heart of old neighbourhoods.

To be sure, this is not a new process. To the north of Paris, the area around Saint-Brice – today a dormitory suburb of the capital – was characterized in the eighteenth century by intense agriculture (cereal crops, vegetables, wine) and forestry before becoming, after the First World War, dominated by apple and pear plantations. Today, occasional fruit trees are all that remain. The process of peri-urbanization has accelerated dramatically since 1950.[26] Threats of urban sprawl have led prominent agronomists and others to seek UNESCO protection for the extraordinarily rich soils near Saint-Brice, around Saclay and Gonesse, which produce 10,000 kilograms of maize and wheat per hectare annually.[27]

Similarly, at the time of the French Revolution, nearby Montmorency, situated on a bluff 13 kilometres north of Paris, was a rural village of fewer than 2,000 people. Once the home of the eminent Montmorency noble family, it was already a retreat from the congestion of Paris: in 1793 it was temporarily renamed Émile in honour of Rousseau, who wrote his treatise on education and the *Social Contract* while there in 1756–62, away from the Paris 'of noise, smoke and mud'. In the nineteenth century, wealthy aristocrats and bourgeois, from the Duchesse de Berry to Richard Wagner, lived in newly constructed mansions on the bluff. Since the 1960s, however, these have been swamped by middle-class housing estates on the plateau of Les Champeaux, and the town of more than 21,000 people is one of many dormitory suburbs ringing the capital.

The effects of peri-urbanization may be seen near every provincial town. In western France, for example, the urban sprawl of Tours has resulted in the loss of 8,000 hectares of agricultural land and 58 per cent of farms in the last thirty years. However, two major vineyards (the AOC of Montlouis and Vouvray) close to Tours have resisted by using the strategies of heritage listing. There have also been some very protracted but successful campaigns to prevent the further extension of infrastructure into rural areas, notably the abandonment in 2018 of the Grand Ouest or Notre-Dame-des-Landes airport near Nantes; another third Paris airport at Chaulnes near Amiens in 2002; and a massive dam on the Loire south of Le Puy in 1991. Other protests have been unsuccessful, such as those against the Somport tunnel under the central Pyrenees, which opened in 2003.[28]

Since 2000, major local decisions about planning have been decentralized through the PLUI ('plan local d'urbanisme intercommunal').[29] These give mayors and their councils extensive powers and responsibilities to accept or reject applications for new construction and renovations, provided the commune has an approved planning overlay in place. The law implementing the code is clear about the responsibilities of mayors in protecting rural landscape values by insisting on new buildings being architecturally and culturally harmonious with the local milieu and protective of existing landscapes, fauna and flora. Such are the complexities of completing an overlay, however, that many small communities have preferred for such decisions to rest with authorities higher up in the administration. Elsewhere, it has been argued that the vulnerability of councils to pressures from vested interests has placed them in invidious positions, leading to approvals which have flouted the principles of the law.

The pressures on precious landscapes have come from elsewhere as well. Among the glories of the French landscape, its eleven national and fifty-six regional parks often suffer from an excess of visitors. At times, the pressures of tourism on beloved landscapes threaten their very viability. The Île Vierge beach on the Crozon promontory in Finistère (Brittany) was classified in 2014 as one of the most beautiful beaches in Europe by European Best Destinations, an organization based in Brussels. So popular was it that its cliffs were eroded by crowds of visitors, and it was closed to the public in May 2020.[30] Another example is Étretat in Normandy, whose famous cliff walks are smothered by up to 10,000 daily visitors in summer, with refuse scattered by birds over a landscape that residents of a small village cannot protect.

The Covid-19 pandemic accelerated the desire to move to a regional centre and with it pressure on existing infrastructure. This was particularly acute in Provence and the southern Alps, where the booming centre of Gap and its irrigated farms, in all 50,000 inhabitants, are reliant on the unpredictable waters of the Canal du Drac, established in 1880 when the population was about 10,000.[31] The increase in tourism after the 're-opening' of France in 2022 after the pandemic forced numerous resorts, from Étretat to the Île de Bréhat in Brittany and the *calanques* near Marseille, to impose limits on daily visitors.[32]

Like all ecosystems, those of France are susceptible to 'biological invasions' accelerated by advanced international trading networks and warming waters. In the Camargue region, for example, the nine species of native heron have switched from a fish diet to the introduced Louisiana crayfish present since 1995, as have bass and other 'exotic' fish. The flourishing of the heron has, however, occurred at the same time as the decline of local amphibians, the preferred diet of the crayfish. In Corsica, just twelve of the thirty-two freshwater fish species are native, and those are vulnerable to introduced predators such as perch and bass. Even apparently benign invaders, such as the Australian wattle *acacia dealbata*, beloved as mimosa in France for its brilliant yellow foliage, may have deleterious effects as they invade woodlands.[33]

On a small scale, the *étang* of Canet-en-Roussillon exemplifies many of the current and future pressures on maritime landscapes. Separated from the Mediterranean by a thin strip of sand dunes, and a small estuary opening (*grau*), the lagoon is just 4 kilometres long and at most 1 metre deep. For many centuries, it supported local fishers (for eel, sole, bass and mullet) and plentiful bird life, some 230 species, including pink flamingoes. While protected from direct encroachment from the urban settlements spreading across the coastal plain, the lagoon is vulnerable to pollution from agricultural run-off and sediment from the streams which feed it, as well as extraction from aquifers for irrigation. The *grau* is mostly open, and rising sea levels inevitably alter the balance of the brackish nature of the water. It is now a paradise for the American blue crabs, which have invaded the western Mediterranean. In the sea, the crabs provide food for octopus and may be contained; in the lagoon at Canet, they devour crustaceans and fish eggs and have almost destroyed the fishing industry. This combination of blue-crab infestation and pesticide pollution will almost certainly threaten the rich lagoons elsewhere along the Mediterranean: in the departments of Aude (*étangs* at Canet, Bages-Sigean, l'Ayrolle, La Palme), of Hérault (Thau, Vic, Méjean, l'Or), then the Berre (Bouches-du-Rhône) and Biguglia in Corsica.[34]

Mounting evidence such as this of the early experience of living through the climatic consequences of the Anthropocene has forced governments to act. In 2007, representatives of government, industry, unions and professional bodies met in the 'Grenelle Environment Round Table' to formulate agreed policies relating to, among other things, climate change and energy, biodiversity and natural resources, health and the environment, and development patterns. Reflecting a new agenda, the Ministry of the Protection of Nature and of the Environment was renamed the Ministry of Ecology and Sustainable Development. It is now the Ministry of Ecological Transition.[35]

Part of the lived experience of climate change has been adjusting to the imperatives of changes to the sources of energy used in everyday life. In 2015, the Paris international climate conference rang the death knell of coal as a major energy source. The replacement of charcoal by coal from the late-eighteenth century had been intrinsic to France's economic transformation and to the experience of the Anthropocene. The coal-mining regions of Nord-Pas-de-Calais and Forez in the Massif Central had developed steelmaking fired by coke and steam engines which would transform the industrial economy, and coal-fired power stations which would power in unprecedented ways the capacity of humans to transform the rural landscape. The post-Second World War agricultural revolution was, however, increasingly powered by gas from the Aquitaine basin, hydroelectricity, and nuclear power, as well as oil and gas from overseas. In 1960 and 1968, government plans plotted the gradual closing of coal mines, as elsewhere in western Europe. The last underground mine in France, at La Houve at Creutzwald in Lorraine, closed in 2004.[36] While in 2020 there were still more than 2,300 coal-fired power stations in China and nearly 600 in India, using coal from Australia and Indonesia, there were to be no new slag heaps on the French landscape. Instead, the mining landscape of the northeast was to be regarded as part of France's heritage (see Figure 7.4). Indeed, they are part of the mines of the Nord-Pas-de-Calais region that in 2013 became the thirty-eighth French site on the list of UNESCO World Heritage Sites as 'a living and changing landscape'.[37]

In the distinctive southern landscape of limestone bluffs, vineyards and Mediterranean shrubs and trees, is another juxtaposition of new and old. On a windswept plateau to the southwest of Narbonne, overlooking the village of Villesèque and a winegrowing estate at Gléon, a large wind farm – twenty-four turbines on 700 hectares – was opened in 2008. In 1830, these battered, largely denuded hillsides were the scene of a bloody battle over the ownership and use of forests, a violent episode in a divisive economic transformation which has scarred the landscape of the region of the Corbières to this day (see Chapter 3). Two centuries ago, wood was the fuel of both daily life and social conflict; today, the wind farm marks the scale of the transition to a new world. Similarly, the juxtaposition of the cooling towers at the nuclear plant at Tricastin in the Rhône valley with a surrounding wind farm marks another shift (see Figure 7.3).

At Piolenc, a small town of 5,000 people to the north of Orange in the department of Vaucluse, two innovations have highlighted the possibilities of solar power confronted with the challenges of climate change. A large surface of water in an unused quarry near the Rhone River has been covered with 50,000 floating photovoltaic panels, producing twice Piolenc's annual power needs. Nearby, the threat posed to vineyards by hotter summers has been responded to by a partnership between the local chamber of agriculture, the French Environment and Energy Management Agency (Ademe) and a private company. About 600 square metres of vines planted with black grenache grapevines were covered by 280 'agrivoltaic' panels, which can be moved in real time using an artificial intelligence algorithm able to determine the ideal tilt of the panels according to the sunshine and water requirements of viticulture, soil quality and weather conditions. Despite such initiatives, however, the expansion of solar power has been slow in France, accounting for just 4 per cent of the energy supply in 2022, or one-third of its neighbours.[38]

The stark choices of living in the Anthropocene dovetail with other fraught issues in the countryside, in particular the tension between environmentalism (including the reintroduction of Pyrenean bears), 'clean' food and remediation of degradation on the one hand and industrial-scale production, 'noxious' pests and animals such as wild boar (*sangliers*), and chemical fertilizers and pesticides on the other.[39]

Much of French agriculture suffers from the vicious cycle of dependence on chemical fertilizers and pesticides. However, dramatic increases in productivity are increasingly measured against the costs of protecting biodiversity (especially the decline in bee populations) and demonstrable medical problems, possibly even Parkinson's disease. One conservative estimate has recently placed these costs at 370 million euros annually.[40] In 2020, the Agency for Food, Environmental and Occupational Health and Safety (ANSES) announced that glyphosate-based products would be phased out by 1 January 2021, except where there were no alternatives to the herbicide. France uses 8,645 tonnes per annum, 19 per cent of Europe's total, especially in sugar beet and wine areas. In orchards and vineyards, for example, farmers would need in future to allow grass to grow around plants and trees or carry out mechanical weeding. The announcement was welcomed by many public-interest and farmers' organizations but was hotly contested by many sugar beet growers and vineyard owners in particular.[41] Despite the plan to ban glyphosate in a majority of agricultural practices by the end of 2020, the sale of the world's most commonly used weedkiller has continued to increase, putting in doubt the feasibility of France's plan to halve the use of pesticides by 2025.[42]

Debates around the use of pesticides are inextricably bound up with contention over access to water and its purity. More than 60 per cent of the water used in France comes from aquifers (*nappes phréatiques*), long regarded as of high quality and symbolized all over the country by the water towers (*châteaux d'eau*), which stud the landscape. The evidence that protracted use of pesticides and herbicides might be endangering the quality of drinking water has been a public shock. In February 2023, ANSES announced measures against the use of the herbicide S-metolachlor, which had been found in groundwater at levels above European limits. Since 2005, some 2,000 tonnes of the herbicide have been used each year.[43]

The impact of industrial-scale agriculture is apparent in the landscape across much of France, and nowhere more so than in Brittany, where vast piggeries dot the landscape in uniform steel buildings which clash with older stone stables nearby. The question of uses of waste from the piggeries is also contentious: the price of sustainable agriculture is at times paid by the landscape. Just as wind farms have been the subject of heated debate between advocates of renewable energy and others horrified by the aesthetic intrusions of massive pylons, so in Brittany the cost of creating biomass from piggeries has been the erection of large, dome-shaped anaerobic digesters.[44] These constructions, made of polyethylene, enable micro-organisms to break down biodegradable waste (see Figure 8.1).

Since the 1990s, there has been a profound recognition of the damage done to biodiversity by the removal of hedgerows in the northwest, as well as the increased exposure to soil erosion and extremes of weather. In the Auvergne-Rhône-Alpes region, farmers have replanted 700 kilometres of hedges since 1996, in all, some 700,000 trees and bushes. Similarly, in the Breton department of Finistère, 760 kilometres of hedges have been replanted since 1991. The changing agricultural politics of the European Union, once so insistent on the advantages of broad-acre industrial farming, have encouraged this reevaluation. Since 2015, the maintenance of ponds, woods and hedgerows has been integral to European policy on subsidies under its 'bonnes conditions agricoles et environnementales' (BCAE) provisions.[45]

But across the country, there are now only 750,000 kilometres of hedges, compared with two million around 1950; 3,500 kilometres of hedges are planted each year, but 11,500 are cleared.[46] In parts of western France, for example, near Bressuire, the population of wild rabbits has almost disappeared because of a virus which has been rendered more deadly because the removal of hedgerows has isolated rabbit populations into small groups.[47] In the tiny Norman village of Camembert, 65 kilometres southeast of Caen, where the cheese was said to

FIGURE 8.1 Industrial-scale raising of animals has changed the landscape in many ways. Here, at Saint-Aignan (Morbihan), anaerobic digesters offer a process to treat biodegradable waste and sewage sludge in piggeries and to reduce the emission of methane. Peter McPhee.

have been invented in 1791, the scattered farm buildings furnish a glaring example of the perils of unplanned change. The financial pressures of contemporary agriculture have led to the removal of many hedgerows, the abandonment of less productive fields, and the erection of large, mass-produced farm buildings alongside deteriorating traditional structures.[48]

Reforestation has been far more successful. So extensive is France's forest cover in the twenty-first century that it is easy to assume that 'nature's raiment' has adorned the country since time immemorial rather than understanding that it has in fact been restored to its place. Most of the great swathes of forest and woodland that cover one-third of France today are the result of a combination of deliberate reforestation and unplanned regeneration since the mid-nineteenth century. The great battle between rural communities dependent on access to forests and the national forest administration reached its peak in the sixty years after the Revolution of 1789. By the 1860s, the administration had triumphed and embarked on ambitious projects of replanting. It was supported in its project by private owners of forest resources, equally determined to restrict access to peasant communities long used to exercising collective rights of access for pastures, fuel, timber and food. Since then, 'old growth' forests in particular, such as the oak forests of Normandy, have been carefully nurtured and highly valued. In August 2021 a sweeping new law identified the fundamental importance of forests for climate change mitigation, biodiversity and water quality, and placed them 'under the protection of the Nation'.[49] They have been protected further by European

Union initiatives and regulations, which have reduced the effects of 'acid rain' so visible across western Europe in the 1990s.

The expansion of tree cover was also due to long-term rural exodus after 1850 from embattled upland areas and the attractions of market specialization on lowlands elsewhere, both of which have allowed hillsides to recover from centuries of overgrazing. In the *garrigues* of the Midi, the expansion of the vineyards in the aftermath of the French Revolution, combined with the collapse of the forges, tanneries and pastoral industry, allowed the slow recovery of the environment from several thousand years of nibbling by sharp teeth.

At times, reforestation has been controversial because of the types of plantations. In 2004, the undulating plateau of Millevaches in the Limousin region became one of the largest national parks in France, renowned for the diversity of its flora and fauna, including otters and endangered birds. Sections of the park are still exploited as pine plantations, which are exotic to the region. For example, the commune of Gentioux-Pigerolles now has 40 per cent of its land covered in forest compared to just 2 per cent a century ago, but 60 per cent of that forest is pine plantation. Not all its inhabitants celebrate the change to the landscape. Elsewhere, too, the expansion of commercial, monocultural plantations is contested by those wishing to see a regeneration of indigenous forest and shrub cover.[50]

Reforestation, whether or not deliberate, has made particular areas more vulnerable to the fiery consequences of climate change because of the prolific vegetation, which for a millennium had been kept cropped by sheep and by peasants seeking fuel.[51] In August 2005, a wildfire destroyed 2,000 hectares of rugged hillsides near the Mediterranean village of Rodès in the eastern Pyrenees, raging through dry coastal shrubs and the dominant tree cover of green and cork oaks (*chêne vert* and *chêne liège*). People used to seeing the familiar Mediterranean *garrigue* landscape were astonished when teams of archaeologists and historians pointed to thousands of years of newly exposed history dating back to Neolithic dolmens. A maze of terracing, pathways to pastures and even an abandoned village highlighted that, until a century ago, the hillsides were intensively cultivated and largely denuded.[52]

This reforestation has allowed the resurgence of large wildlife, which was almost exterminated in the nineteenth century with the depletion of forests and the extension of farmed areas. Deer and boar populations have increased rapidly, in the latter case ruinously, while wolves have deliberately been reintroduced.[53] Other animals have been less fortunate: it is estimated that a staggering 194 million birds and 29 million animals are killed by cars each year on Europe's roads. French car drivers have become used to seeing more than 1,800 new wildlife passages or *écoponts* constructed above roads to facilitate the movement of animals between habitats; less obvious are fish ladders and underground tunnels to enable similar passages through human obstacles across rivers and land.[54] While drivers may take some reassurance from the sight of such corridors, what they cannot see are the impact on nocturnal animal, bird and insect life of the floodlit networks of roadways that disrupt, often fatally, foraging and reproduction which depends on dark skies.

One of the most preciously guarded peasant triumphs of the Revolution, the right to hunt, was extended by the 'loi Verdeille' of 1964 into the right of access of departmental hunting associations to all rural property. There are one million *chasseurs* in France today: 196 for every 10,000 people, against a European Union average of 122.[55] Even though active hunters are a small minority of the population, their political influence remains powerful, as exemplified by the decision of the government in January 2023 to step away from a proposal to have one hunting-free day per week across France.[56] These hunters kill about 22 million animals each year, 80 per cent of them birds. The most numerous are pheasants (about 3 million) and partridges (2.2 million), most raised commercially, pigeons (5 million), thrushes (2 million) and ducks (2 million). Among the mammals are 2 million rabbits and hares, 600,000 deer and more than 700,000 boars. Most concerning are the significant numbers of threatened species of birds: turtle doves, teals, snipes and curlews.[57] In the Sologne region south of Orléans, the 3,000 ponds and surrounding woodlands, now mostly in the hands of wealthy individuals, have been divided with between 3,000 and 5,000 kilometres of mesh fencing, creating closed hunting reserves described by some locals as 'live target practice' and by others as 'butchery'.[58]

Much more controversial have been decisions about the 'rewilding' of upland areas from which wolves in particular were exterminated early in the twentieth century. In the heart of the Massif Central is Mont Lozère, the source of the River Tarn and the highest point on the Robert Louis Stevenson walking path, which follows the route he travelled in 1878 and described in *Travels with a Donkey in the Cévennes* (1879).[59] The path follows a *draille* (shepherds path) across the mountain, marked by *montjoies* (standing stones). These stones mark one dimension of an ancient pastoral economy linking lowlands and highlands: milk production and cheese making, textiles and meat. The *bories* (drystone huts) which dot the upper hillsides were used in winter to shelter shepherds against storms; in summer, the larger ones were for men to milk Salers cattle and make the distinctive hard cheeses of the region. North of Mont Lozère is the tiny village of Auvers. Today, about 50 people still live there, and in 1770 there were about 400. In the heart of the village is the statue of Marie-Jeanne Valet, the servant of the priest Dumont de Paulhac, who on 11 August 1765, fought off the infamous 'Bête du Gévaudan', a monstrous beast alleged to have killed scores of peasants. It was probably a wolf, and there were about 3,000 fatal wolf attacks in France from the late sixteenth to the early-nineteenth century; some estimates are that the true number may have been three times greater. The Gévaudan wolf became extinct in the 1930s, but in the 1990s, wolves from Italy, which were common in the French Alps, reappeared in the region, much to the delight of many but to the consternation of farmers.[60]

As with wolves and bears, there is a precious balance with vultures. Many farmers in the Cévennes and Massif Central have adapted to their increasing presence by erecting platforms on which dead livestock is placed as a particularly easy way of encouraging bird life while disposing of carcasses. For others, there is now an imbalance. In the words of one:

> with its 100,000 sheep, the Aveyron is the premier ovine department in France. On the bovine side, Aubrac cattle, which had almost disappeared twenty-five years ago, have totally renewed the region's economy. Now the vultures have upset things, and I just want a new balance which will allow us to set off alarms when they come near herds, and to be able to control their density.[61]

Today, there is a precarious peace between wolves and pastoralists, where authorities claim that an equilibrium can be maintained with culling while farmers bemoan the loss of animals. There were fewer attacks in 2021 than in 2020, but more than 10,000 sheep were killed across the forty-eight departments where wolves are now present. Authorities argue that annual culling of about 20 per cent of the more than 900 wolves will maintain an equilibrium; many farmers instead demand eradication. The issue is now fraught. The peace has been broken occasionally when wolves and vultures have been poisoned. Elsewhere, the *chat forestier* or European wild cat, the predecessor of domestic cats, is increasingly present in rural and upland areas, although interbreeding with feral domestic cats threatens their integrity as a species.[62]

While debate has raged about the reintroduction of wolves and bears into the Pyrenees and Alps, and the potential threat to livestock, far more serious for the rural landscape has been the extraordinary proliferation of wild boar (*sangliers*). Once threatened because hunting had reduced their number and those of their predators, boar have proliferated with the deliberate feeding of grain to lure them by hunters keen to show their prowess and to have them butchered for their lean and strongly flavoured meat. There were 36,000 killed by hunters in 1973, but 747,000 in 2019. The French rural landscape today has a distinctive Sunday morning aural atmosphere, of the mechanical whirring of bicycle chains punctuated by shotgun blasts – far more common than the pealing of church bells. Hunters and wild boar have developed a symbiotic relationship, since hunters can now claim that they are controlling a crisis (largely of their own making). There are up to 1.5 million boars in France today, and their destruction of crops has become a major problem, particularly in winegrowing areas, necessitating the banning of bait-laying close to farms.[63]

The landscape of France therefore remains the source of pride and friction, as it has for centuries. But new sensibilities and practices are continuing to remake its appearance, often in unexpected ways. Just 40 kilometres west of Paris, in the undulating landscape of the Haute Vallée de Chevreuse nature park, the village of Lévis-Saint-Nom is home to a new enterprise which claims to be the world's largest agricultural campus. 'Hectar' covers more than 600 hectares of agricultural land and forest and offers students an eclectic mix of courses ranging from an introduction to farming to the use of artificial intelligence and land regeneration. The school defines itself as an innovative response to climate change to secure a new generation of farmers as more farms fall vacant and to confront ecological challenges.[64]

The new environmental sensibilities have even affected one of the most distinctive characteristics of the entries into towns and villages across the French countryside, the proud proclamation that the visitor is entering one of France's floral communities ('villes et villages fleuris'). Since the annual awards were established in 1959, 4,462 communes out of the current 34,968 have earned the title. Now, rather than ubiquitous hanging baskets and traffic roundabouts with their annual bursts of colour, these villages and towns are encouraged to privilege biodiversity, durability and alignment with local ecosystems.[65]

Even in Paris itself, there are signs of renewed appreciation of landscapes buried for centuries under urban construction and reconstruction, in particular the attention being paid to the Bièvre, a 35-kilometre-long stream running from Guyancourt, south of Versailles, to the Seine near the Jardin des Plantes. It was Paris' second natural waterway until it was buried under the city and its surrounding suburbs in a long process that started in the thirteenth century and ended in the mid-twentieth century. The river was heavily industrialized with mills, which led to the straightening of the river. Tanneries, butcher shops and dyemakers were built along its banks, leading to serious pollution concerns. The Gobelins workshop had been on its banks in the *faubourg* Saint-Marcel since the fifteenth century. Then, starting in the eighteenth century, the river was gradually diverted into culverts. Much of the neglected stream – beloved of creative minds from Antoine Watteau, Victor Hugo and Joris-Karl Huysmans to Odilon Redon, Eugène Atget and Louise Bourgeois – had become a drain.

By the end of the twentieth century, the entire urban section from Antony to the Seine was underground under concrete slabs or rubble, and the stream was simply an underground wastewater course. Since its disappearance, urban projects to unearth the river have consistently surfaced: the most recent was endorsed by the City of Paris in 2020 and promises to 'cool and regreen' the dense and polluted city by reclaiming its forgotten waterway. Today, it meanders through the countryside, then urban parks, as far as a reservoir and nature reserve in Antony, where it disappears underground. Then, in 2003, 200 metres of the Bièvre were re-opened in the Parc des Prés in Fresnes. At the same time, over twenty direct wastewater connections to the Bièvre were eliminated. Another section of the Bièvre between Massy and Verrières was re-opened in 2006. Most impressively, a 600-metre section was opened at Arcueil in 2022 after more than two years of work removing concrete slabs and roads covering a drain. Today, a clear stream winds through a verdant slice of flourishing vegetation in the urban landscape, on a small scale as impressive as the ambitions to clean the River Seine as the centrepiece of the 2024 Olympics (see Plate 16).[66]

Such initiatives seemed to shrivel in the reality of the hot, dry summer of 2022, which brought many of the consequences of climate change together. The French weather bureau defines heatwaves (*jours aux températures caniculaires*) as periods of at least three consecutive days where maximum temperatures are 5 degrees above average. Since 1945, there have been forty-six heatwaves, but across these seventy-five years, the number of heatwave days has increased ninefold. The summer of 2022 was the second hottest on record after that of 2003, in which heatwaves claimed 15,000 lives. The accompanying drought led to three-quarters of the country being registered at the highest, 'crisis' level of water supply and led to scores of southern villages relying on water tanker deliveries.

The searing 2022 summer reduced the harvest of lavender and other perfume flower crops around Grasse by half, and the remainder of the crop was of poor quality.[67] In 2023, communes in the *pays de Fayence* north of Fréjus announced that they would have to suspend all building permits because of the combination of inadequate water supplies and increasing tourism. Some winegrowers in Roussillon began harvesting muscat grapes as early as 3 August; around Bordeaux, the harvest began in mid-August, one month earlier than average.[68]

Almost 600 kilometres of canals were closed in eastern France and people could wade across the Loire near Orléans. Deaths of mature oaks from drought were reported in the forest of Chantilly when 2,000 of them had already been committed to rebuild 'la forêt' (the roof beams) in the Cathedral of Notre Dame.[69] Wildfires consumed 50,000 hectares of forest, particularly in the Landes region. Campers were threatened not only by the proximity of many of these fires to the mass camping grounds of the southwest: news emerged that half of France's six hundred camping sites along coastlines are threatened with closure due to coastal erosion and vulnerability to storm surges.

The parched summer of 2022 was followed by a dry winter with comparatively little snow, leading to twelve departments imposing water restrictions and doubts about the capacity of the Canal du Midi to welcome summer tourists.[70] Further south, the ancient irrigation systems of the fertile plain of Roussillon which feed the rich market gardens (*horts*) and orchards and are intrinsic to its landscape, dried up following the winter of 2023. Villages began to run out of drinking water while farmers sought to dig deeper into the dwindling water table. The first wildfire of the year was reported on 16 April.[71]

CONCLUSION

Underpinning this story of the making of the French landscape across 250 years has been the complex relationship – sometimes nurturing, sometimes rapacious – between humans and the rural environment. For many, the 'taming' of rivers, wetlands and hillsides has been an imperative in the name of progress; for others, the environment has been a legacy to be curated and sustained. The imperative to control 'nature' in the interests of the progress of cultivation and productivity has often resulted in nature's revenge in the form of floods, wildfires and the pollution of precious resources of soil and water. In this age of the Anthropocene, never before have humans had such weapons at their disposal to alter or remediate the landscape; nor has there ever been such depth of concern and expertise about the impact of such weapons if poorly directed.[1]

Today, the French countryside has never been so valued by visitors, but for those who work within it, its use and appearance have in many regions changed dramatically since the Second World War. This has not always been for the better for the landscape. Industrial-scale agriculture has turned much of the Paris basin and Champagne into treeless plains of cereal crops; swathes of the Loire valley seem covered in plastic hothouses; vast metal piggeries stud the Breton countryside. Everywhere there is evidence of 'rurbanization', where villages within commuting distance of a major urban centre have become 'dormitory' suburbs. The villages close to cities have been revitalized, but the built landscape around towns has become dominated by suburban housing developments and shopping malls. Sprawling suburbs and commercial precincts are creating a 'peri-urban' ring, which disrupts the aesthetic affinity between old urban centres and their rural hinterland.

In the eighteenth century, every community of necessity had its most fertile land set aside for the production of foodstuffs, particularly vegetables, in plots often labelled *horts* from the Latin *hortus* for garden. Major urban centres such as Bourges and Amiens had developed where vast wetlands enabled intensively farmed *hortillons* to support large populations. Even in Paris, the rue des Maraîchers (market gardeners) in the 20th *arrondissement* in the east of the city signals a time well into the nineteenth century when the daily needs of the capital were largely supplied from its margins.[2] Today, the successive transport revolutions which since 1830 have integrated France into national and international supply chains have meant that local produce is valued only as a specialized and often more expensive product. The fertile river flats that once supported local populations everywhere are largely part of the urban sprawl, except where they are particularly prized, as in Amiens.

One French family in seven now owns a 'résidence secondaire', many of them old family houses in villages but increasingly near the sea. Apart from the largest Alpine ski resorts, all the forty-five towns with more than 7,000 holiday residences are on the coasts. At the same time, land seen as marginal for production has been allowed to revert to *friches*, abandoned fields overrun with weeds and exotic plants. It has been millennia since so few people have tilled the soil, but never have so few produced so much. The cost of this bounty in areas of industrial agriculture has been the degradation of the soil and waterways and the continued shrinking of biodiversity.

A government agency founded in 2009, the Office Français de la Biodiversité, recently published a summary of its key indicators across the ten-year period 2012–22. There were some heartening improvements: a 19 per cent increase in indigenous trees in forests in 2007–17; more forests supporting genuine biodiversity; and a doubling of migratory birds along shorelines since 1980. But more alarming was the steep decline in the numbers of birds in farmland areas (36 per cent since 1989) and in the numbers of bees and bats, and only 6 per cent of wetlands were in prime condition. Frogs are especially vulnerable to any degradation of the quality of water as well as to a warming climate.[3] Western Europe is one of the most intensive regions of artificial lighting in the world, with all the consequences this represents for animal life dependent on dark skies for movement, reproduction and feeding.[4] For humans, too, this means that very few French people ever see a night sky, as their ancestors did all the time.

In contrast, cultural values of landscape beauty, quiet forests and the harmony of built and natural environments have never been so powerful. The concept of 'heritage' to be protected has changed across time, just as have the values imputed to particular landscapes. In 1839, the poet Prosper Mérimée, then inspector of historic monuments, wrote to the prefects of France's eighty-three departments, asking them to submit a list of monuments to be protected. Of the 1,082 nominated, 934 were buildings, almost all churches, *châteaux* and Roman ruins. None were landscapes. Today, there are more than 45,000 on the list, including industrial sites being constructed during the period in which Mérimée was working.[5] What has changed most dramatically, however, is the place of landscapes as protected sites, whether the most protected *sites classés* or less protected *sites inscrits*. Under a law of 21 April 1906, the Île de Bréhat, near Paimpol on the north coast of Brittany, was the first to be designated a *site classé*. Today, there are about 6,700 classified sites, together covering more than 2.5 million hectares or 4 per cent of France.

The classified sites are an extraordinary natural heritage, but equally revealing is what is deemed to be worthy of protection. The lists are dominated by the dramatic and picturesque: gorges, mountains, forests, islands and lakes. There are very few protected sites distinguished by a particular agricultural or pastoral configuration: some areas of *bocage* in the northwest, the mountain plateau pastures (Hautes Chaumes) in the Forez mountains and the peat bog of Longéroux on the Millevaches plateau in Corrèze.[6] There are other categories, including since 1993 the less protected rural and urban 'remarkable patrimonial sites' (*sites patrimoniaux remarquables*) and 'sites of community importance' designated by Natura 2000 at a European level. The National Inventory of Natural Patrimony lists almost 1,800 locations of 'riches of ecology, fauna and flora, geology, mineralogy and paleontology'.[7]

The new appreciation of public responsibility for safeguarding the richness of the landscape is symbolized at Versailles itself. There, the most spectacular human remaking of the environment to that time, the creation by Louis XIV, until his death in 1715, of the *château* and its eight hundred hectares of gardens and waterworks, transformed a swampy plain into an awe-inspiring monument to royal authority. Today, while Versailles continues to arouse awe among more than seven million tourists annually, it also houses the National School of Landscape (École Nationale Supérieure de Paysage), with another branch at Marseille.

Many recent developments – the acceleration of the rural exodus, the peri-urbanization of formerly agricultural areas, the spread of national parks and forests, the hollowing out of rural cultures, 'touristification' – have outraged those for whom an idealized (and illusory) world of self-sufficient peasant households was a golden age. Many farmers have accused urban elites of imposing ever more stringent environmental and heritage controls while failing to appreciate their labours and care for the countryside, even of 'agribashing'.[8] The spread of American fast-food outlets and Australian broad-acre farming practices is seen by others as the death knell of a whole way of life.[9] Agronomists and historians, in particular, have been sympathetic to the complaints of the shrinking numbers of agricultural producers. In 1991, a special issue of a leading academic journal devoted to rural studies, *Études rurales*, brought together eminent scholars who lamented the net impact of these changes, where the landscape had become an object of urban leisure and devoid of farmers: the transition from 'agriculture to landscape'.[10]

This epochal change from 'agriculture to landscape' – at least in the minds of urban visitors to the countryside – has been reflected in the intensification of interest in preservation and environmental protection. While about 20 per cent of French people still live in rural communities, fewer than 900,000 (or 1.4 per cent) of France's sixty-five million people now work in agriculture. In the 1770s, this figure was closer to 80 per cent, given that all members of peasant households made a contribution to the family's survival. As the rural landscape has slowly been drained of people across two centuries, so urban sensibilities have focused more on valuing and protecting 'the world we have lost'. ·

The place of landscape in the rich legacy of French painting has reflected this history. Eighteenth-century landscape painters had used idealized, Italianate rococo scenes of 'nature' as background to aristocrats at play, as in the work of Fragonard and Boucher, or revelled in ruins (Hubert Robert) or occasionally painted *châteaux* and great domains to illustrate power. After 1815, the romanticized landscapes of the post-revolutionary decades by Georges Michel and others used menacing skies and stormy seas to evoke the emotions and perils of revolutionary upheaval. While the Barbizon school, exemplified by Camille Corot, mostly sought after 1840 to capture the play of light on forests and water, it was one of their number, Jean-François Millet, who from 1847 would focus on the countryside as a landscape of work, producing scores of stylized portraits of men and women working the soil, tending animals, preparing food and raising children. Gustave Courbet gave Millet's 'naturalism' a harder realist edge: his landscapes were not only places of labour but sites of social relations, even class conflict. After 1880, however, as the countryside was slowly transformed by rural exodus of the poorest peasants and by the specialization and mechanization of agriculture, such 'realist' portraits of rural work and life were superseded. Impressionist painters (notably Auguste Renoir, Claude Monet and Vincent van Gogh) focused their skills on the evocation of the senses aroused by the landscape. Rural people disappeared from their landscapes altogether.

In contrast, across the decades 1860–1900, a legion of lesser painters (notably Jules Breton, Jules Bastien-Lepage, and Julien Dupré) used a sentimentalized nostalgia to present an idealized rural world of honest toil by hearty rural folk, ideal for the urban drawing rooms of the very wealthy. Still others created rich regional schools of landscape art, such as Eugène Le Poittevin at Étretat, Georges Bradberry and Charles Frechon in the countryside around Rouen, Ludovic-Napoléon Lepic and Francis Tattegrain along the Picard coast, Louis-René Boulanger, Léon Dallemagne and Louis Carrand in the Bresse, Étienne Martin, Henri Jaubert, Théodore Jourdan and Théodore Décanis in Provence, Achille Laugé and Paul Sibra around Carcassonne, and Jeanne-Marie Barbey and Henry Moret in Brittany. These were skilled craftspeople with a deep passion for their *pays* and who preferred to capture its 'traditions' in a realist style rather than experiment with subject or form. Today, such 'realist' landscape painting is the most democratic and popular of artistic forms, as evidenced by its ubiquity in art galleries catering for the tourist market and reflecting the profound popular resonance of environmental and landscape values. In contrast, contemporary professional artists have largely eschewed the landscape genre, despite the brilliance of some abstract works such as Raoul Ubac's *Terre rouge* (1971) and Philippe Cognée's *Paysage* (1994).[11]

This book has argued that the imprint of human activity is present everywhere on the French landscape, evident along the course of the greatest of its rivers, the Loire, which flows like a great artery through the heart of the land. It still has its wild sections as it travels northwest in a great arc from its source on the Gerbier du Jonc in the Massif Central 1,120 kilometres to its mouth near Saint-Nazaire, where it enters the sea 70 metres below France's longest bridge. It has its rapids and gorges south of Roanne, marshes and forests in the Sologne region and is home to 250 species of birds, otters (reintroduced in the 1970s), beavers and water voles and plentiful animals. It flows past nuclear power stations and oil refineries, as well as fabled châteaux, through lower reaches polluted by agricultural run-off and drained by drought and irrigation – and yet still vulnerable to flooding.

It is not surprising that the river has attracted some of France's greatest novelists, from George Sand and Honoré de Balzac in the nineteenth century to Colette and Julien Gracq in the twentieth. Gracq's subtle evocations of the nature of the 'deep, black' Èvre, a 'dark corridor' tributary which enters the Loire near his home village of Saint-Florent-le-Vieil, were published as *Les Eaux étroites* in 1976.[12] The river's source of vitality is contested along every stretch: the ponds, streams and forests of the Sologne, immortalized in 1913 by the local boy Alain-Fournier in *Le Grand Meaulnes*, were a primary site for Napoleon III's urge to bring 'wilderness' into productive use in the 1850s and are fought over today by environmentalists and owners of private hunting permits.[13]

The creation of the French rural landscape has also been a process of the imagination and not just for artists and novelists. Urban dwellers and tourists have been conditioned to see rural France as 'traditional', even unchanging, with its extraordinary variety reduced to a few trademarks or *appellations*. The great diversity of landscapes created by human action and at times open conflict has been flattened by the homogeneous language of tourist brochures into timeless, beautiful and quaint rusticity.[14] Autoroutes and the TGV have not only transformed travellers' views of the landscape but have furnished new ways of envisaging that landscape, reducing its scale and complexity through the speed of traversing it. Indeed, French autoroute companies have developed a set of wayside symbols to reduce whole regions to single objects: a new 'Catalan village' for the Roussillon, medieval knights for the Corbières, a cluster of grapes for Burgundy.[15]

A visitor from the eighteenth century to rural France today would be most impressed by the lattice-like network of paved roads and highways but no less startled by the spread of railway lines, power lines and buildings across the best agricultural land in the country. The power of seigneurs and religious was inscribed in the eighteenth-century landscape: the most imposing structures in the daily experience of rural people were the parish church and the village *château*. Both still exist, of course, but are unable to compete for height and bulk with high-voltage power lines and new castles, the *châteaux d'eau*. The price of domestic amenity and immediate access to the outside world has been paid by the aesthetic qualities of rural landscapes.

The nineteenth century witnessed an extraordinary development of roads and canals, then railway networks, followed in the late-twentieth century by autoroutes and high-speed railway lines. Improvements to major roads by the 1780s had placed Lyon within five days of Paris by coach; Marseille was only eight days away. Two hundred years later, Lyon could be reached by a TGV in less than two hours, Marseille in three hours. The almost 30,000 kilometres of railway lines still in use mostly paralleled major road routes until, with the opening of the first TGV lines from 1981, the engineering specifications, noises and dangers of TGVs required fenced swathes through rural areas that could not be traversed. New 'sugar beet' stations – so named because the first was built among *betterave* or sugar beet fields in Picardy – have been constructed well outside urban areas. As with autoroutes, new TGV lines have almost always generated dismay and protest among those most affected by the stark change to local landscapes. But rare was the victory at Vouvray in the Loire Valley that in 1990 forced a TGV line underground for 1,500 metres to preserve 'chenin blanc' vineyards.[16]

In part, this history of the French rural landscape has been the story of successive frameworks of massive infrastructure imposed on the countryside, from railways to autoroutes and from mining slag heaps to nuclear power stations. Most recent – and just as controversial – has been the rapid growth in the number of wind farms. By the end of 2023, France had up to 1,400 turbines, each about 90 metres high, dotted across most of its regions. While welcomed for their contribution to renewable energy (currently producing about 4 per cent of France's needs), their size and location also make them unpopular, especially in valued landscapes. A new wind farm of twenty-two turbines on the hillsides of the villages of Artigues and Ollières, on the lower slopes of the Montagne Sainte-Victoire, east of Aix-en-Provence, has been particularly contested in this land of Paul Cézanne. New laws giving mayors stronger powers to refuse permits for new turbines have served to accentuate local conflicts.[17] A new TGV rail tunnel – of which 80 per cent of the load will be freight – from Lyon to Turin has posed a similar question: does the destruction of swathes of mountain landscape and the use of polluting methods of construction outweigh the long-term benefits of a significant shift away from road transport?[18]

There was never a 'golden age' of the French landscape in the sense of a close alignment between human uses of its resources and the richness of biodiversity. Certainly, the decades between 1850 and 1880, which have also been labelled 'the pinnacle of peasant civilization', were a time when the widest range of regional produce was created without artificial fertilizers and pesticides. The hedgerows (*bocage*) of the northwest and elsewhere were at their most extensive. However, this richness coincided with the greatest extent of deforestation in French history and the spread of phylloxera through southern vineyards. There were minimal constraints on the urban waste that was routinely deposited in waterways. There was little sign of the popular environmental sensibilities which today sustain many thousands of community groups which enjoy the landscape or work to protect it.

Now, a new rural landscape is emerging across France in the context of the challenges of genetically modified crops, diseases linked to industrial production of foodstuffs, climate change and pollution.[19] In 1770, no less than about ten million of the twenty-four million hectares of arable land were in fallow to allow exhausted soil a chance to recover. By 1900, the land that could be considered fallow had fallen by 75 per cent.[20] Today, the extent of uncultivated land is again increasing, due to a combination of more productive use of the best soils, the continuing exodus from the most marginal farms, and European Union policies setting quotas on production and requiring farmers to set aside a percentage of land to encourage biodiversity.

In the process, some regional landscapes that were dramatically altered in the past have now become 'iconic' and deemed worthy of preservation. This is the case, for example, in the *landes* region of the Médoc north of Bordeaux, where there had been draining and forestation of the swampy lowlands, just as in the Landes de Gascogne to the south. Others with a deeper understanding of the history of the region are now actively restoring wetlands, reintroducing wild cattle and even the dung beetles that thrived on their manure, for example, around the beautiful Étang de Cousseau in the west of the Médoc.[21] There are few if any regional landscapes in France which have not continued to evolve. Even what appears to be the most historically intact landscape – the hedgerows and pastures of the Charolais-Brionnais *bocage* in southern Burgundy – has continued to change as markets for its high-quality beef have extended beyond France.[22]

Other aspects of the landscape have endured but fill very different functions. In certain regions (Sologne, Dombes, Bresse, Poitou, Somme and elsewhere), ponds or *étangs* have dotted the landscape for hundreds of years, covering perhaps 70,000 hectares in total. Often, they were created to both drain marshlands for arable fields and to create fishponds. Around urban centres such as Rochefort, Saint-Omer, Amiens and Bourges, they were invaluable for market gardens. Hundreds of hectares of *hortillonages* around Amiens are still there, far more valued than they were in times of 'modernization' but much more likely to be prized for fishing, hunting and 'green tourism'.[23]

In the Dombes region east of Lyon, more than one thousand *étangs* covering 11,000 hectares – created by religious orders as fish ponds many centuries ago – have mostly survived the pressures of agricultural entrepreneurs keen to expand broad-acre farming. Many are still part of an ancient cycle of filling (*l'évolage*), draining, harvesting fish, cropping (*l'assec*) and refilling, despite the lure of lucrative but thirsty crops such as maize. Today, the Dombes is home to more than 130 bird species, including swans, herons, grebes, pochards, coots and gulls. Since March 2023, the region has been designated a RAMSAR site, one of twenty-two in France. Others include the bay at the mouth of the Somme, the Camargue, the gulf of Morbihan and the great *étang* of Salses-Leucate between Narbonne and Perpignan.

Everywhere, access to and control of clean water resources has become central to debates over the landscape and its uses. The dry winter of 2022–3 exacerbated tensions. At the same time that media attention across the globe was captured by angry protests against the Macron government's decision to push through an increase in the retirement age from sixty-two to sixty-four years, a violent clash in the west of France in March 2023 between 3,000 police and 6,000 protesters left hundreds wounded, according to protesters. Here the issue was proposed new dams at Sainte-Soline and Mauzé-sur-le-Mignon (department of Deux-Sèvres), two of sixteen which the government had agreed to subsidize in the area, subject to farmers adopting ecological farm practices. The drought had pushed some farmers to walk away from these commitments while insisting that the dams go ahead. In the words of the sociologist Jean Viard, 'the question is how to save nature. On the one side are those who want to save agriculture because it captures a lot of carbon and on the other those who say we must go back to a state of nature'.[24]

Epitomizing the dilemmas of industrial-scale agriculture is the highly productive plain of Limagne near Clermont-Ferrand. The black soil had been effectively 'tamed' by drainage systems by the mid-twentieth century and transformed from small-scale polyculture into broad-acre cereal and maize cropping. In a region hitherto vulnerable to stagnant pools of water after summer thunderstorms, maize farmers now have to resort to irrigation for their crops. The massive Limagrain cooperative has become one of the world's largest suppliers of seed (see Figure 7.1), but the proud achievements of local farmers have been mired in controversy over the company's support for genetically modified crops and, more recently, for two new dams – dubbed *mégabassines* by opponents – covering 33 hectares, two of more than 300 currently being considered across France.[25]

So the landscape of France has been created since 1770 by a series of rural revolutions: the slow and incomplete victory of private property over collective use; the victory of monocultures and mechanization over polyculture and small holdings; the return of arable land to fallow. These changes have been overlaid by transport infrastructure and traces of war. The layers of landscape history are visible everywhere, although nowhere in more concentrated form than northeast of Saint-Quentin (Aisne). Here, the village of Vadencourt presents the image of bucolic permanence around its *château*, its ancient church steeple and the ruins of a Cistercian abbey. Its population of about five hundred is about the same as it was in the eighteenth century; its 12 square kilometres are still covered in farmland. The sense of permanence is symbolized by the presence of two remarkable houses dating from 1775, the property of the master stonemason Nicolas Grain (1750–1823), a writer and sculptor active during the French Revolution. But a closer look at its landscape reveals evidence of many of the key themes of this book. The destruction of the old feudal system after 1789 left its mark on the abbey, which was sold off and its cloister converted into a textile factory. The territory of Vadencourt is crossed by two rivers – the Noirieu and the Oise – but in 1834–9, a major canal was constructed across the village from the Sambre to the Oise to facilitate the transport of coal from Belgium to Paris, with a major turning basin in Vadencourt itself. More dramatically, the village was traversed in the second half of the nineteenth century by no fewer than three separate railway lines: from Bohain to Guise (on rails of 1 metre) to transport sugar beet and workers towards Bohain; from Guise to Busigny (on rails of 1.435 metres); and from Saint-Quentin to Guise (on similar rails). All three lines are now closed. Vadencourt was also in the line of fire during the First World War, as evidenced by the presence of a major cemetery with 760 allied soldiers buried (mainly British but also Australian, Canadian and Indian). The nearby hamlet of Bohéries has a memorial to local members of the Resistance killed in the Second World War.

Another example of the layers of change is the Breton village of Saint-Aignan, lovingly photographed between the wars by the progress-minded Paul Lotz, as we saw in Chapter 6. Superficially, it is much the same as when he was mayor in 1904–47. As then, about two-fifths of its land is in forests or uncultivated *landes*, and the rest is under pasture and crops. In every other way, it is radically different. In the interwar years, its 1,200 people mostly lived a precarious existence: cereals grew with difficulty; only apple and pear trees flourished. Today, its population is half what it was, and there are very few farmers. A *remembrement* that was finalized in 1990 drastically reduced the number of parcels of land in the interests of more efficient production. The Porh Antoine section to the west of the village had had 363 separate parcels when the first cadastral survey was completed in 1836. After the 1990 consolidation, there were just eighty-eight. Today, most of the fertilized fields are used for cereal crops and are devoid of the hedgerows that feature in Lotz's photographs (see Figure 6.3). Instead of the farm animals that dotted the landscape before the proliferation of tractors after 1950, there are humans walking and cycling the maze of tracks through Saint-Aignan's forests and hills and appreciating the four classified monuments inside the village church.[26]

Lotz's great pride, the hydroelectric dam on the river Blavet, has become a major source of income from holidaymakers who enjoy camping and water sports in a forest setting. It is also a source of angry division between those who support an expensive new crossing along the wall over the Guerlédan dam to facilitate booming tourism and those for whom the passage and its associated carparks and construction would benefit commerce but create congestion and threaten rich birdlife. It is a test case of the virtues of 'slow tourism' opposed to the lure of attracting more visitors. So heated had community meetings become in late 2022 that the mayor and some of the council resigned in disgust.[27]

*   *   *

In 1789, a great shift occurred in the very meaning of 'property'. Most of the land in the kingdom had had one legal owner but was subject to other 'rights': of rural communities to collective rights to graze and glean on others' lands, and of the king and privileged orders of clergy and nobility to claim 'rights' over peasant produce and labour. From 1789, all property was to have a single owner unless it was the 'commons' in some regions, and only the state could claim 'rights' over its owners. Today, the notion of rural property ownership as a purely private 'right' is moribund. A combination of environmental challenges, European Union subsidies and regulation, and sensitivity to local identity have made governments more protective of the ancient collective rights and practices which they for so long dismissed as archaic.

Ever since the Revolution, and particularly since 1900, the French state has been forced to intervene in the uses made of private property, whether to protect valued but vulnerable landscapes, to impose environmental controls or to protect regional commercial interests. In the process, private property has become subject to the claims – and protections – of the state, the European Union and even of global institutions. The revolutionary proposition of 1789, that individual property owners should be able to use their private resources as they wished within the bounds of the law, has been constrained by the claims of many others with an interest in protecting landscapes. Across France, 9 per cent of forests belong to the state and 16 per cent to local communities; 75 per cent of forests are in private hands, but such are the competing demands and rights of others that it would be simplistic to see this as purely 'private' property.

Nor is it only the government of France and its citizens who insist that landscapes are subject to multiple claims and different purposes. European and even global institutions have vested interests as well. One wonders what the revolutionaries of 1789, who boldly articulated the untrammelled rights of private property owners, would make of the 'terroirs' of Bourgogne, Champagne and Saint-Émilion, and the pastures of the Causses and Cévennes, being listed on a World Heritage Register as part of humanity's shared patrimony.

Some have argued accordingly that it is time for a new, 'multi-usage' cadastral survey based on rural land as a 'common good' – but this would unleash a new wave of tensions between those who see farms as rural enterprises and those who advance public interest claims on the countryside. As *Le Monde* posed the question in 2012, referring to the increasing presence of wolves in the Jura and elsewhere, how can we 'keep the wolf without losing the sheep?' How can the precious landscapes of France be maintained as sites of productive labour and viable rural communities while at the same time being preserved as part of a shared national and international patrimony?[28]

NOTES

Introduction

1 For example, in 1981 a cluster of villages started the prestigious 'Les Plus beaux villages de la France' association: https://www.tripsavvy.com/most-beautiful-villages -of-france-1517869.

2 *Forêt et paysage, Xe-XXIe siècle*, ed. Andrée Corvol (Paris: L'Harmattan, 2011), 7. See the discussion in Graham Robb's captivating 'historical guidebook', *The Discovery of France* (London: Picador, 2007), ch. 2.

3 *Le Paysage, entre art et nature*, ed. Jean-Noël Bret and Yolaine Escande (Rennes: Presses universitaires de Rennes, 2017). A beautifully illustrated geological perspective is by Georges Feterman and Marc Giraud, *Paysages de France en bord de chemin* (Paris: Éditions Delachaux et Niestlé, 2021).

In the collection of essays by Jean-Pierre Deffontaines, Jean Ritter, Benoît Deffontaines and Denis Michaud, *Petit guide de l'observation du paysage* (Paris: INRA, 2006), a geologist, a botanist, an agronomist and an agriculture teacher offer different perspectives on the same mountain landscape.

4 George Seddon, *Sense of Place: A Response to an Environment* (Perth: University of Western Australia Press, 1972), Foreword. See too Penelope Lively, *The Presence of the Past: An Introduction to Landscape History* (London: Collins, 1976).

5 Michael Roth and Dietwald Gruehn, 'Landscape, an Area as Perceived by People: Measuring Perceived Forest Landscape Aesthetics using Internet Survey Methodologies', in Corvol, *Forêt et paysage*, 377–90. Key texts on the meaning of landscape include Augustin Berque, *Écoumène: Introduction à l'étude des milieux humains* (Paris: Belin, 2001); John Wylie, *Landscape* (London and New York: Routledge, 2007); *Foundation Papers in Landscape Ecology*, ed. J. A. Wiens, M. R. Moss, M. G. Turner and D. J. Mladenoff (New York: Columbia University Press, 2007); *Key Topics in Landscape Ecology*, ed. J. Wu and R. Hobbs (Cambridge: Cambridge University Press, 2007); Stéphane Frioux, *The Environment, an Object of History – Encyclopedia of the Environment* (encyclopedie-environnement.org).

6 The most influential recent overview in French, by Jean-Robert Pitte in 1983, is a masterpiece of erudition and breadth, although criticized for assuming that, despite great regional diversity, there is in some sense one *French* landscape, and as old-fashioned in its assumption that there is a direct relationship between the viewer and the object: *Histoire du paysage française*, 2 vols (Paris: Tallandier, 1983).

7 Henri Lefebvre, *The Production of Space*, trans. D. Nicholson-Smith (1974. Oxford: Oxford University Press, 1991), 110.

8 Alain Corbin, *L'Homme dans le paysage. Entretien avec Jean Lebrun* (Paris: Éditions Textuel, 2001), 11, 42. Literary constructions of the English countryside are famously explored in Raymond Williams, *The Country and the City* (London: Chatto and Windus, 1973).

9 Marcel Roncayolo, 'The Scholar's Landscape', in *Rethinking France. Les Lieux de mémoire*, vol. 2, *Space*, ed. Pierre Nora (Chicago, IL: University of Chicago Press, 2006), 343, 376.

10 Fabien Gaveau, *Propriété, cadastre et usages locaux dans les campagnes françaises (1789–1960). Histoire d'une tension légale* (Besançon: Presses universitaires de Franche-Comté, 2021), 318–19.

11 Wetlands in nearby Saint-Omer are just as old but not as attentively maintained. The *marais* in Bourges had originally been part of the town's defences but were leased out to market gardeners.

12 Jacques Blondel, James Aronson, Jean-Yves Bodiou, and Gilles Bœuf, *The Mediterranean Region. Biological Diversity in Space and Time*, 2nd edn (Oxford: Oxford University Press, 2010), 202 and ch. 10.

13 Jean-François Blanc, 'Landscape Typology of French Agrarian Terraces', in *World Terraced Landscapes: History, Environment, Quality of Life*, ed. Mauro Varotto, Luca Bonardi and Paulo Tarolli (Cham: Springer, 2019), 63–77. https://doi.org/10.1007/978 -3-319-96815-5_5; Romana Harfouche, *Histoire des paysages méditerranéens terrassés: aménagements et agriculture* (Oxford: BAR Publishing, 2007).

14 Fernand Braudel, *The Identity of France*, vol. 1, *History and Environment* (London: Collins, 1988); vol. 2, *People and Production*, trans. S. Reynolds (London: Collins, 1990). His remarks on his relationship with France are in vol. 1, Introduction.

15 Fernand Braudel, *The Mediterranean and the Mediterranean World in the Age of Phillip II*, trans. S. Reynolds (London: HarperCollins, 1992).

16 Braudel, *People and Production*, 674.

17 Ibid., 410 and ch. 10. A similar argument was made by Gordon Wright, *Rural Revolution in France; the Peasantry in the Twentieth Century* (Stanford, CA: Stanford University Press, 1964).

18 Braudel, *People and Production*, 465.

19 The key statement was Paul J. Crutzen and Eugene F. Stoermer, 'The Anthropocene', *IGPB (International Geosphere-Biosphere Programme)* Newsletter 41 (2000): 17, and the 2002 article by Crutzen in *Nature*: www.nature.com/nature/journal/v415 /n6867/full/415023a.html (accessed 18 August 2021). See too Will Steffen, Paul J. Crutzen and John R. McNeill, 'The Anthropocene: Are Humans Now Overwhelming the Great Forces of Nature?', *Ambio* 36, no. 8 (2007): 614–21; Carolyn Merchant, *The Anthropocene and the Humanities. From Climate Change to a New Age of Sustainability* (New Haven, CT and London: Yale University Press, 2020), Intro.

20 John McNeill and Peter Engelke, *The Great Acceleration: An Environmental History of the Anthropocene since 1945* (Cambridge, MA: Harvard University Press, 2014).

21 See *Anthropocene or Capitalocene? Nature, History, and the Crisis of Capitalism*, ed. Jason W. Moore (Oakland, CA: PM Press, 2016).

22 Tom Griffiths, 'The Planet Is Alive. Radical Histories for Uncanny Times', *Griffith Review* 63 (2019): 61–72. See too Dipesh Chakrabarty, 'The Climate of History: Four Theses', *Critical Inquiry* 35 (2009): 197–222. For a French perspective, see Fabien Locher and Grégory Quenet, 'L'Histoire environnementale: origines, enjeux et perspectives d'un nouveau chantier', *Revue d'histoire moderne et contemporaine* 56, no. 4 (2009): 7–38.

23 Charles Tilly, *The Vendée* (Cambridge, MA: Harvard University Press, 1964); Peter McPhee, *Revolution and Environment in Southern France: Peasant, Lords, and Murder in the Corbières, 1780–1830* (Oxford: Clarendon Press, 1999).

24 See, for example, the recent European Environment Agency report on https://www .eea.europa.eu/soer-2015/countries/france.

25 Braudel, *History and Environment*, 146–7. On the history of forests, see Corvol, *Forêt et paysage*; and *L'Homme aux bois: histoire des relations de l'homme et de la forêt (XVIIe–XXe siècle)* (Paris: Fayard, 1987); and the beautifully produced overview by Stéphanie Thiébault, *La Forêt. Histoire, usages, représentations et enjeux* (Paris: CNRS, 2023). There have also been fine case-studies in English, notably Kieko Matteson, *Forests in Revolutionary France: Conservation, Community, and Conflict 1669–1848* (Cambridge: Cambridge University Press, 2014); and Tamara Whited, *Forests and Peasant Politics in Modern France* (New Haven, CT: Yale University Press, 2000).

Chapter 1

1 Braudel, *History and Environment*, 37.

2 Arthur Young, *Travels in France during the years 1787, 1788 and 1789* (1790. Cambridge: Cambridge University Press, 1929), 4, 15–16. See the discussion in Hugh Clout, *Agriculture in France on the Eve of the Railway Age* (London: Croom Helm, 1980), ch. 1.

3 Young, *Travels in France*, 271–2; P. Charbonnier et al., *Auvergne* (Chamalières: Éditions Christine Bonneton, 1985), 331–7.

4 Robert Specklin, 'L'Achèvement des paysages agraires', in *France rurale*, ed. Georges Duby and Armand Wallon, vol. 3, 255–305. See Roncayolo, 'The Scholar's Landscape', 366–79. Roger Dion added a fourth category, the village-based landscapes of the centre and west: *Essai sur la formation du paysage rural français* (Tours: Arrault, 1934).

5 Peter McPhee, *Une communauté languedocienne dans l'histoire: Gabian 1760–1960* (Nîmes: Lacour, 2001), ch. 1.

6 Lawrence Wylie, *Chanzeaux: A Village in Anjou* (Cambridge, MA: Harvard University Press, 1966), ch. 1; Tilly, *The Vendée*, 28–36, 83–8.

7 Albert Dauzat and Charles Rostaing, *Dictionnaire étymologique des noms de lieu en France* (Paris: Librairie Guénégaud, 1979); Jean-Pierre Jessenne, *Pouvoir au village et révolution: Artois, 1760–1848* (Lille: Presses universitaires de Lille, 1987).

8 Clout, *Agriculture in France*, 69–71.

9 David Bruce Young, 'A Wood Famine? The Question of Deforestation in Old Regime France', *Forestry* 49 (1976): 45–56; P.W. Bamford, *Forests and French Sea Power, 1660–1789* (Toronto: University of Toronto Press, 1956).

10 Martine Acerra, 'Marine militaire et bois de construction. Essai d'évaluation (1779–1789)', in *Révolution et espaces forestiers. Colloque des 3 & 4 juin 1987, Groupe d'histoire des forêts françaises,* ed. Denis Woronoff (Paris: L'Harmattan, 1988), 114.

11 Jean de Cayeux, *Le Paysage en France de 1750 à 1815* (Saint-Remy-en-l'Eau: Éditions Monelle, Hayot, 1997), 101–8; Bret and Escande (eds), *Le Paysage;* Émilie Beck Saiello, Laurent Châtel, and Élisabeth Martichou (eds), *Écrire et peindre le paysage en France et en Angleterre, 1750–1850* (Rennes: Presses universitaires de Rennes, 2021).

12 The aural landscape is captured in Anne Zink's study of southwestern France, *Clochers et troupeaux: les communautés rurales des Landes et du sud-ouest avant la Révolution* (Bordeaux: Presses Universitaires de Bordeaux, 1997).

13 P. M. Jones, *The Peasantry in the French Revolution* (Cambridge: Cambridge University Press, 1988), ch. 1.

14 Georges Duby and Armand Wallon (eds), *Histoire de la France rurale,* vol. 2 (Paris: Seuil, 1975), 440–1.

15 Ibid.

16 J. Delaspre, 'La Naissance d'un paysage rural au XVIIIe siècle sur les hauts plateaux de l'Est du Cantal et du Nord de la Margeride', *Revue de Géographie Alpine* 40 (1952): 493–7.

17 Duby and Wallon (eds), *France rurale,* vol. 2, 417 and 393–441.

18 Nicolas-Edme Restif de La Bretonne, *Monsieur Nicolas ou le cœur humain dévoilé* (Paris: Gallimard 1989), vol. 1, part 3.

19 Robert Forster, *The Nobility of Toulouse in the Eighteenth Century* (Baltimore, MD: Johns Hopkins University Press, 1960), 193–5.

20 Michèle Merger, 'Voies navigables et paysages en France', in *Les Sources de l'histoire de l'environnement. Le XIXe siècle,* ed. Andrée Corvol (Paris: L'Harmattan, 1999), 85.

21 Joël Cornette (ed.), *Atlas de l'histoire de France, 481–2005* (Paris: Belin, 2012), 304–5.

22 Marcel Moreau, *L'Abbaye de Noirlac au XVIIIe siècle* (Paris: Bernard Royer, 1990). On the geographic 'centre', see Robb, *Discovery of France,* 348–9.

23 Marquis de Turbilly, *Mémoire sur les défrichemens* (Paris, 1760); Archives Nationales [herafter AN], Procès-verbaux des Comités d'Agriculture.

24 AN, Recueil général des anciennes lois, AD IV, 4; Archives Départementales [hereafter AD] Aude 10C 22, 23; Léon Dutil, *L'État économique du Languedoc à la fin de l'Ancien Régime* (Paris: Hachette, 1911), 106–30; Jones, *Peasantry,* 11, 144. On Colbert's ordinance, see Simon Schama, *Landscape and Memory* (New York: Vintage, 1995); Andrée Corvol (ed.), *La Forêt. Actes du 113e Congrès national des sociétés savantes, Strasbourg 1988* (Paris: Éditions du CTHS, 1991). For case studies of Languedoc, see McPhee, *Revolution and Environment,* 47–8, 141–7; Noelle Plack, 'Agrarian Reform and Ecological Change During the Ancien Régime: Land Clearance, Peasants and Viticulture in the Province of Languedoc', *FH* 19 (2005): 189–210.

25 Christian Lassure, 'Master Class: les cabanes aka "village des bories", at Gordes, Vaucluse', https://thestonetrust.org/master-class-les-cabanes/; Pierre Viala, *Le Village des bories à Gordes dans le Vaucluse* (Gordes: Éditions le Village des bories, 1976).

26 Albert Soboul, *Les Campagnes montpelliéraines à la fin de l'ancien régime: propriété et culture d'après les compoix* (Paris: Presses universitaires de France, 1958); E. A. Allen, 'Deforestation and Fuel Crisis in Pre-Revolutionary Languedoc', *FHS* 13 (1984): 466; McPhee, *Revolution and Environment*, 21–4.

27 Gilbert Larguier, *Le Drap et le grain en Languedoc. Narbonne et Narbonnais 1300–1789* (Perpignan: Presses universitaires de Perpignan, 1999), ch. 13.

28 *L'Aubrac. Étude ethnologique, linguistique, agronomique et économique d'un établissement humain*, vol. 2 (Paris: Éditions du CNRS, 1971), 39–45.

29 Larguier, *Le Drap et le grain*; Christopher H. Johnson, *The Life and Death of Industrial Languedoc, 1700–1920* (New York: Oxford University Press, 1995); Claude Marquié, *L'Industrie textile carcassonnaise au XVIIIe siècle. Étude d'un groupe social: les marchands-fabricants* (Carcassonne: Société d'études scientifiques de l'Aude, 1993); J. K. J. Thomson, *Clermont-de-Lodève, 1633–1789: Fluctuations in the Prosperity of a Languedocian Cloth-Making Town* (Cambridge: Cambridge University Press, 1982).

30 Gwynne Lewis, *The Advent of Modern Capitalism in France 1770–1840: The Contribution of Pierre-François Tubeuf* (Oxford: Clarendon Press, 1993), Intro., ch. 1.

31 Thiébault, *La Forêt*, 109.

32 M. de Genssane, *Histoire naturelle de la province de Languedoc*, 5 vols (Montpellier, 1778–9), vol. 2, 160. See also Young, 'A Wood Famine?'.

33 *Cahiers de doléances des bailliages des généralités de Metz et de Nancy pour les États-Généraux de 1789*, vol. 4 (Nancy: Ministère de l'Instruction publique, 1907), 62–3, 70, 87; *Cahiers de doléances des sénéchaussées de Quimper et de Concarneau pour les États-Généraux de 1789* (Rennes: Ministère de l'Instruction publique, 1927), 109–10.

34 See Gilbert F. LaFreniere, 'Rousseau and the European Roots of Environmentalism', *Environmental History Review* 14 (1990): 41–72; Clarence J. Glacken, *Traces on the Rhodian Shore: Nature and Culture in Western Thought from Ancient Times to the End of the Eighteenth Century* (Berkeley and Los Angeles: University of California Press, 1967), 698–702.

35 Paul Butel, 'Défrichements en Guyenne au XVIIIe siècle', *Annales du Midi* 72 (1965): 195.

36 Peter McPhee, '"The misguided greed of peasants"? Popular attitudes to the environment in the Revolution of 1789', *FHS* 24 (2001): 247–69; McPhee, *Revolution and Environment*, 122–6, 182–4; Michel Noël, *L'Homme et la forêt en Languedoc-Roussillon. Histoire et économie des espaces boisés* (Perpignan: Presses universitaires de Perpignan, 1996), esp. 61–9.

37 *Cahiers de doléances de la sénéchaussée de Nîmes pour les États-Généraux de 1789*, 2 vols. (Nîmes: Ministère de l'Instruction publique, 1908–9), vol. 1, 131.

38 *Cahiers de doléances de la sénéchaussée de Cahors pour les États-Généraux de 1789* (Cahors: Ministère de l'Instruction publique, 1908), 327–8.

39 Ibid., 198.

40 *Cahiers de doléances du bailliage d'Amont*, vol. 1 (Besançon: J. Dodivers, 1918), 286; vol. 2, 75. On the environmental impact of rural industry in eastern France, see Jean-Marie Schmitt, 'De la proto-industrie à la révolution industrielle: la vallée de Saint-Amarin, région pionnière au XVIIIe siècle', *Historiens et géographes* 86 (1995): 207–10; Jean-Paul Jacob and Michel Mangin (eds), *De la mine à la forge en Franche-Comté, des origines au XIXe siècle: approche archéologique et historique* (Besançon: Annales littéraires de l'Université de Besançon, 1990); François Vion-Delphin, 'Forêts et cahiers de doléances: l'exemple de la Franche-Comté', in Woronoff (ed.), *Révolution et espaces forestiers*, 11–22.

41 *Cahiers de doléances des bailliages des généralités de Metz et de Nancy*, vol. 1, 13, 43. See Jean-Pierre Husson, 'Les Paysages forestiers lorrains, rôle et impact de l'épisode révolutionnaire (étude de géographie historique)', in Woronoff (ed.), *Révolution et espaces forestiers*, 63–70.

42 *Cahiers de doléances des bailliages des généralités de Metz et de Nancy*, 130–1.

43 Alain Chenevez, *La Saline d'Arc-et-Senans: de l'industrie à l'utopie* (Paris: Éditions L'Harmattan, 2006).

44 *Cahiers de doléances des sénéchaussées de Quimper et de Concarneau pour les Etats-Généraux de 1789*, 37. See Michel Duval, 'Besoins de guerres et forêts bretonnes', in Woronoff (ed.), *Révolution et espaces forestiers*, 119–26; Alain Le Bloas, 'La Question du domaine congéable', *AHRF* 331 (2003): 1–27.

45 Gilbert Shapiro and John Markoff, *Revolutionary Demands: A Content Analysis of the Cahiers de Doléances of 1789* (Stanford, CA: Stanford University Press, 1998), esp. ch. 14 and Appendix I; John Markoff, *The Abolition of Feudalism: Peasants, Lords, and Legislators in the French Revolution* (University Park, PA: Pennsylvania State University Press, 1996).

Chapter 2

1 There is a massive literature on the origins of the Revolution. See, for example, Peter Campbell (ed.), *The Origins of the French Revolution* (Basingstoke: Palgrave Macmillan, 2006); Thomas E. Kaiser and Dale K. Van Kley (eds), *From Deficit to Deluge: The Origins of the French Revolution* (Stanford, CA: Stanford University Press, 2011).

2 Geneviève Koubi (ed.), *Propriété et Révolution: Actes du colloque de Toulouse, 1989* (Paris: CNRS, 1990); Rafe Blaufarb, *The Great Demarcation. The French Revolution and the Invention of Modern Property* (New York and Oxford: Oxford University Press, 2016).

3 See the overview by Laurent Brassart, Grégory Quenet, and Julien Vincent, 'Révolution et environnement: état des savoirs et enjeux historiographiques', *AHRF* 399 (2020): 3–18.

4 Anne Jollet, *Terre et société en Révolution. Approche du lien social dans la région d'Amboise* (Paris: Éditions du CTHS, 2000), 25–6.

5   Some 66 of Shapiro and Markoff's sample of 748 parish *cahiers* expressed their
    concerns about wild or 'destructive animals'. Gilbert Shapiro, FRAS: The French
    Revolution Analysis System. A Portable Data Archive, Version 1.

6   Young, *Travels in France*, 226.

7   McPhee, *Revolution and Environment*, 126. See Geoffroy de Gislain, 'Chasse et
    nuisibles dans les cahiers de doléances', in *La Nature en Révolution. Colloque
    Révolution, nature, paysage et environnement*, ed. Andrée Corvol (Paris: Harmattan,
    1993), 86–93.

8   Jacques Bernet (ed.), *Le Journal d'un maître d'école d'Île-de-France (1771–1792):
    Silly-en-Multien de l'Ancien Régime à la Révolution* (Villeneuve-d'Asq: Presses
    universitaires du Septentrion, 2000), 194, 199–207.

9   Gaveau, *Propriété, cadastre et usages locaux*, 45–6; Peter Jones, *Liberty and Locality
    in Revolutionary France: Six Villages Compared, 1760–1820* (Cambridge: Cambridge
    University Press, 2003), 100.

10 Comte de Courchamps, *Souvenirs de la marquise de Créquy de 1710 à 1803*, 10 vols
    (Paris: Garnier Frères, 1865), vol. 9, 107–8.

11 *Histoire de l'administration française. Les Eaux et forêts du 12ᵉ au 20ᵉ siècle* (Paris:
    Éditions du CNRS, 1987), 213; Woronoff (ed.), *Révolution et espaces forestiers*;
    Matteson, *Forests in Revolutionary France*, 69–70. Metropolitan France's area today
    is almost 552,000 square kilometres. Allowing for the later additions of Comtat-
    Venaissin, Savoie and Nice, France would have been about 420,000 square kilometres
    in 1790.

12 Markoff, *Abolition of Feudalism*, 255; Noelle L. Plack, *Common Land, Wine and
    the French Revolution. Rural Society and Economy in Southern France, c1789–1820*
    (Farnham, Surrey and Burlington, VT: Ashgate, 2009), ch. 2; McPhee, *Revolution and
    Environment*, ch. 5.

13 Young, *Travels in France*, 227–8.

14 Archives parlementaires, 11 December 1789.

15 *Instruction de l'Assemblée Nationale concernant les fonctions des assemblées
    administratives* 12–20 août 1790, 297; AN, AD IV 19.

16 AD Ain, Archives Communales de Bourg, Registre des délibérations du Conseil
    Municipal, 2 December 1790.

17 Fernand Gerbaux and Charles Schmidt, *Procès-verbaux des comités d'agriculture et
    de commerce de la Constituante, de la Législative et de la Convention*, 5 vols (Paris:
    Imprimerie nationale, 1906–37), vol. 2, 171.

18 Nadine Vivier, *Propriété collective et identité communale. Les Biens communaux en
    France 1750–1914* (Paris: Publications de la Sorbonne, 1998), 20, 32, and ch. 2.

19 Markoff, *Abolition of Feudalism*, 255; Vivier, *Propriété collective et identité communale*,
    162–74, 212–24.

20 Vivier, *Propriété collective et identité communale*, 97–8 and chs 3–4; Georges Bourgin,
    *Le Partage des biens communaux. Documents sur la préparation de la loi du 10 juin
    1793* (Paris: Imprimerie nationale, 1908), 22–3.

21 Vivier, *Propriété collective et identité communale*, 175–8, and chs 3–4.

22 Gerbaux and Schmidt, *Procès-verbaux des comités d'agriculture et de commerce*, vol. 1,
    686.

23 Xavier de Massary, 'Les Usages de l'arrondissement de Château-Thierry: l'époque révolutionnaire', *Fédération des sociétés d'histoire et d'archéologie de l'Aisne. Memoires* 34 (1989): 21–43.

24 McPhee, *Revolution and Environment*, 122–3.

25 Françoise Fortunet, 'Le Code rural ou l'impossible codification', *AHRF* 247 (1982): 95–112.

26 The tortured legislative attempts to reimpose control over the forests are recounted in Jean-Baptiste Fressoz, 'Les Politiques de la nature au début de la Révolution. Sens et fonctions de l'alerte environnementale, 1789–1793', *AHRF* 399 (2020): 19–38; *Histoire de l'administration française*, Book III; Corvol, *L'Homme aux bois*, ch. 6; Andrée Corvol and Isabelle Richefort (eds), *Nature, paysage et environnement. L'héritage révolutionnaire* (Paris: L'Harmattan, 1995).

27 François Rouvière, *Histoire de la Révolution française dans le département du Gard*, 4 vols (Nîmes: Librairie ancienne A. Catélan, 1887–9), vol. 2, ch. 4.

28 Plack, *Common Land, Wine and the French Revolution*, ch.3; Vivier, *Propriété collective et identité communale*, chs 3–4.

29 Jones, *Peasantry*, 137–54.

30 Vivier, *Propriété collective et identité communale*, 161–2.

31 AD Meurthe-et-Moselle, L 1876; Jean-Pierre Gross, *Fair Shares for All: Jacobin Egalitarianism in Practice* (Cambridge and New York: Cambridge University Press, 1997), 102–18; Robert Parisot, *Histoire de Lorraine*, vol. 2 (Paris: Auguste Picard, 1924), 171.

32 Matteson, *Forests in Revolutionary France*, 135; Anatoli Ado, *Paysans en Révolution. Terre, pouvoir et jacquerie 1789–1794* (Paris: SÉR, 1996), 373–9; McPhee, *Revolution and Environment*, 129–31; Plack, *Common Land, Wine and the French Revolution*, 72–6.

33 Vivier, *Propriété collective et identité communale*, 135–7, 305–7.

34 Gerbaux and Schmidt, *Procès-verbaux des comités d'agriculture et de commerce*, 138–9, 165–6.

35 Reynald Abad, *La Conjuration contre les carpes. Enquête sur les origines du décret de dessèchement des étangs du 14 frimaire an II* (Paris: Fayard, 2006).

36 Félix Mourlot, *Recueil des documents d'ordre économique contenus dans les registres de délibérations des municipalités du district d'Alençon, 1788-An IV* (London: Forgotten Books, 2018), 404.

37 Tilly, *The Vendée*; Claude Petitfrère, 'The Origins of the Civil War in the Vendée', *FH* 2 (1988): 187–207.

38 Alain Corbin, *Village Bells: Sound and Meaning in the 19th-Century French Countryside*, trans. M. Thom (New York: Columbia University Press, 1998), 12–23; Bernard Richard, *Cloches et querelles de cloches dans l'Yonne. La Cloche entre maire et curé, XVIIIe-XXe* (Villeneuve-sur-Yonne: Les Amis du Vieux Villeneuve, 2010).

39 Corbin, *Village Bells*, 32–40.

40 *De la nature. Paysages de Poussin à Courbet dans les collections du musée Fabre* (Montpellier: Musée Fabre, 1996), 27–31; Saiello, Châtel and Martichou (eds), *Écrire et peindre le paysage*. The paintings by Dunouy, Swebach and Vallin are in the Musée de la Révolution française at Vizille.

41 AN AD IV 19. Coupé may have been referring to the comments in Pliny, *Natural History*, trans. H. Rackham (London, 1942), Book III. iv. See, too, J.-B. Rougier de la Bergerie, *Mémoire et observations sur les abus des défrichemens et la destruction des bois et forêts; avec un projet d'organisation forestière* (Auxerre: An IX), 3.

42 Pierre Chevallier and Marie-José Couailhac, 'Sauvegarde des forêts de montagne en France au XIXe siècle (l'exemple du Dauphiné)', in Corvol, *La Forêt*, 334; Pitte, *Histoire du paysage*, vol. 2, 87.

43 AD Aude L 2194.

44 Historians have often averred that the Revolution was an unparalleled disaster for the forests: see, for example, Pierre Gresser et al., *Les Hommes et la forêt en Franche-Comté* (Paris: Bonneton, 1990), 103; Schama, *Landscape and Memory*, 179–80.

45 Abbé Maxime Seguin de Pazzis, *Mémoire statistique sur le Département du Vaucluse* (Carpentras, 1808), 236.

46 Claude-Joseph Trouvé, *États de Languedoc et département de l'Aude*, 2 vols (Paris: Didot, 1818), vol. 2, 530–2.

47 Rougier de la Bergerie, *Mémoire et observations*, 6–11. On Rougier see Caroline Ford, *Natural Interests. The Contest over Environment in Modern France* (Cambridge, MA and London: Harvard University Press, 2016), 47–52.

48 Amans-Alexis Monteil, *Description du département de l'Aveyron* (Rodez: An X), 32. Note the comments on Monteil by Peter Jones in *Peasantry*, 248–51.

49 Bernard Bodinier and Éric Teyssier, 'L'Événement le plus important de la Révolution': *la vente des biens nationaux en France et dans les territoires annexés, 1789–1867* (Paris: SÉR, 2000); Bodinier, 'La Révolution française et la question agraire: un bilan national en 2010', *Histoire et sociétés rurales* 33 (2010): 7–47; Jones, *Liberty and Locality*, 245–50.

50 Robert Forster, 'The French Revolution and the "New" Elite, 1800–1850', in *The American and European Revolutions, 1776–1848*, ed. J. Pelenski (Iowa City: University of Iowa Press, 1980), 182–207.

51 T. J. A. Le Goff and D. M. G. Sutherland, 'The Revolution and the Rural Economy', in *Reshaping France: Town, Country and Region during the French Revolution*, ed. Alan Forrest and P. M. Jones (Manchester: Manchester University Press, 1991).

52 Georges Lefebvre, 'La Révolution française et les paysans', in *Études sur la Révolution française* (Paris: PUF, 1954), 257; P. M. Jones, 'Agricultural Modernization and the French Revolution', *Journal of Historical Geography* 16 (1990): 38–50; Le Goff and Sutherland, 'The Revolution and the Rural Economy'.

53 Ado, *Paysans en Révolution*, 6, Conclusion; Florence Gauthier, *La Voie paysanne dans la Révolution française: l'exemple picard* (Paris: François Maspero, 1977); Paul T. Hoffman, *Growth in a Traditional Society: The French Countryside, 1450–1815* (Princeton, NJ: Princeton University Press, 1996); Peter McPhee, 'The French Revolution, Peasants, and Capitalism', *AHR* 94 (1989): 1265–80; McPhee, *Revolution and Environment*, ch. 7; James Livesey, 'Material Culture, Economic Institutions and Peasant Revolution in Lower Languedoc 1770–1840', *Past and Present* 182 (2004): 143–73.

54 Peter McPhee, *Liberty or Death: The French Revolution* (New Haven and London: Yale University Press, 2016), 76, 165, 308, figures 11, 12, 13, 33.

55 Koubi (ed.), *Propriété et Révolution*; Blaufarb, *Great Demarcation*.

Chapter 3

1 Marie-Noëlle Bourguet, *Déchiffrer la France: la statistique départementale à l'époque napoléonienne* (Paris: Éditions des archives contemporaines, 1989); Isser Woloch, *Napoleon and his Collaborators: The Making of a Dictatorship* (New York: W. W. Norton, 2001); Robb, *Discovery of France*, ch. 9.

2 Josef Konvitz, *Cartography in France, 1660–1848: Science, Engineering, and Statecraft* (Chicago, IL: University of Chicago Press, 1987), chs 1–2; *Histoire de la population française*, ed. Jacques Dupâquier et al. (Paris: PUF, 1988), vol. 3, 16–36.

3 Gaveau, *Propriété, cadastre et usages locaux*, 154–7.

4 Woronoff (ed.), *Révolution et espaces forestiers*; Corvol (ed.), *La Nature en Révolution*; Matteson, *Forests in Revolutionary France*, 187–98; McPhee, *Revolution and Environment*, ch. 6.

5 See, for example, Raymond Viney, 'L'Ordonnance forestière de Colbert et les législateurs de la Révolution française', *Revue forestière française* 21 (1969): 607–10. On the *légende noire*, see Fréréric Ogé, 'Héritage révolutionnaire: les forêts pyrénéennes, enjeux de conflis États-communautés', in Corvol, *La Nature en Révolution*, 156; Denis Woronoff, 'La "Dévastation révolutionnaire" des forêts', in Woronoff (ed.), *Révolution et espaces forestiers*, 52; Whited, *Forests and Peasant Politics*, 21–6.

6 Jean-Baptiste Huet de Coetlizan, *Recherches économiques . . . sur le département de la Loire-Inférieure* (Paris: L'Imprimerie des sourds-muets), An X, 22, 89; Jean Charles and Joseph Laumond, *Statistique du département du Bas-Rhin* (Paris: L'Imprimerie des sourds-muets), An X, 29.

7 Clout, *Agriculture in France*, 63 and ch. 5.

8 Livesey, 'Material Culture', 164.

9 Albert Soboul, 'Concentration agraire en pays de grande culture: Puiseux-Pontoise (Seine-et-Oise) et la propriété Thomassin', in *Problèmes paysans de la Révolution (1789–1848)* (Paris: François Maspero, 1976), ch. 11. See too Jean-Marc Moriceau and Gilles Postel-Vinay, *Ferme, entreprise, famille: grande exploitation et changements agricoles: les Chartier: XVIIᵉ-XIXᵉ siècles* (Paris: ÉHSS, 1992).

10 Olwen Hufton, *Bayeux in the Late Eighteenth Century: A Social Study* (Oxford: Oxford University Press, 1967), 37–8, 283.

11 G. Debien, *Avant la révolution agricole: les prairies artificielles dans le sud du Haut-Poitou (XVIe- XIXe siècle)* (Dakar: Université de Dakar, Publications de la section d'histoire, no. 6, 1964).

12 McPhee, *Revolution and Environment*, ch. 5. See, for example, AD Aude B 540, 590, 1239, 1240–2; L 1431.

13 McPhee, *Revolution and Environment*, ch. 8.

14 Marquié, *L'Industrie textile*; Serge Chassagne, 'L'Industrie lainière en France à l'époque révolutionnaire et impériale, 1790–1810', in *Voies nouvelles pour l'histoire de la Révolution française*, ed. Albert Soboul (Paris: Bibliothèque nationale, 1978), 143–67.

15 AD Aude 13 M 397–400; Trouvé, *États de Languedoc*, vol. 2, ch. xiv; Chassagne, 'L'Industrie lainière'; McPhee, *Revolution and Environment*, ch. 7.

16 McPhee, *Revolution and Environment*, 196–8.

17 Plack, *Common Land, Wine and the French Revolution*, 145–6; Raymond Dugrand, *La Garrigue montpelliéraine. Essai d'explication d'un paysage* (Paris: PUF, 1964).

18 Gilles Postel-Vinay, 'A la recherche de la Révolution économique dans les campagnes (1789–1815)', *Revue économique* 6 (1989): 1015–45; Marcel Lachiver, *Vins, vignes et vignerons. Histoire du vignoble français* (Paris: Fayard, 1988), 368–93.

19 AD Aude 13M 61, 263–70; Trouvé, *États de Languedoc*, vol. 2, ch. vii; Jacques Pech de Laclause, 'La Vigne dans les Basses-Corbières depuis le XVIIIe siècle' (Thèse pour le doctorat en droit, Université de Toulouse, 1959).

20 See: https://www.brech.fr/a-voir/le-patrimoine-historique/le-champ-des-martyrs -et-sa-chapelle-expiatoire/le-champ-des-martyrs-et-sa-chapelle-expiatoire/. Long afterwards, in 1902, the victor, General Lazare Hoche, was commemorated in a statue by Jules Dalou on an eponymous square in Quiberon itself.

21 G. Garry, *La Baie de Somme et le canal de la Somme* (Abbeville: Imprimerie F. Paillart, 1920).

22 Reed G. Geiger, *Planning the French Canals: Bureaucracy, Politics, and Enterprise under the Restoration* (Newark, NJ: University of Delaware Press, 1994); Georges Reverdy, *Les Travaux publics en France 1817–1847 – trente années glorieuses* (Paris: Presses de l'école nationale des Ponts et Chaussées, 2003); Robb, *Discovery of France*, ch. 12.

23 Robb, *Discovery of France*, ch. 11.

24 Laurent Brassart, 'Planter des arbres le long des routes. La Politique horticole impériale et ses contradictions (1800–1815)', *AHRF* 399 (2020): 179–210.

25 https://lestetardsarboricoles.fr/wordpress/2016/07/07/les-platanes-revolutionnaires -de-caunes-minervois-aude/ (accessed 22 September 2021).

26 David Edwards-May, *Inland Waterways of France* (St Ives: Imray, 2010), 247–9. The link from the Sambre to the Oise was closed in 2006 but was fully restored and re-opened to navigation in 2021.

27 M. Estancelin, *Observations sur le canal de la Basse-Somme d'Abbeville à Saint-Vallery* (Paris: Imprimerie A. Pinard, 1833), 48.

28 Edward Duyker, *Dumont d'Urville: Explorer and Polymath* (Dunedin: Otago University Press, 2014).

29 Lewis, *Advent of Modern Capitalism*.

30 T. W. Margadant, 'Tradition and Modernity in Rural France during the Nineteenth Century', *JMH* 56 (1984): 667–97.

31 Jean-Luc Mayaud, *Les Paysans du Doubs au temps de Courbet: étude économique et sociale des paysans du Doubs au milieu du XIXe siècle* (Paris: Les Belles-Lettres, 1979); A. Chatelain, 'Problèmes ruraux en Bugey au milieu du XIXe siècle', *Revue de géographie de Lyon* 27 (1952): 155–63; Duby and Wallon (eds.), *France rurale*, vol. 3, 107–41.

32 *Madame Bovary* (1856), part II, chapter 8.

33 Maurice Agulhon, 'La Crise dans un département méditerranéen: le cas du Var', in Ernest Labrousse (ed.), *Aspects de la crise et de la dépression de l'économie française au milieu du XIXe siècle, 1848–1851, Études* 19 (1956): 316–56.

34 *Grasse: portrait d'une ville provençale* (Nice: Serre, 1981).

35 Gaveau, *Propriété, cadastre et usages locaux*, 329–30.

36 Prosper Mérimée, *Notes d'un voyage en Auvergne* (1838. Paris: Hachette, 2012).

37 Charbonnier et al., *Auvergne*, 352–5.

38 Ford, *Natural Interests*, ch. 1.

39 Cayeux, *Le Paysage en France*, 151–64. See too Steven Adams, *Landscape Painting in Revolutionary France: Liberty's Embrace* (New York and London: Routledge, 2020).

40 Saiello, Châtel, and Martichou (eds), *Écrire et peindre le paysage*, 151–62.

41 Alain Corbin, *The Lure of the Sea: The Discovery of the Seaside in the Western World, 1750–1840*, trans. J. Phelps (Berkeley and Los Angeles: University of California Press, 1994); Richard Taws, 'A Storm is Coming: Georges Michel in the Wind', in *Time, Media, and Visuality in Post-Revolutionary France*, ed. Iris Moon and Richard Taws (London: Bloomsbury, 2021).

42 Ford, *Natural Interests*, ch. 4.

43 Hugh D. Clout, 'Agricultural Progress and Environmental Degradation in the Pyrénées-Orientales during the nineteenth century', *Bulletin de la Société royale de géographie d'Anvers* 83 (1972–3): 31–53.

44 https://www.fousdetoc.com/2020/04/04/legislation-et-organisation-de-la-peche-en -eau-douce-en-france-a-travers-les-siecles/.

45 On the forest codes of 1827 and 1846, see Matteson, *Forests in Revolutionary France*, ch. 6; Jean-François Soulet, *Les Pyrénées au XIXe siècle*, 2 vols (Toulouse: Privat, 1987), vol. 2, ch. 11.

46 Peter McPhee, *The Politics of Rural Life: Political Mobilization in the French Countryside 1846–1852* (Oxford: Clarendon Press, 1992), 83.

47 Ibid., 271–2. A superb study of the exodus is by Patrice L. R. Higonnet, *Pont-de-Montvert: Social Structure and Politics in a French Village, 1700–1914* (Cambridge, MA: Harvard University Press, 1971), ch. 5.

Chapter 4

1 R. D. Price, 'The Onset of Labour Shortage in French Agriculture', *English Historical Review* 28 (1975): 260–79. The uneven nature of the 'exodus' is examined in Philippe Pinchemel, *Structures sociales et dépopulation rurale dans les campagnes picardes de 1836 à 1936* (Paris: A. Colin, 1957).

2 Alain Guillemin, 'Patrimoine foncier et pouvoir nobiliaire: la noblesse de la Manche sous la Monarchie de Juillet', *Études rurales* 63–4 (1976): 136.

3 Duby and Wallon (eds) *Histoire de la France rurale*, vol. 3, 464.

4 Pierre Bozon, *La Vie rurale en Vivarais* (Paris: Éditions du CNRS, 1961), 371–90, 509–15.

5 John M. Merriman, *The Stones of Balazuc: a French Village in Time* (New York: Norton, 2002), chs 4–5. See also W. G. Sebald, *The Rings of Saturn*, trans. M. Hulse (London: The Harvill Press, 1998), ch. 10.

6   Blanc, 'French Agrarian Terraces'; Jancis Robinson (ed.), *Oxford Companion to Wine*, 3rd edn (Oxford: Oxford University Press, 2006).

7   For an interesting regional study of this process, see John W. Shaffer, *Family and Farm: Agrarian Change and Household Organization in the Loire Valley, 1500–1900* (Albany, NY: State University of New York Press,1982), chs 7–10.

8   See https://www.visorando.com/randonnee-les-capitelles-de-conques-sur-orbiel/; Christian Lassure, '*Baraques* et *cortals* du Roussillon ou le mythe des "capitelles" et des "orris"', *L'Architecture rurale en pierre sèche*, suppl. No 1, 1977, https://www .pierreseche.com/terminologie_Roussillon.html.

9   See Pierres Sèches (free.fr).

10   Jean-Pierre Jessenne and Dominique Rosselle, 'L'Histoire rurale de la France du nord de la fin du Moyen Âge au XXe siècle', *Revue du Nord* 375–6, no. 2–3 (2008): 303–33.

11   Pierre Boisard, *Camembert: A National Myth*, trans. R. Miller (Berkeley, CA: University of California Press, 2003).

12   Blanc, 'French Agrarian Terraces'.

13   Jean-Paul Barbier, *Nicolas Appert: inventeur et humaniste* (Paris: Royer, 1994); Zachary Nowak, *Truffle: A Global History* (London: Reaktion Books, 2015).

14   Raymond Viney, 'L'Œuvre forestière du Second Empire', *Revue forestière française* 6 (1962): 532–43; Paul Arnould, 'Les Forêts industrielles (Landes, Sologne)', in Corvol, *Le XIXe siècle*, 3–9. Since 2006 the Château de Saint-Maurice has served as the headquarters of the French Equestrian Federation.

15   Louis Girard, *La Politique des travaux publics du Second Empire* (Paris: A. Colin, 1952).

16   Jacques Sargos, *Histoire de la forêt landaise. Du désert à l'âge d'or* (Bordeaux: L'Horizon chimérique, 1998); Caroline Ford, 'The Environmental Transformation of "Empty Space": From Desert to Forest in the *Landes* of Southwestern France', *Comparative Studies in Society and History* (2023): 422–45, doi:10.1017/ S0417522000482.

17   Ford, *Natural Interests*, 138–63; William G. Pooley, *Body and Tradition in Nineteenth-Century France. Félix Arnaudin and the Moorlands of Gascony, 1870–1914* (Oxford: Oxford University Press, 2019).

18   Alice Garner, *A Shifting Shore: Locals, Outsiders, and the Transformations of a French Fishing Town, 1823–2000* (London: Cornell University Press, 2005); Helen M. Davies, *Émile and Isaac Pereire: Bankers, Socialists and Sephardic Jews in Nineteenth-Century France* (Manchester: Manchester University Press, 2016), ch. 5; Corbin, *Lure of the Sea*. A brilliant novel drawing on this history is Gregory Day's *A Sand Archive* (Sydney: Picador, 2018). Of course, even railway lines have lifespans, and their demise may open up other uses for landscape. One of Eiffel's first railway bridges was a small iron structure in 1873 on the branch line 15 kilometres from Bazas to Villandraut, 60 kilometres south of Bordeaux. The railway line is long gone, now a beautiful bike path through forest, and Eiffel's bridge is known locally just as the *pont bleu*.

19   Blondel, Aronson, Bodiou, and Bœuf, *The Mediterranean Region*, 300–1.

20 Ford, *Natural Interests*, ch. 3; Denis Cœur, 'Les Inondations de mai-juin 1856 en France: dommages et conséquences', *La Houille blanche* 93, no. 2 (2007): 44–51, doi:10.1051/lhb:2007016; Denis Cœur and Abdelatif Djerboua, 'La Crue de 1856: reconstitution et analyse d'un événement hydrologique de référence', *La Houille blanche* 93, no. 2 (2007): 27–37, doi:10.1051/lhb:2007014.

21 Whited, *Forests and Peasant Politics*.

22 Gaveau, *Propriété, cadastre et usages locaux*, 297–8.

23 Ibid., 283–4.

24 Garrett Hardin, 'The Tragedy of the Commons', *Science* 162 (1968): 1243–8. Hardin later qualified his argument: 'The Tragedy of the Unmanaged Commons', *Trends in Ecology & Evolution* 9, no. 5 (1994): 199. A detailed discussion is by Fabien Locher, 'Cold War Pastures. Garrett Hardin and the "Tragedy of the Commons"', *Revue d'histoire moderne et contemporaine* vol. 60 (2013): 7–36.

25 Ford, *Natural Interests*, ch. 6; Andrea E. Duffy, *Nomad's Land: Pastoralism and French Environmental Policy in the Nineteenth-Century Mediterranean World* (Lincoln, NA: University of Nebraska Press, 2019), ch. 4.

26 Frédéric Thomas, 'Protection des forêts et environnementalisme colonial: Indochine, 1860–1945', *Revue d'histoire moderne et contemporaine* 56, no. 4 (2009): 104–36.

27 Peasant attitudes to their *milieux* are explored in James Lehning, *Peasant and French: Cultural Contact in Rural France in the Nineteenth Century* (Cambridge: Cambridge University Press, 1995). 'The peak of rural civilization' is used by Duby and Wallon (eds) *Histoire de la France rurale*, vol. 3.

28 See Timothy J. Clark, *Image of the People: Gustave Courbet and the 1848 Revolution* (Berkeley, CA: University of California Press, 1999); Timothy J. Clark, *The Absolute Bourgeois: Artists and Politics in France 1848–1851* (London: Thames and Hudson, 1973); John Berger, *About Looking* (New York: Random House, 1980); Robert L. Herbert, 'City Vs. Country: The Rural Image in French Painting from Millet to Gauguin', *Artform* 8 (1970): 44–55.

29 Ford, *Natural Interests*, ch. 4; Nicholas Green, *The spectacle of nature: landscape and bourgeois culture in nineteenth-century France* (Manchester: Manchester University Press, 1990); Théodore Rousseau (FranceArchives). Accessed 25 May 2023.

30 *De la nature. Paysages de Poussin à Courbet*, 36–40; Gustave Cahen, *Eugène Boudin* (Paris, 1899); Pierre Miquel, *Eugène Isabey: 1803–1886: la marine au XIXe siècle* (Maurs-la-Jolie: Éditions de la Martinelle, 1980).

31 Caroline Ford, 'Landscape and Environment in French Geographical and Historical Thought: New Directions', *FHS* 24, no. 1 (2001): 125–34; Eugen Weber, *Peasants into Frenchmen: The Modernization of Rural France, 1870–1914* (Stanford, CA: Stanford University Press, 1976), ch. 18; Pierre Nora (ed.), *Les Lieux de mémoire*, vol. 1, *La République* (Paris: Gallimard, 1984).

32 Maurice Agulhon, *Marianne into Battle: Republican Imagery and Symbolism in France, 1789–1880*, trans. J. Lloyd (Cambridge: Cambridge University Press, Paris, 1981), ch. 7.

33 Robert Specklin, 'L'Achèvement des paysages agraires', in Duby and Wallon (eds) *Histoire de la France rurale*, vol. 3, 255–305.

34 'Économie - Bocage breton. La difficile renaissance', *Le Télégramme* (letelegramme.fr), 15 July 2019 (accessed 5 April 2023).

35 Pitte, *Histoire du paysage*, vol. 2, 88–91.

36 Charbonnier et al., *Auvergne*, 100–1.

37 Leo Loubère, *The Wine Revolution in France* (Princeton, NJ: Princeton University Press, 1990); Geneviève Gavignaud-Fontaine, *Le Languedoc viticole, la Méditerranée et l'Europe au siècle dernier* (Montpellier: Presses de l'Université Paul Valéry, 2000).

38 Jean-Marc Moriceau, *Histoire du méchant loup: la question des attaques sur l'homme en France, xvᵉ-xxᵉ siècle* (Paris: Pluriel, 2016); Éric Fabre, 'La Destruction des loups au XIXe siècle. La Technique, l'État et les milieux naturels en France', *Revue d'histoire du XIXe siècle* (2017): 81–94. doi:10.4000/rh19.5188.

Chapter 5

1 The outlook of Freycinet's generation is explored by, among others, Sanford Elwitt, *The Making of the Third Republic: Class and Politics in France, 1868–1914* (Baton Rouge, LA: Louisiana State University Press, 1975); Judith F. Stone, *Sons of the Revolution: Radical Democrats in France, 1862–1914* (Baton Rouge, LA: Louisiana State University Press, 1996).

2 Charles de Freycinet, *Souvenirs 1878–1893*, vol. 2 (Paris: Ch. Delagrave, 1913), ch. 1.

3 *Le Patrimoine de la SNCF et des chemins de fer français* (Paris: Flohic éditions, 1999), 103–10. One tonne/kilometre is one metric ton carried for one kilometre.

4 Hugh McKnight, *Cruising French Waterways*, 4th edn (London: Bloomsbury Publishing, 2013); Michèle Merger, 'La Concurrence rail-navigation intérieure en France 1850–1914', *Histoire, économie et société* 9 (1990): 65–94; Martin Garrett, *The Loire. A Cultural History* (Oxford: Oxford University Press, 2010), 49.

5 https://e-monumen.net/patrimoine-monumental/monument-au-comte-de -chambord-sainte-anne-dauray/.

6 Jean Ibanès, 'La Répartition des exploitations dans l'agriculture française à la fin du XIXe et au début du XXe siècle', *Revue économique* 25 (1974): 706–34; Jean-Luc Mayaud, *La Petite exploitation rurale triomphante, France XIXe siècle* (Paris: Belin, 1999), 56–68; Ronald Hubscher, *L'Agriculture et la société rurale dans le Pas-de-Calais du milieu du XIXe siècle à 1914* (Arras: Mémoires de la CDMH du Pas-de-Calais, 1979), vol. 2, 738–49.

7 Pitte, *Histoire du paysage français*, vol. 2, 55–6.

8 Jean Meyer, *Histoire du sucre* (Paris: Desjonquères, 1989).

9 Étienne Baux, *Agriculture et vie rurale en Quercy au XIXe siècle, 1789–1914* (Cahors: Archives du Lot, 1982).

10 https://www.legifrance.gouv.fr/loda/id/LEGITEXT000006071118.

11 Laura Frader, *Peasants and Protest: Agricultural Workers, Politics, and Unions in the Aude, 1850–1914* (Berkeley, CA: University of California Press, 1994); J. Harvey Smith, 'Work Routine and Social Structure in a French Village: Cruzy in the Nineteenth Century', *Journal of Interdisciplinary History* 5 (1975): 357–82.

12 Duby and Wallon (eds), *Histoire de la France rurale*, vol. 3, 429–51.

13 Whited, *Forests and Peasant Politics*.

14 AD Alpes-de-Haute-Provence 29 Fi 0001 – 29 Fi 1878 preserves more than 2,000 glass plates of mountain areas prior to reforestation.

15 Thiébault, *La Forêt*, 122–8; Annick Douguédroit, 'Reafforestation in the French Southern Alps', *Mountain Research and Development* 1, no. 3–4 (1981): 245–52. *JSTOR*, https://doi.org/10.2307/3673061. Accessed 20 June 2023.

16 Duffy, *Nomad's Land*.

17 Aimé Perpillou, *Cartographie du paysage rural limousin. Essai d'utilisation rationnelle des documents cadastraux* (Chartres: Imprimerie Durand, 1940).

18 Gaveau, *Propriété, cadastre et usages locaux*, 294–303.

19 Alain Corbin, *The Foul and the Fragrant: Odor and the French Social Imagination*, trans. M. Kochan, R. Porter, and C. Prendergast (Cambridge, MA: Harvard University Press, 1986), esp. 154–6, 186–95.

20 *Bulletin de la Société pour la protection des paysages de France* – Year available 1902 – Gallica (bnf.fr).

21 Gaveau, *Propriété, cadastre et usages locaux*, 318–19; Corbin, *L'Homme dans le paysage*, 151–73.

22 Ford, *Natural Interests*, 111.

23 AD Aude 50 W 46–663. On Cros-Mayrevielle, see http://www.garae.fr/spip.php?article414.

24 Laura Lee Downs, *Childhood in the Promised Land: Working-Class Movements and the Colonies de Vacances in France, 1880–1960* (Durham, NC and London: Duke University Press, 2002).

25 Corbin, *L'Homme dans le paysage*, 164.

26 *La Vagabonde*, in *Oeuvres de Colette*, 3 vols (Paris: Flammarion, 1960), vol. 1, 830; Jane Gilmour, *Colette's France. Her Lives, her Loves* (London and Melbourne: Hardie Grant, 2013), 86.

27 Bill and Carol McGann, *The Story of the Tour de France*, vol. 1 (Indianapolis, IN: Dog Ear Publishing, 2006).

28 Alain Corbin, 'Naissance de la politique du paysage en France', *Revue des deux mondes* (March 2002): 9–13. Stable URL:https://www.jstor.org/stable/44189610.

29 Michel Fleury and Pierre Valmar, 'Les Progrès de l'instruction élémentaire de Louis XIV à Napoléon III, d'après l'enquête de Louis Maggiolo (1877–1879)', *Population* 12 (1957): 71–92.

30 AD Meuse 118 Tp 86; AD Haute-Garonne, BH br 4° 366; AD Lozère 1 T 681–2; AD Mayenne MS 80 14-2. In general, see François Ploux, *Une Mémoire de papier. Les Historiens de village et le culte de petites patries rurales* (Rennes: Presses universitaires de Rennes, 2011); 'Les sentiers de la mémoire. Site d'histoire locale: monographies instituteurs' (gilbert-delbrayelle.fr).

31 *The Memoirs of Frédéric Mistral*, trans. G. Wickes (New York: New Directions Publishing, 1986), ch. 9 ('progress' is capitalized in the original); Arno J. Mayer, *The Persistence of the Old Régime: Europe to the Great War* (London: Pantheon Books, 1981), esp. Introduction.

32 Jean Anglade, *Le Massif central au XIXe siècle* (Paris: Hachette, 1971), ch. 16.

33 Peter McPhee, 'Social Change and Political Conflict in Mediterranean France: Canet in the Nineteenth Century', *FHS* 12 (1981): 68–97.

34 Overviews in English include Margadant, 'Tradition and Modernity'. Among many fine regional studies, see P. M. Jones, *Politics and Rural Society: The southern Massif Central c. 1750–1880* (Cambridge: Cambridge University Press, 1985); Johnson, *Life and Death of Industrial Languedoc*; Raymond A. Jonas, *Industry and Politics in Rural France: Peasants of the Isère, 1870–1914* (Ithaca, NY: Cornell University Press, 1994).

35 François Michaud, 'Parcs et jardins des châteaux du vignoble biterrois du milieu du XIXe siècle à nos jours', ESO Travaux et documents, 15 March 2001 (cnrs.fr).

36 Roger Thabault, *Mon village: ses hommes, ses routes, son école. 1848–1914, l'ascension d'un peuple* (1944) (Paris: Presses de la Fondation nationale des sciences politiques, 1982).

37 Higonnet, *Pont-de-Montvert*, 102–4; Robert Louis Stevenson, *Travels with a Donkey in the Cévennes and Selected Travel Writings* (1879. Oxford: Oxford University Press, 1993).

38 McPhee, *Gabian*, 110.

39 Jean-Louis Bordes, 'Les Barrages en France du XVIIIe à la fin du XXe siècle', *Comité Français des Barrages et Réservoirs* 9 (2010). https://www.barrages-cfbr.eu/IMG/pdf/barrages-jlb.pdf (accessed 22 August 2023).

40 Jean Butaud, *Bourganeuf, ville médiévale* (Bourganeuf: Imprimerie Rebière, 1944).

41 Émile Zola, *Germinal*, trans. H. Ellis (London: J.M. Dent & Sons, 1885), ch. 1. See too *La Terre* (1887).

42 https://www.rouleur.cc/blogs/the-rouleur-journal/arenberg-part-one-the-making-of -a-paris-roubaix-legend (accessed 14 February 2023).

Chapter 6

1 Edith Wharton, *A Motor-Flight through France* (1908. New York: Atlas & Co., 2008), 9–13.

2 Edith Wharton, *Fighting France: From Dunkerque to Belport* (New York: Charles Scribner's Sons, 1918), 94, 140–1, 165–6.

3 Wharton, *A Motor-Flight through France*, 196–7.

4 Franck Meyer, *Verdun: des ravages à la renaissance, 1915–1929*, 2 vols (Verdun: Connaissance de la Meuse, 2006–7); Alain Nolibos, *Arras: de Nemetucam à la communauté urbaine* (Lille: La Voix du Nord, 2003).

5 https://www.chemindesdames.fr/fr/ (accessed 17 August 2021).

6 Christina Holstein, *Fort Douaumont*, revised edition (Barnsley: Pen and Sword Books, 2010).

7 Daniel J. Sherman, *The Construction of Memory in Interwar France* (Chicago, IL: University of Chicago Press, 1999).

8 Andrée Corvol and Jean-Paul Amat (eds), *Forêt et guerre* (Paris: L'Harmattan, 1994); Tamara Whited, *A History of State Forestry in France – Arboriculture* (wordpress .com); Thiébault, *La Forêt*, 129–38.

9 Hugh Clout, *After the Ruins. Restoring the Countryside of Northern France after the Great War* (Exeter: University of Exeter Press, 1996), chs 1–2.

10 Jean-Paul Amat, 'L'Impact de la Grande Guerre: paysages dévastés et voies de la reconstruction', in *Les Sources de l'histoire de l'environnement. Tome III: Le XXe siècle*, ed. Andrée Corvol (Paris: L'Harmattan, 2003), 3–14.

11 Chris Pearson, *Mobilizing Nature: The Environmental History of War and Militarization in Modern France* (Manchester: Manchester University Press, 2016), ch. 1.

12 Pearson, *Mobilizing Nature*, ch. 4; Hugh Clout, 'Rural Revival in Marne, 1914–1930', *The Agricultural History Review* 42 (1994), 144. See too Stéphane Audoin-Rouzeau, Gerd Krumeich, and Jean Richardot, *Cicatrices: la Grande Guerre aujourd'hui* (Paris: Éditions Tallandier, 2008).

13 There is a vast literature on the battles of the Somme, including Simon Jones, *Underground Warfare 1914–1918* (Barnsley: Pen & Sword Books, 2010).

14 Clout, *After the Ruins*, 276–7, 287; Philippe Boulanger, 'Le Paysage de guerre dans le canton de Lassigny (Oise)', *Ruralia* 8 (2001), http://journals.openedition.org/ruralia /216 (accessed 30 August 2022).

15 Jean-Charles Cappronnier, 'La Restauration des châteaux et des manoirs en Picardie après la Grande Guerre', in *Les Malheurs de la guerre*, vol. 2, *De la guerre réglée à la guerre totale*, ed. André Corvisier and Jean Jacquart (Paris: Éditions du CTHS, 1997), 147–60.

16 Gaveau, *Propriété, cadastre et usages locaux*, 336–7.

17 Major overviews of these decades are Serge Berstein and Pierre Milza, *Histoire de la France au XXe siècle*, 3 vols (Paris: Perrin, 2009), vols 1–2; Nicolas Beaupré, *Les Grandes guerres 1914–1945* (Paris: Belin, 2012).

18 F. Patrix and E. Massué, 'L'Assainissement de la Limagne' and 'Le Remembrement en Limagne', in *Clermont-Ferrand et sa région. Association française pour l'avancement des sciences, 68ᵉ Congrès*, 1949, 191–202; Raoul Reynaud, *L'Assainissement de la Limagne*, Ennezat mémoire et patrimoine, no. 3 (2017).

19 Duby and Wallon (eds), *Histoire de la France rurale*, vol. 4, 195–6, 204, 315–19.

20 Ibid., 212–16, 324–5.

21 RTE - Gestionnaire du Réseau de Transport d'Electricité (wikiwix.com).

22 More than 400 of the glass-plate negatives are preserved in the AD Morbihan, Series 8 Fi 1–419.

23 Nowak, *Truffle: A Global History*.

24 Christian Manable, *Rainneville. Histoire d'un village picard*, n.p. (1984).

25 McPhee, *Gabian*, chs. 6–7.

26 Bozon, *Vivarais*, 343.

27 Ford, *Natural Interests*, ch. 4; *Bulletin de la Société pour la protection des paysages de France*, Gallica (bnf.fr). The political divisions of the Vichy regime made the reconstitution of the society difficult after the Second World War. It merged with another association to become the Société pour la Protection des Paysages et de l'Esthétique de la France in February 1956. It continues its work more modestly today.

28 Brevets, marques, dessins et modèles. Évolution des protections de propriété industrielle au XIXe siècle en France (openedition.org); Article 1 – Loi du 28 juillet 1824 relative aux altérations ou suppositions de noms sur les produits fabriqués – Légifrance (legifrance.gouv.fr); https://www.wine-law.org/index.php/protection-de-lappellation-champagne-le-premier-jugement-des-1844/.

29 Kolleen M. Guy, *When Champagne Became French: Wine and the Making of a National Identity* (Baltimore, MD: John Hopkins University Press, 2003).

30 Gaveau, *Propriété, cadastre et usages locaux*, 308.

31 Boisard, *Camembert*; Sylvie Vabre, *Le Sacre du Roquefort. L'Émergence d'une industrie agroalimentaire* (Rennes: Presses universitaires de Rennes, 2015).

32 'La Dimension patrimoniale des appellations' (u-bourgogne.fr); Gaveau, *Propriété, cadastre et usages locaux*, 305–14.

33 https://www.world-nuclear-news.org/Articles/Macron-clarifies-French-energy-plans (accessed 25 August 2023).

34 William Allcorn, *The Maginot Line 1928–45* (Oxford: Osprey Publishing, 2003); J. E. Kaufmann, H. W. Kaufmann, A. Jancovič-Potočnik, and Patrice Lang, *The Maginot Line: History and Guide* (Havertown, PA: Pen and Sword, 2011).

35 Rudolph Chelminski, 'The Maginot Line', *Smithsonian*, June 1997: 90–100.

36 Sarah Farmer, *Martyred Village: Commemorating the 1944 Massacre at Oradour-sur-Glane* (Oakland, CA: University of California Press, 2000); Jean-Jacques Fouché, *Massacre at Oradour: France, 1944; Coming to Grips With Terror*, trans. D. Sices and J. B. Atkinson (De Kalb, IL: Northern Illinois University Press, 2004); Robert Pike, *Silent Village: Life and Death in Occupied France* (Cheltenham: The History Press, 2021).

37 Gary Sterne, *The Cover-up at Omaha Beach* (New York: Skyhorse Publishing, 2014).

38 Pearson, *Mobilizing Nature*, 179–82.

39 Hugh Clout, 'From Utah Beach toward Reconstruction: Revival in the Manche *département* of Lower Normandy after June 1944', *Journal of Historical Geography* 35 (2009): 154–77.

40 Chris Pearson, *Scarred Landscapes. War and Nature in Vichy France* (Basingstoke: Palgrave Macmillan, 2008), ch. 6.

41 Bertram M. Gordon, *War Tourism: Second World War France from Defeat and Occupation to the Creation of Heritage* (Ithaca, NY, and London: Cornell University Press, 2018).

42 Pearson, *Mobilizing Nature*, 215; https://www.memorialcamprivesaltes.eu/.

43 Pearson, *Scarred Landscapes*, ch. 5.

44 Alain Collomp, *La Découverte des gorges du Verdon: histoire du tourisme et des travaux hydrauliques* (Aix-en-Provence: Édisud, 2002).

45 Jean Gravier, *Paris et le désert française* (Paris: Flammarion, 1947). An account of the impact of the installation of the military camp is Annie Bruel, *De la terre et des larmes* (Gap: Éditions Aubéron, Gap, 2005).

46   Pearson, *Mobilizing Nature*, 2–3, ch. 8.

47   François Jarrige and Thomas Le Roux, *The Contamination of the Earth A History of Pollutions in the Industrial Age*, trans. Janice Egan and Michael Egan (Cambridge, MA: MIT Press, 2020).

Chapter 7

1   Jean Fourastié, *Les Trente Glorieuses, ou la révolution invisible de 1946 à 1975* (Paris: Fayard, 1979). See too John Ardagh, *France in the New Century: Portrait of a Changing Society* (New York: Viking, 1999).

2   Wright, *Rural Revolution in France*. There is an interesting collection of recoloured photographs of post-war mechanization in Jean-Marc Moriceau, *Les Couleurs de nos campagnes, 1880–1960* (Paris: Les Arènes, 2020), part 4.

3   Braudel, *People and Production*, 674.

4   Ibid., 675.

5   Ibid., 676; Armand Frémont, 'The Land', in *Realms of Memory: Rethinking the French Past*, vol. 2, *Traditions*, trans. A. Goldhammer, ed. Pierre Nora (New York: Columbia University Press, 1997), ch. 1.

6   François Clerc, 'Les Étapes de la révolution verte', in Corvol, *Le XXe siècle*, 63–4; Sarah Farmer, *Rural Inventions: The French Countryside after 1945* (New York: Oxford University Press, 2020), 12–18. For the international context of agricultural change, see Stephen Forbes (ed.), *A Cultural History of Plants in the Modern Era*, vol. 6 of *A Cultural History of Plants* (London: Bloomsbury Academic, 2022).

7   Gaveau, *Propriété, cadastre et usages locaux*.

8   Stephen J. Miller, 'Peasant Farming in Eighteenth and Nineteenth-Century France and the Transition to Capitalism under Charles De Gaulle', in *Case Studies in the Origins of Capitalism*, ed. Xavier LaFrance and Charles Post (London: Palgrave Macmillan, 2019), 87–109.

9   Venus Bivar and Tamara L. Whited, 'Industrial French Food and its Critics', *Modern & Contemporary France* 28, no. 2 (2020): 129–39, doi:10.1080/09639489.2019.16762 18. Bivar, *Organic Resistance: The Struggle over Industrial Farming in Postwar France* (Chapel Hill, NC: University of North Carolina Press, 2018), Intro., describes French agriculture as essentially unchanging before 1950, and dismisses claims of high-quality produce as 'largely vacuous'.

10   Florent Allais, Honorine Lescieux-Katir, and Jean-Marie Chauvet, 'The Continuous Evolution of the Bazancourt–Pomacle site Rooted in the Commitment and Vision of Pioneering Farmers', *EFB Bioeconomy Journal* 1 (2021). https://doi.org/10.1016/j .bioeco.2021.100007.

11   Fabien Liagre, *Les Haies rurales: rôles, création, entretien* (Paris: France Agricole Editions, 2006).

12   *Le Monde*, 9 April, 23–24 May 2021.

13   Le Charolais-Brionnais, paysage culturel de l'élevage bovin - UNESCO Centre du patrimoine mondial.

14   https://spectrum.ieee.org/wine-is-going-out-of-stylein-france. The peak was 136 litres in 1926.

15   Origine Cévennes accueil - Oignons doux des Cévennes (oignon-doux-des-cevennes .fr).

16   Blanc, 'Landscape Typology of French Agrarian Terraces'.

17   Germaine Berthon, interview with the author in 1998.

18   George Kish, 'Hydroelectric Power in France: Plans and Projects', *Geographical Review* 45, no. 1 (1955): 81–98. https://doi.org/10.2307/211731.

19   Gabrielle Hecht, *The Radiance of France: Nuclear Power and National Identity after World War II*, 2nd edn (Cambridge, MA: The MIT Press, 2009).

20   https://web.archive.org/web/20130124025211/http://docs.nrdc.org/nuclear/files/nuc _01009601a_006.pdf.

21   Dominique Barjot, 'Les Industries de la construction et la transformation des paysages', in Corvol, *Le XXe siècle*, 27–39.

22   Spencer Segalla, *Empire and Catastrophe: Decolonization and Environmental Disaster in North Africa and Mediterranean France since 1954* (Lincoln, NE: University of Nebraska Press, 2020), ch. 3. Open Access: http://library.oapen.org/handle/20.500 .12657/37329

23   Brian Perren, *TGV handbook*, 2nd edn (Harrow Weald: Capital Transport, 2000); Claude Soulié and Jean Tricoire, *Le Grand livre du TGV* (Paris: La Vie du Rail, 2002).

24   Duby and Wallon (eds), *Histoire de la France rurale*, vol. 4, 281; Farmer, *Rural Inventions*, 31–5.

25   https://www.lejdd.fr/Societe/cest-quoi-une-journee-rouge-sur-les-routes-405962262; https://www.guinnessworldrecords.com/world-records/ 903-longest-traffic-jam.

26   Guillaume Fabras, *Histoire d'Amiens* (Montigny-lès-Metz: Feuilles de menthe, 2008); Gérard Devaux, *Les hortillonnages d'Amiens* (Amiens: Centre régional de documentation pédagogique d'Amiens, 1984).

27   Giacomo Parrinello and Renaud Bécot, 'Regional Planning and the Environmental Impact of Coastal Tourism: The Mission Racine for the Redevelopment of Languedoc-Roussillon's Littoral', *Humanities* 8 (2019), article 13; doi:10.3390/ h8010013.

28   *Travels Through France and Italy*, 1766, Letter XIII; Julian Hale, *The French Riviera. A Cultural History* (Oxford: Oxford University Press, 2009), ch. 10.

29   Farmer, *Rural Inventions*, 31–5.

30   Steve Hagimont, *Pyrénées. Une histoire environnementale du tourisme* (Ceyzérieu: Champ Vallon, 2022), chs 5–6.

31   *L'Aubrac. Étude ethnologique, linguistique, agronomique et économique d'un établissement humain*, vol. 2 (Paris: Éditions du CNRS, 1971), 127–65.

32   Farmer, *Rural Inventions*, 24–9. Farmer's book is a fine analysis of the cultural resonances and appeal of the changing French countryside.

33   AD Morbihan 2179 W 1–17 – Agréments d'association au titre du code de l'urbanisme et du code rural 1971–2011.

34   *Le Monde*, 26 October 1977.

35   https://books.google.com/ngrams/graph?content=paysage&year_start=1770&year
     _end=2019&corpus=fr-2019&smoothing=3.

36   K. Suter, 'The Club of Rome: The Global Conscience', *Contemporary Review* 275
     (1999): 1–5.

37   Farmer, *Rural Inventions*, ch. 4.

38   Pierre-Jakez Hélias, *The Horse of Pride: Life in a Breton Village*, trans. J. Guicharnaud
     (New Haven, CT: Yale University Press, 1978), 324.

39   François Mauriac, *Thérèse*, trans. G. Hopkins (1927. London: Penguin Books, 2002),
     70.

40   Susan Carol Rogers, *Shaping Modern Times in Rural France: The Transformation and
     Reproduction of an Aveyronnais Community* (Princeton, NJ: Princeton University
     Press, 1991), ch. 2.

41   Claire Delfosse, *La France fromagère (1850–1990)* (Paris: La Boutique de l'histoire
     éditions, 2007); Ernest Mignon, *Les Mots du général* (Paris: A. Fayard, 1962).

42   Gaveau, *Propriété, cadastre et usages locaux*, 320–1.

43   Pitte, *Histoire du paysage français*, vol. 2, 132–41.

44   Michael Bess, *The Light-Green Society: Ecology and Technological Modernity in France,
     1960–2000* (Chicago, IL: University of Chicago Press, 2003). Note Bess' discussion of
     climate change in *Planet in Peril: Humanity's Four Greatest Challenges and How We
     Can Overcome Them* (Cambridge: Cambridge University Press, 2022).

45   La contribution des pêcheurs à la loi sur l'eau de 1964 (openedition.org). The Musée
     de la Chasse et de la Nature, founded in 1967 in two mansions in the Marais district
     of Paris, displays an extraordinary array of paintings, hunting rifles and stuffed
     animals in sumptuous – some would say grotesque – settings.

46   Alexandre Brun et al., 'Les Conséquences écologiques et sociales de l'aménagement
     de la Reyssouze dans l'Ain (années 1850-années 2000)', in *Aménagement et
     environnement. Perspectives historiques*, ed. Patrick Fournier and Geneviève Massard-
     Guilbaud (Rennes: Presses universitaires de Rennes, 2018), 179–92, https://books
     .openedition.org/pur/44409; Stéphane Marette and Alexandre Brun, 'Le Bilan d'un
     contrat de rivière: le cas de la Reyssouze', *Économie rurale* 275 (2003): 30–50. 10.3406/
     ecoru.2003.5412.

47   Pierre Cornu, 'Déprise agraire et reboisement. Le Cas des Cévennes (1860–1970)',
     Histoire et sociétés rurales 20, no. 2 (2003): 173–201.

48   Peter H. Amann, *The Corncribs of Buzet: Modernizing Agriculture in the French
     Southwest* (Princeton, NJ: Princeton University Press, 1990).

49   http://www.absconsulting.com/resources/Catastrophe_Reports/Lothar-Martin
     Report.pdf (accessed 16 September 2021); Looking Back, Looking Forward: Anatol,
     Lothar and Martin Ten Years Later | AIR Worldwide (air-worldwide.com) (accessed 3
     September 2023).

50   See https://web.archive.org/web/20190605091924/http://quaternary.stratigraphy.org/
     working-groups/anthropocene/.

Chapter 8

1 Hugh Clout, 'Rural France in the New Millennium: Change and Challenge', *Geography* 91, no. 3 (2006): 205–17. *JSTOR*, http://www.jstor.org/stable/40574160 (accessed 27 April 2023).

2 See https://www.ecologie.gouv.fr/politique-des-sites#scroll-nav__4.

3 See, for example, https://www.burgundy-tourism.com/sit/la-moutarderie-fallot-parcours-decouvertes (accessed 19 August 2022).

4 Blanc, 'Landscape Typology of French Agrarian Terraces'.

5 *Le Monde*, 9–10 October 2022; Jean-Philippe Martin, *Des paysans écologistes: politique agricole, environnement et société depuis les années 1960* (Ceyzérieu: Champ Vallon, 2023).

6 See Susanne Freidberg, *French Beans and Food Scares. Culture and Commerce in an Anxious Age* (Oxford: Oxford University Press, 2004), ch. 5.

7 One example is the series of sumptuous and detailed volumes produced by the Conseil Départemental de l'Isère in Grenoble, for example, *Cent lieux. Paysages et patrimoine en Isère* (Grenoble: Département de l'Isère, 2016). See https://collections.isere.fr/fr/museum/page/patrimoine-in-situ/f4020ca4-c7be-45cf-9a38-399118b5c6b2.

8 T. Labbé, C. Pfister, S. Brönnimann, D. Rousseau, J. Franke, and B. Bois, 'The Longest Homogeneous Series of Grape Harvest Dates, Beaune 1354–2018, and its Significance for the Understanding of Past and Present Climate', *Climate of the Past* 15 (2019): 1485–1501, https://doi.org/10.5194/cp-15-1485-2019, 2019.

9 *Le Monde*, 9 September 2021.

10 Ibid., 7–8 November 2021.

11 Blondel, Aronson, Bodiou, and Bœuf, *The Mediterranean Region*, 282.

12 Ibid., 288–9; 'Vacances d'été 2023', 31 July 2023 *20 Minutes*, [archive] (accessed 5 October 2023). There is a vast literature on 'sustainable tourism': a brief introduction is https://www.shutterstock.com/blog/regenerative-travel-future-of-tourism.

13 Sandrine Aubié and Jean-Pierre Tastet, 'Coastal Erosion, Processes and Rates: An Historical Study of the Gironde Coastline, Southwestern France', *Journal of Coastal Research* 16, no. 3 (2000): 756–67. See the excellent study by Stephen L. Harp, *The Riviera, Exposed: An Ecohistory of Postwar Tourism and North African Labour* (Ithaca and London: Cornell University Press, 2022).

14 *Le Monde*, 12 April 2023.

15 'Forestiers d'Alsace – La santé des forêts' (forestiersdalsace.fr); 'Ravaging Bark Beetles Take a Bite out of France's Softwood Market', *Forestry & Carbon* (forestry-carbon.com) (accessed 4 January 2024).

16 https://www.lemonde.fr/a-la-une/article/2012/09/15/superficie-du-vignoble-francais-en-milliers-d-hectares_1760912_3208.html; https://www.nationmaster.com/nmx/timeseries/france-wine-consumption-per-capita; https://www.statista.com/statistics/434726/wine-consumption-in-france-per-person/ (accessed 24 September 2021).

17 *Le Monde*, 21 June 2023.

18 Joseph Bohling, *The Sober Revolution: Appellation Wine and the Transformation of France* (Ithaca, NY and London: Cornell University Press, 2018).

19 https://www.securite-routiere.gouv.fr/actualites/1972-2012-les-francais-et-la-securite-routiere-40-annees-de-route-commune (accessed 24 September 2021). The road toll was later revised to 18,034.

20 Philippe Madeline, 'L'Évolution du bâti agricole en France métropolitaine: un indice des mutations agricoles et rurales', *Information géographique* 70 (2006): 33–49.

21 *Le Monde*, 30 July 2021.

22 https://www.insee.fr/fr/statistiques/4806694.

23 https://saint-nolff.bzh/environnement-2/ (accessed 31 May 2023).

24 https://www.bruded.fr/wp-content/uploads/2017/08/fiche-saint-nolff_ecocite _prevert.pdf; https://www.construction21.org/france/city/h/eco-city-of-the-green -meadow-in-st-nolff-en.html.

25 Pierre Dérioz, 'Naissance, extension et mutations des paysages périurbains pavillonnaires dans le sud-est de la France', in Corvol (ed.), *Le XXe siècle*, 93–117.

26 Hugues Neveux, 'Un paysage rural d'Île-de-France au XVIIIe siècle: Saint-Brice vers 1760–1780', in *Paris et ses campagnes sous l'Ancien Régime*, ed. Michel Balard, Jean-Claude Hervé and Nicole Lemaître (Paris: Éditions de la Sorbonne, 1994).

27 *Le Monde*, 14 September 2022.

28 Graeme Hayes, *Environmental Protest and the State in France* (Basingstoke: Palgrave Macmillan, 2002).

29 https://www.legifrance.gouv.fr/loda/id/LEGITEXT000005630252.

30 *Le Monde*, 25–26 July 2021. Similar pressures are felt on the coast at Étretat: *Le Monde*, 9–11 April 2023.

31 Ibid., 4 December 2022.

32 Ibid., 9–11 April, 20 June 2023.

33 Blondel, Aronson, Bodiou, and Bœuf, *The Mediterranean Region*, 269, 272–3.

34 *Le Monde*, 20 September 2022, 8–9; 'Étang de Canet' (pole-lagunes.org) (accessed 21 September 2022). The particular fragility of the Mediterranean was documented at the 22nd Conference of Parties to the United Nations Framework Convention on Climate Change (COP22) in Marrakesh in 2016: see *The Mediterranean Region under Climate Change. A scientific update: Abridged English/French Version*, ed. Jean-Paul Moatti and Stéphanie Thiébault (Marseille: IRD éditions, 2018). doi:10.4000/books. irdeditions.24549.

35 http://www.ecologiste.org/contents/fr/p96.html.

36 Disruptions to power supply due to the war in Ukraine led to two small coal-fired power stations remaining active in 2023, at Saint-Avold in eastern France and Cordemais in the west.

37 Hubert Bonin, 'Le Charbon, de la glorification à la diabolisation', *Histoire*, 7 June 2021; Virginie Debrabant and Gérard Dumont, *Les Trois Ages de la mine*. vol. I, *Le Temps des pionniers, 1720–1830*, vol. 2, *L'Ère du charbon roi, 1830–1914*, vol. 3,

De l'apogée au déclin, 1914–1990 (Leuwarde-Lille: Centre historique minier-La Voix du Nord, 2007); http://www.france.fr/en/news/mines-nord-pas-de-calais-make-their -debut-unesco-world-heritage-site (accessed 14 February 2023).

38 'O'MEGA1: first floating solar power plant in France', *Bouygues Energies & Services* (bouygues-es.com); https://s.campbellsci.com/documents/eu/case-studies/france _dynamic_agri-voltaism.pdf (accessed 17 August 2021); *Le Monde*, 14 March 2023.

39 See, for example, the recent European Environment Agency report on https://www .eea.europa.eu/soer-2015/countries/france.

40 *Le Monde*, 25 November 2022; 21 January 2023. Causes of Parkinson's disease are analysed in L. M. de Lau and M.M. Breteler, 'Epidemiology of Parkinson's disease', *The Lancet. Neurology* 5 (2006): 525–35. doi:10.1016/S1474-4422(06)70471-9.

41 'France announces partial ban on glyphosate', *Farmers Weekly* (fwi.co.uk) 12 October 2020; 'Où en est-on de l'interdiction du glyphosate, cet herbicide controversé?' (msn.c om) 14 October 2021.

42 *Le Monde*, 25 March 2022.

43 Ibid., 16 February 2023.

44 https://www.researchgate.net/publication/264161664_Effect_of_on-farm_biogas _production_on_impacts_of_pig_production_in_Brittany_France.

45 Liagre, *Les Haies rurales*; Philippe Bardel, Jean-Luc Maillard, and Gilles Pichard, *L'Arbre et la haie: mémoire et avenir du bocage* (Rennes: Presses universitaires de Rennes, 2008); Dominique Soltner, *Planter des haies: brise-vent, bandes boisées* (Angers: Imprimerie Siraudeau, 1984).

46 *Le Monde*, 12–13 September 2021.

47 https://france3-regions.francetvinfo.fr/nouvelle-aquitaine/deux-sevres/deux-sevres -lapin-garenne-plus-plus-rare-campagnes-1657350.html.

48 Philippe Madeline, 'Les Constructions agricoles dans les campagnes françaises. Héritages et dynamiques actuelles d'évolution', *Histoire et Sociétés Rurales* 26 (2006): 53–93; *Autour de Camembert: de l'an mille à l'an 2000: quatre années de recherches interdisciplinaires*, ed. Jean-Marc Moriceau, Roger Calmès and Philippe Madeline (Caen: Presses Universitaires de Caen, 1999), 173–86.

49 Thiébault, *La Forêt*, 114.

50 Claire Labrue, 'Habiter la forêt: du rêve de s'enfermer à la réalité enfermante. Le plateau de Millevaches', in Corvol (ed.), *Forêt et paysage*, 95–110. The village is famous for its First World War memorial depicting an orphan and the words 'Maudite soit la guerre' (Cursed be war).

51 See Thiébault, *La Forêt*, ch. 6; Kieko Matteson, 'The Revival of Tradition in France's Forests', Al Jazeera, 10 March 2013.

52 *Archéologie d'une montagne brûlée: massif de Rodès, Pyrénées-Orientales*, ed. Olivier Passarrius, Aymat Catafau, and Michel Martzluff (Perpignan: Éditions Trabucaire, 2009).

53 Fabre, 'Destruction des loups'.

54 https://www.nouvelobs.com/animaux/20201202.OBS36896/des-millions-d-animaux -se-font-tuer-sur-les-routes-voici-comment-stopper-l-hecatombe.html; *Le Monde*, 3 September 2021.

55 Ibid., 17 November 2021.

56 Ibid., 10 January 2023.

57 *Libération*, 8 November 2021.

58 *Le Monde*, 3 February 2021.

59 Stevenson, *Travels with a Donkey in the Cévennes*.

60 Tom Griffiths, 'At Dusk in the Gévaudan', *Australian Book Review* no. 354 (2013); Jay M. Smith, *Monsters of the Gévaudan* (Cambridge, MA: Harvard University Press, 2011); Jean-Marc Moriceau, *Histoire du Méchant Loup* (Paris: Fayard, 2007).

61 *Le Monde*, 29–30 August 2021.

62 Ibid., 3 February, 20–21 March, 31 March, 11 October 2022; 20 September 2023.

63 Ibid., 16–17 April 2023; 'Pourquoi les sangliers envahissent-ils les jardins et les champs?' (biojardinservices.com); David Servenay, 'Les chasseurs deviennent des viandards: la prolifération des sangliers hors de contrôle', *Le Monde*, 18 July 2020.

64 Its detractors point to the college's ownership by a prominent telecommunications magnate linked to the wealthiest family in France and its undermining of established qualifications pathways into farming. 'Yvelines. Le patron de Free, Xavier Niel, finance une école des métiers agricoles à Lévis-Saint-Nom', *78actu*, 4 March 2021.

65 *Le Monde*, 1–2 August 2021.

66 https://www.nationalgeographic.com/travel/article/in-paris-conservation-effort-is-recovering-lost-river (accessed 16 September 2021); *Le Monde*, 17 August 2023.

67 https://www.theguardian.com/world/2023/feb/18/climate-crisis-brings-whiff-of-danger-to-french-perfume-capital.

68 *Le Monde*, 11, 14–16 August 2022, 1 April 2023.

69 Ibid., 25 June 2022.

70 Ibid., 8 March 2023.

71 Ibid., 23–24 April 2023.

Conclusion

1 An expert overview of the landscape since 1950 is by Élisabeth Trotignon, *Il Faut sauver nos campagnes* (Paris: Delachaux et Niestlé, 2021).

2 Chantal Gaulin, 'Horticulteurs et maraîchers parisiens de la seconde moitié du XIXe siècle à la première guerre mondiale', *Journal d'agriculture traditionnelle et de botanique appliquée* 34 (1987): 113–23.

3 'La biodiversité française en déclin: 10 ans de chiffres-clés' (ofb.fr).

4 https://education.nationalgeographic.org/resource/light-pollution/ (accessed 17 September 2023).

5 Prosper Mérimée, *Rapport au ministre de l'Intérieur* (Paris: Imprimerie royale, 1840).

6 See two government websites: Portail de la France and Portail de la conservation de la nature.

7 https://inpn.mnhn.fr/accueil/a-propos-inpn.

8 'Pourquoi tout le monde se retourne contre nous?: le profond désarroi du monde agricole face à "l'agribashing"', Le Monde, 7 November 2019: https://www.lemonde.fr/societe/article/2019/11/07/commentaires-malveillants-intrusions-nocturnes-querelles-de-voisinage-le-profond-desarroi-du-monde-agricole_6018297_3224.html.

9 For example, from a 'social Catholic' point of view, see Geneviève Gavignaud-Fontaine, *Villageois sans agriculture! Observations sur la société rurale contemporaine* (Montpellier: Publications de la Méditerranée, 2007); *La Révolution rurale dans la France contemporaine, XVIIIᵉ–XXᵉ siècle* (Paris: L'Harmattan, 1996).

10 Note in particular the contributions of Yves Luginbühl, Didier Bouillon, Martine Berlan-Darqué, and Bernard Kalaora to 'De l'agricole au paysage', special issue of *Études rurales* no. 121–4 (1991): 197–205. Stable URL: https://www.jstor.org/stable/20125262.

11 The latter two works are in the Musée de Picardie in Amiens.

12 *Les Eaux étroites* (Paris: José Conti, 1976); published in translation as *The Narrow Waters* (New York: Turtle Point Press, 2004).

13 *Le Grand Meaulnes* (Paris: Éditions Émile-Paul Frères, 1913); Garrett, *The Loire*. In 2008 the writer and jurist Camille de Toledo, the heritage archaeologist Virginie Serna and others established a 'parliament' to oversee the wellbeing of the Loire: https://projetcoal.org/en/sharing/the-loire-parliament-hearings-negotiating-in-an-inter-species-context/.

14 Susan Carol Rogers, 'Which Heritage? Nature, Culture, and Identity in French Rural Tourism', *FHS* 25 (2002): 475–503.

15 Jacques Houlet, 'Les Autoroutes et le paysage', in *Le Paysage: sauvegarde et création*, ed. Gilbert Pons (Seyssel: Champ Vallon, 1999): 63–86.

16 A. Thomas and G. Lemoine, 'Le Tunnel de Vernou-Vouvray du TGV Atlantique', *Travaux* 634 (1988): 1–11.

17 'New rules could make it harder to install wind turbines in France' (wind-watch.org); *Le Monde*, 3 November 2021 (accessed 5 November 2021).

18 Ibid., 18–19 June 2023.

19 François Clerc, 'Les Étapes de la révolution verte', in Corvol (ed.), *Le XXe siècle*, 66–70.

20 Ibid., 59–60.

21 Ford, 'The Environmental Transformation of "Empty Space"', *The Guardian* 30 April 2023: Patrick Greenfield, 'Field of fresh cow pats welcomes first dung beetles to be rewilded in France', *The Guardian*, 30 April 2023.

22 https://www.patrimoinecharolaisbrionnais.fr/le-paysage-culturel-de-l-elevage-bovin/un-bocage-faconne-par-l-homme.html.

23 Jean-Michel Derex, 'Les Étangs: du déclin à la renaissance. Traditions et nouvelles vocations', in Corvol (ed.), *Le XXe siècle*, 83–92.

24 *L'Express*, 25 March, 28 March, 9–11 April 2023.

25 'Mégabassines: en Auvergne, le nouveau champ de bataille' (reporterre.net) (accessed 21 August 2023).

26 AD Morbihan 3P 246 4; 1854W 165/4. In Morbihan, the 'Napoleonic' cadastral survey took from 1807 to 1901; the post-war *remembrement* took from 1953 to 2009.

27 https://actu.fr/bretagne/saint-aignan_56203/lac-de-guerledan-entre-huees-et -applaudissements-la-passerelle-de-la-division-de-saint-aignan_54241742.html.

28 'Garder le loup sans perdre l'agneau': Gaveau, *Propriété, cadastre et usages locaux*, 371. Such questions are at the heart of the collection of articles edited by Fabien Locher, *La Nature en communs. Ressources, environnement et communautés (France et Empire français XVIIe-XXIe siècle)* (Ceyzérieu: Champ Vallon, 2020).

SELECT BIBLIOGRAPHY

This is a bibliography of those printed and digital sources most useful for this book. Other references are cited in footnotes, as are references to some of the manuscript material used from the Archives Nationales and departmental archives in Bourg-en-Bresse (Ain), Bar-le-Duc (Meuse), Carcassonne (Aude), Digne (Alpes-de-Haute-Provence), Laval (Mayenne), Mende (Lozère), Nancy (Meurthe-et-Moselle), Toulouse (Haute-Garonne), and Vannes (Morbihan).

Adams, Steven. *Landscape Painting in Revolutionary France: Liberty's Embrace*. New York and London: Routledge, 2020.

Allen, Edward A. 'Deforestation and Fuel Crisis in Pre-Revolutionary Languedoc'. *FHS* 13 (1984): 455–73.

Amann, Peter H. *The Corncribs of Buzet: Modernizing Agriculture in the French Southwest*. Princeton, NJ: Princeton University Press, 1990.

Anglade, Jean. *Le Massif central au XIXe siècle*. Paris: Hachette, 1971.

Aubié, Sandrine and Jean-Pierre Tastet. 'Coastal Erosion, Processes and Rates: An Historical Study of the Gironde Coastline, Southwestern France'. *Journal of Coastal Research* 16, no. 3 (2000): 756–67.

L'Aubrac. Étude ethnologique, linguistique, agronomique et économique d'un établissement humain. vol. 2, Paris: Éditions du CNRS, 1971.

Bamford, Paul W. *Forests and French Sea Power, 1660–1789*. Toronto: University of Toronto Press, 1956.

Bardel, Philippe, Jean-Luc Maillard, and Gilles Pichard. *L'Arbre et la haie: mémoire et avenir du bocage*. Rennes: Presses universitaires de Rennes, 2008.

Baux, Étienne. *Agriculture et vie rurale en Quercy au XIXe siècle, 1789–1914*. Cahors: Archives du Lot, 1982.

Beaupré, Nicolas. *Les Grandes guerres 1914–1945*. Paris: Belin, 2012.

Bernet, Jacques (ed.). *Le Journal d'un maître d'école d'Île-de-France (1771–1792): Silly-en-Multien de l'Ancien Régime à la Révolution*. Villeneuve-d'Asq: Presses universitaires du Septentrion, 2000.

Berque, Augustin. *Écoumène: introduction à l'étude des milieux humains*. Paris: Belin, 2001.

Berstein, Serge and Pierre Milza. *Histoire de la France au XXe siècle*. 3 vols. Paris: Perrin, 2009.

Bess, Michael. *The Light-Green Society: Ecology and Technological Modernity in France, 1960–2000*. Chicago, IL: University of Chicago Press, 2003.

Bivar, Venus. *Organic Resistance: The Struggle over Industrial Farming in Postwar France*. Chapel Hill, NC: University of North Carolina Press, 2018.

Bivar, Venus and Tamara L. Whited. 'Industrial French Food and its Critics'. *Modern & Contemporary France* 28, no. 2 (2020): 129–39, https://doi.org/10.1080/09639489.2019.1676218.

Blanc, Jean-François. 'Landscape Typology of French Agrarian Terraces'. In *World Terraced Landscapes: History, Environment, Quality of Life*, edited by Mauro Varotto, Luca Bonardi, and Paulo Tarolli, 63–77. Cham: Springer, 2019. https://doi.org/10.1007/978-3-319-96815-5_5.

Blaufarb, Rafe. *The Great Demarcation. The French Revolution and the Invention of Modern Property*. New York: Oxford University Press, 2016.

Blondel, Jacques, James Aronson, Jean-Yves Bodiou, and Gilles Bœuf. *The Mediterranean Region. Biological Diversity in Space and Time*. 2nd edn. Oxford: Oxford University Press, 2010.

Bodinier, Bernard and Éric Teyssier. *'L'Événement le plus important de la Révolution': la vente des biens nationaux en France et dans les territoires annexés, 1789–1867*. Paris: SÉR, 2000.

Bohling, Joseph. *The Sober Revolution: Appellation Wine and the Transformation of France*. Ithaca, NY and London: Cornell University Press, 2018.

Boisard, Pierre. *Camembert: A National Myth*. Trans. R. Miller. Berkeley, CA: University of California Press, 2003.

Boulanger, Philippe. 'Le Paysage de guerre dans le canton de Lassigny (Oise)'. *Ruralia* [En ligne] 8 (2001). http:// journals.openedition.org/ruralia/216 (accessed 1 May 2019).

Bourgin, Georges. *Le Partage des biens communaux. Documents sur la préparation de la loi du 10 juin 1793*. Paris: Imprimerie nationale, 1908.

Bozon, Pierre. *La Vie rurale en Vivarais*. Paris: Éditions du CNRS, 1961.

Brassart, Laurent. 'Planter des arbres le long des routes. La Politique horticole impériale et ses contradictions (1800–1815)'. *AHRF*, no. 399 (2020): 179–210.

Brassart, Laurent, Grégory Quenet, and Julien Vincent. 'Révolution et environnement: état des savoirs et enjeux historiographiques'. *AHRF*, no. 399 (2020): 3–18.

Braudel, Fernand. *The Identity of France*. 2 vols. Trans. S. Reynolds. London: Collins, 1990.

Bret, Jean-Noël and Yolaine Escande (eds). *Le Paysage, entre art et nature*. Rennes: Presses universitaires de Rennes, 2017.

Bulletin de la Société pour la protection des paysages de France (1902–39).

Cayeux, Jean de. *Le Paysage en France de 1750 à 1815*. Saint-Rémy-en-l'Eau: Éditions Monelle, Hayot, 1997.

Chakrabarty, Dipesh. 'The Climate of History: Four Theses'. *Critical Inquiry* 35 (2009): 197–222.

Charbonnier, Pierre et al. *Auvergne*. Chamalières: Éditions Christine Bonneton, 1985.

Chassagne, Serge. 'L'Industrie lainière en France à l'époque révolutionnaire et impériale, 1790–1810'. In *Voies nouvelles pour l'histoire de la Révolution française*, edited by Albert Soboul, 143–67. Paris: Bibliothèque nationale, 1978.

Chastel, André. 'The Notion of Patrimony'. Trans. N. Turpin. In *Rethinking France. Les Lieux de mémoire*. vol. 3, *Legacies*, edited by Pierre Nora. Chicago: University of Chicago Press, 2009, ch. 1.

Chouquer, Gérard. *L'Étude des paysages. Essais sur leurs formes et leur histoire*. Paris: Errance, 2000.

Clermont-Ferrand et sa région. Association française pour l'avancement des sciences, 68e Congrès, 1949.

Clout, Hugh. 'Agricultural Progress and Environmental Degradation in the Pyrénées-Orientales during the Nineteenth Century'. *Bulletin de la Société royale de géographie d'Anvers* 83 (1972–3): 31–53.

Clout, Hugh. *Agriculture in France on the Eve of the Railway Age*. London: Croom Helm, 1980.

Clout, Hugh. *After the Ruins. Restoring the Countryside of Northern France after the Great War*. Exeter: University of Exeter Press, 1996.

Clout, Hugh. 'Rural France in the New Millennium: Change and Challenge'. *Geography* 91, no. 3 (2006): 205–17. http://www.jstor.org/stable/40574160 (accessed 27 April 2023).

Clout, Hugh. 'From Utah Beach toward Reconstruction: Revival in the Manche *département* of Lower Normandy after June 1944'. *Journal of Historical Geography* 35 (2009): 154–77.

Cœur, Denis. 'Les Inondations de mai–juin 1856 en France: dommages et conséquences'. *La Houille blanche* 93 (2007): 44–51, https://doi.org/10.1051/lhb :2007016.

Cœur, Denis and Abdelatif Djerboua. 'La Crue de 1856: reconstitution et analyse d'un événement hydrologique de référence'. *La Houille blanche* 93 (2007): 27–37, https://doi .org/10.1051/ lhb:2007014.

Corbin, Alain. *The Foul and the Fragrant: Odor and the French Social Imagination*. Trans. M. Kochan, R. Porter, and C. Prendergast. Cambridge, MA: Harvard University Press, 1986.

Corbin, Alain. *The Lure of the Sea: The Discovery of the Seaside in the Western World, 1750–1840*. Trans. J. Phelps. Berkeley and Los Angeles: University of California Press. 1994.

Corbin, Alain. *Village Bells. The Culture of the Senses in the Nineteenth-Century French Countryside*. Trans. M. Thom. New York: Columbia University Press, 1998.

Corbin, Alain. *L'Homme dans le paysage. Entretien avec Jean Lebrun*. Paris: Éditions Textuel, 2001.

Corbin, Alain. 'Naissance de la politique du paysage en France'. *Revue des deux mondes* (March 2002): 9–13. https://www.jstor.org/stable/44189610.

Corbin, Alain. *La Douceur de l'ombre: l'arbre, source d'émotions, de l'antiquité à nos jours*. Paris: Fayard, 2013.

Cornu, Pierre. 'Déprise agraire et reboisement. Le Cas des Cévennes (1860–1970)'. *Histoire et Sociétés Rurales* 20, no. 2 (2003): 173–201.

Corvisier, André and Jean Jacquart (eds). *Les Malheurs de la guerre*, vol. 2, *De la guerre réglée à la guerre totale*. Paris: Éditions du CTHS, 1997.

Corvol, Andrée. *L'Homme aux bois. Histoire des relations de l'homme et de la forêt, XVIIe–XXe siècle*. Paris: Fayard, 1987.

Corvol, Andrée (ed.). *La Forêt. Actes du 113e Congrès national des sociétés savantes, Strasbourg 1988*. Paris: Éditions du CTHS, 1991.

Corvol, Andrée (ed.). *La Nature en Révolution. Colloque Révolution, nature, paysage et environnement*. Paris: L'Harmattan, 1993.

Corvol, Andrée (ed.). *Les Sources de l'histoire de l'environnement. Le XIXe siècle*. Paris: L'Harmattan, 1999.

Corvol, Andrée (ed.). *Les Sources de l'histoire de l'environnement. Tome III: Le XXe siècle*. Paris: L'Harmattan, 2003.

Corvol, Andrée (ed.). *Forêt et paysages, Xe–XXIe siècle*. Paris: L'Harmattan, 2011.

Corvol, Andrée and Jean-Paul Amat (eds). *Forêt et Guerre*. Paris: L'Harmattan, 1994.

Corvol, Andrée and Isabelle Richefort (eds). *Nature, paysage et environnement. L'Héritage révolutionnaire*. Paris: L'Harmattan, 1995.

Davies, Helen. *Émile and Isaac Pereire. Bankers, Socialists and Sephardic Jews in Nineteenth-Century France*. Manchester: Manchester University Press, 2015.

Debrabant, Virginie and Gérard Dumont. *Les Trois Ages de la mine*. vol. 1, *Le Temps des pionniers,1720–1830*, vol. 2, *L'Ère du charbon roi, 1830–1914*, vol. 3, *De l'apogée au déclin, 1914-1990*. Leuwarde-Lille: Centre historique minier-La Voix du Nord, 2007.

De la nature. Paysages de Poussin à Courbet dans les collections du musée Fabre. Montpellier: Musée Fabre, 1996.

Delaspre, Jean. 'La Naissance d'un paysage rural au XVIIIe siècle sur les hauts plateaux de l'Est du Cantal et du Nord de la Margeride'. *Revue de Géographie Alpine* 40 (1952): 493–7.

Delfosse, Claire. *La France fromagère (1850–1990)*. Paris: La Boutique de l'histoire éditions, 2007.

Dion, Roger. *Essai sur la formation du paysage rural français*. Tours: Arrault, 1934.

Douguédroit, Annick. 'Reafforestation in the French Southern Alps'. *Mountain Research and Development* 1, no. 3–4 (1981): 245–52. https://doi.org/10.2307/3673061 (accessed 20 June 2023).

Duby, Georges and Armand Wallon (eds). *Histoire de la France rurale*. vol. 2, *L'Age classique des paysans de 1340 à 1789*. Paris: Seuil, 1975; vol. 3, *Apogée et crise de la civilisation paysanne de 1789 à 1914*. Paris: Seuil, 1976; vol. 4, *La fin de la France paysanne, de 1914 à nos jours*. Paris: Seuil, 1976.

Duffy, Andrea E. *Nomad's Land: Pastoralism and French Environmental Policy in the Nineteenth-Century Mediterranean World*. Lincoln, NE: University of Nebraska Press, 2019.

Dupâquier, Jacques et al. (eds). *Histoire de la population française*. Paris: PUF, 1988.

Durand, Georges. 'Vine and Wine'. Trans. H. Glagov. In *Rethinking France. Les Lieux de mémoire*. vol. 3, *Legacies*, edited by Pierre Nora. Chicago: University of Chicago Press, 2009, ch. 6.

Fabre, Éric. 'La Destruction des loups au XIXe siècle. La Technique, l'État et les milieux naturels en France'. *Revue d'histoire du XIXe siècle* 54 (2017): 81–94.

Farmer, Sarah. *Martyred Village: Commemorating the 1944 Massacre at Oradour-sur-Glane*. Oakland, CA: University of California Press, 2000.

Farmer, Sarah. *Rural Inventions: The French Countryside after 1945*. New York: Oxford University Press, 2020.

Feterman, Georges and Marc Giraud. *Paysages de France en bord de chemin*. Paris: Éditions Delachaux et Niestlé, 2021.

Ford, Caroline. 'Landscape and Environment in French Geographical and Historical Thought: New Directions'. *FHS* 24, no. 1 (2001): 125–34.

Ford, Caroline. 'Reforestation, Landscape Conservation, and the Anxieties of Empire in French Colonial Algeria'. *AHR* 113, no. 2, (2008): 341–62.

Ford, Caroline. *Natural Interests. The Contest over Environment in Modern France*. Cambridge, MA and London: Harvard University Press, 2016.

Ford, Caroline. 'The Environmental Transformation of "Empty Space": From Desert to Forest in the *Landes* of Southwestern France'. *Comparative Studies in Society and History* 65, no. 2 (2023): 422–45, https://doi.org/10.1017/S0010417522000482.

Fortunet, Françoise. 'Le Code rural ou l'impossible codification'. *AHRF*, no. 247 (1982): 95–112.

Fouché, Jean-Jacques. *Massacre At Oradour: France, 1944. Coming To Grips With Terror*. Trans. D. Sices and J. B. Atkinson. De Kalb, IL: Northern Illinois University Press, 2004.

Frankopan, Peter. *The Earth Transformed: An Untold History*. London: Bloomsbury, 2023.

Freidberg, Susanne. *French Beans and Food Scares. Culture and Commerce in an Anxious Age*. Oxford: Oxford University Press, 2004.

Frémont, Armand. 'The Land'. In *Realms of Memory: Rethinking the French Past*. vol. 2, *Traditions*, edited by Pierre Nora. Trans. A. Goldhammer. New York: Columbia University Press, 1997, ch. 1.

Fressoz, Jean-Baptiste. 'Les Politiques de la nature au début de la révolution. Sens et fonctions de l'alerte environnementale, 1789–1793'. *AHRF*, no. 399 (2020): 19–38.

Frioux, Stéphane, *The Environment, an Object of History – Encyclopedia of the Environment*. encyclopedie-environnement.org.

Garner, Alice. *A Shifting Shore: Locals, Outsiders, and the Transformations of a French Fishing Town, 1823–2000*. London: Cornell University Press, 2005.

Garrett, Martin. *The Loire. A Cultural History*. Oxford: Oxford University Press, 2010.

Garry, G. *La Baie de Somme et le canal de la Somme*. Abbeville: Imprimerie F. Paillart, 1920.

Gaulin, Chantal. 'Horticulteurs et maraîchers parisiens de la seconde moitié du XIXe siècle à la première guerre mondiale'. *Journal d'agriculture traditionnelle et de botanique appliquée* 34 (1987): 113–23.

Gaveau, Fabien. *Propriété, cadastre et usages locaux dans les campagnes françaises (1789–1960). Histoire d'une tension légale*. Besançon: Presses universitaires de Franche-Comté, 2021.

Gavignaud-Fontaine, Geneviève. *La Révolution rurale dans la France contemporaine, XVIIIe–XXe siècle*. Paris: L'Harmattan, 1996.

Gavignaud-Fontaine, Geneviève, 'Usages, propriété, environnement: les mutations du paysage rural contemporain'. In *Le Paysage rural et ses acteurs. Première journée d'étude du Centre de recherches historiques sur les sociétés méditerranéennes*, edited by Aline Rousselle and Marie-Claude Marandet, 379–45. Perpignan: Presses universitaires de Perpignan, 1998.

Gavignaud-Fontaine, Geneviève. *Le Languedoc viticole, la Méditerranée et l'Europe au siècle dernier*. Montpellier: Presses de l'Université Paul Valéry, 2000.

Gavignaud-Fontaine, Geneviève. *Villageois sans agriculture! Observations sur la société rurale contemporaine*. Montpellier: Publications de la Méditerranée, 2007.

Geiger, Reed G. *Planning the French Canals: Bureaucracy, Politics, and Enterprise under the Restoration*. Newark, NJ: University of Delaware Press, 1994.

Genssane, M. de. *Histoire naturelle de la province de Languedoc*. 5 vols. Montpellier, 1778–9.

Gerbaux, Fernand and Charles Schmidt. *Procès-verbaux des comités d'agriculture et de commerce de la Constituante, de la Législative et de la Convention*. 5 vols. Paris: Imprimerie nationale, 1906–37.

Girard, Louis. *La Politique des travaux publics du Second Empire*. Paris: A. Colin, 1952.

Glacken, Clarence J. *Traces on the Rhodian Shore: Nature and Culture in Western Thought from Ancient Times to the End of the Eighteenth Century*. Berkeley and Los Angeles, CA: University of California Press, 1967.

Gordon, Bertram M. *War Tourism: Second World War France from Defeat and Occupation to the Creation of Heritage*. Ithaca, NY and London: Cornell University Press, 2018.

Green, Nicholas. *The Spectacle of Nature: Landscape and Bourgeois Culture in Nineteenth-Century France*. Manchester: Manchester University Press, 1990.

Gresser, Pierre, et al. *Les Hommes et la forêt en Franche-Comté*. Paris: Bonneton, 1990.

Griffiths, Tom. 'At Dusk in the Gévaudan'. *Australian Book Review*, no. 354, September 2013.

Griffiths, Tom. 'The planet is alive. Radical histories for uncanny times'. *Griffith Review* 63 (2019): 61–72.

Guy, Kolleen M. *When Champagne Became French: Wine and the Making of a National Identity*. Baltimore, MD: John Hopkins University Press, 2003.

Hagimont, Steve. *Pyrénées. Une histoire environnementale du tourisme*. Ceyzérieu: Champ Vallon, 2022.

Hale, Julian. *The French Riviera. A Cultural History*. Oxford: Oxford University Press, 2009.

Harfouche, Romana. *Histoire des paysages méditerranéens terrassés: Aménagements et agriculture*. Oxford: BAR Publishing, 2007.

Harp, Stephen L. *The Riviera Exposed: An Ecohistory of Postwar Tourism and North African Labour*. Ithaca and London: Cornell University Press, 2022.

Hartley, Daniel. 'Against the Anthropocene'. *Salvage*, 31 August 2015.

Hayes, Graeme. *Environmental Protest and the State in France*. Basingstoke: Palgrave Macmillan, 2002.

Hecht, Gabrielle. *The Radiance of France: Nuclear Power and National Identity after World War II*. 2nd edn. Cambridge, MA: The MIT Press, 2009.

Hélias, Pierre-Jakez. *The Horse of Pride: Life in a Breton Village*. Trans. J. Guicharnaud. New Haven, CT: Yale University Press, 1978.

Higonnet, Patrice L. R. *Pont-de-Montvert: Social Structure and Politics in a French Village, 1700–1914*. Cambridge, MA: Harvard University Press, 1971.

Hoffman, Paul T. *Growth in a Traditional Society: The French Countryside, 1450–1815*. Princeton, NJ: Princeton University Press, 1996.

Holmes, Katie, Andrea Gaynor, and Ruth Morgan. 'Doing Environmental History in Urgent Times'. *History Australia* 17 (2020): 230–51. https://doi.org/10.1080/14490854.2020.1758579

Hubscher, Ronald. *L'Agriculture et la société rurale dans le Pas-de-Calais du milieu du XIXe siècle à 1914*. 2 vols. Arras: Mémoires de la CDMH du Pas-de-Calais, 1979.

Ibanès, Jean. 'La Répartition des exploitations dans l'agriculture française à la fin du XIXe et au début du XXe siècle'. *Revue économique* 25 (1974): 706–34.

Ives, Colta. *Public Parks, Private Gardens. Paris to Provence*. New York: Metropolitan Museum of Art, 2018.

Jarrige, François and Thomas Le Roux. *The Contamination of the Earth. A History of Pollutions in the Industrial Age*. Trans. J. Egan and M. Egan. Cambridge, MA: MIT Press, 2020.

Jessenne, Jean-Pierre. *Pouvoir au village et Révolution: Artois, 1760–1848*. Lille: Presses universitaires de Lille, 1987.

Jessenne, Jean-Pierre. *Les Campagnes françaises entre mythe et histoire (XVIIIe–XXIe siècle)*. Paris: Armand Colin, 2006.

Jessenne, Jean-Pierre and Dominique Rosselle. 'L'Histoire rurale de la France du nord de la fin du Moyen Âge au XXe siècle'. *Revue du Nord* 375–6, no. 2–3 (2008): 303–33.

Johnson, Christopher H. *The Life and Death of Industrial Languedoc, 1700–1920*. New York: Oxford University Press, 1995.

Jollet, Anne. *Terre et société en Révolution. Approche du lien social dans la région d'Amboise*. Paris: Éditions du CTHS, 2000.

Jones, Peter M. *The Peasantry in the French Revolution*. Cambridge: Cambridge University Press, 1988.

Jones, Peter M. *Liberty and Locality in Revolutionary France: Six Villages Compared, 1760–1820*. Cambridge: Cambridge University Press, 2003.

Kish, George. 'Hydroelectric Power in France: Plans and Projects'. *Geographical Review* 45, no. 1 (1955): 81–98.

Koubi, Geneviève (ed.). *Propriété et Révolution: Actes du Colloque de Toulouse, 12–14 Octobre, 1989*. Paris: CNRS, 1990.

Labrousse, Ernest (ed.). 'Aspects de la crise et de la dépression de l'économie française au milieu du XIXe siècle, 1848–1851'. *Bibliothèque de la Révolution de 1848* 19 (1956).

Lachiver, Marcel. *Vins, vignes et vignerons. Histoire du vignoble français*. Paris: Fayard, 1988.

Larguier, Gilbert. *Le Drap et le grain en Languedoc. Narbonne et Narbonnais 1300–1789*. Perpignan: Presses universitaires de Perpignan, 1999.

Lefebvre, Henri. *The Production of Space*. Trans. D. Nicholson-Smith. 1974. Oxford: Oxford University Press, 1991.

Lehning, James R. *The Peasants of Marlhes. Economic Development and Family Organization in Nineteenth-Century France*. London: Macmillan, 1980.

Lehning, James R. *Peasant and French: Cultural Contact in Rural France in the Nineteenth Century*. Cambridge: Cambridge University Press, 1995.

Le Monde, 2019–23.

Le Patrimoine de la SNCF et des chemins de fer français. Paris: Flohic éditions, 1999.

Lewis, Gwynne. *The Advent of Modern Capitalism in France 1770–1840: The Contribution of Pierre-François Tubeuf*. Oxford: Clarendon Press, 1993.

Liagre, Fabien. *Les Haies rurales: Rôles, création, entretien*. Paris: France Agricole Éditions, 2006.

Locher, Fabien. 'Cold War Pastures. Garrett Hardin and the "Tragedy of the Commons"'. *Revue d'histoire moderne et contemporaine* 60 (2013): 7–36.

Locher, Fabien (ed.). *La Nature en communs. Ressources, environnement et communautés (France et Empire français XVIIe–XXIe siècle)*. Ceyzérieu: Champ Vallon, 2020.

Locher, Fabien and Grégory Quenet. 'L'Histoire environnementale: origines, enjeux et perspectives d'un nouveau chantier'. *Revue d'histoire moderne et contemporaine* 56, no. 4 (2009): 7–38.

Loubère, Leo. *The Wine Revolution in France*. Princeton, NJ: Princeton University Press, 1990.

Madeline, Philippe and Jean-Marc Moriceau. *Acteurs et espaces de l'élevage (XVIIe–XXIe siècles). Évolution, structuration, spécialisation*. Caen: Presses universitaires de Caen, 2006.

Madeline, Philippe and Jean-Marc Moriceau. *Les Paysans (1870–1970). Récits, témoignages et archives de la France agricole*. Paris: Éditions les Arènes, 2013.

Margadant, Ted W. 'Tradition and Modernity in Rural France during the Nineteenth Century'. *JMH* 56 (1984): 667–97.

Martin, Jean-Philippe. *Des paysans écologistes: politique agricole,environnement et société depuis les années 1960*. Ceyzérieu: Champ Vallon, 2023.

Matteson, Kieko. *Forests in Revolutionary France: Conservation, Community, and Conflict, 1669–1848*. Cambridge: Cambridge University Press, 2015.

Mayaud, Jean-Luc. *La Petite exploitation rurale triomphante, France XIXe siècle*. Paris: Belin, 1999.

McNeill, John R., *Something New Under the Sun. An Environmental History of the Twentieth-Century World*. New York: Norton, 2000.

McNeill, John R. and Peter Engelke. *The Great Acceleration: An Environmental History of the Anthropocene since 1945*. Cambridge, MA: Harvard University Press, 2014.

McNeill, John R. and Alan Roe. *Global Environmental History. An Introductory Reader*. London: Routledge, 2012.

McPhee, Peter. 'Social Change and Political Conflict in Mediterranean France: Canet in the Nineteenth Century'. *FHS* 12 (1981): 68–97.

McPhee, Peter. *Revolution and Environment in Southern France: Peasant, Lords, and Murder in the Corbières, 1780–1830*. Oxford: Clarendon Press, 1999.

McPhee, Peter. '"The Misguided Greed of Peasants"? Popular Attitudes to the Environment in the Revolution of 1789'. *FHS* 24 (2001): 247–69.

McPhee, Peter. *Une communauté languedocienne dans l'histoire: Gabian 1760–1960*. Nîmes: Lacour, 2001.

McPhee, Peter. *A Social History of France, 1780–1914*. 2nd edn. London and New York: Palgrave Macmillan, 2004.

McPhee, Peter. '"Cette anarchie dévastatrice": The *légende noire* of the French Revolution'. In *Invaluable Trees. Cultures of Nature, 1660–1830*, edited by Laura Auricchio, Elizabeth Cook, and Giulia Pacini, 73–85. Oxford: Studies in Voltaire and the Eighteenth Century, 2012.

McPhee, Peter. *Liberty or Death: The French Revolution*. New Haven, CT and London: Yale University Press, 2016.

Merchant, Carolyn. *The Anthropocene and the Humanities. From Climate Change to a New Age of Sustainability*. New Haven, CT and London: Yale University Press, 2020.

Merger, Michèle. 'La Concurrence rail-navigation intérieure en France 1850–1914'. *Histoire économie et société* 9 (1990): 65–94.

Merriman, John M. *The Stones of Balazuc: A French Village in Time*. New York: Norton, 2002.

Meyer, Jean. *Histoire du sucre*. Paris: Desjonquères, 1989.

Miller, Stephen J. 'Peasant Farming in Eighteenth and Nineteenth-Century France and the Transition to Capitalism under Charles De Gaulle'. In *Case Studies in the Origins of Capitalism*, edited by Xavier LaFrance and Charles Post, 87–109. London: Palgrave Macmillan, 2019.

Moatti, Jean-Paul and Stéphanie Thiébault (eds). *The Mediterranean Region under Climate Change. A scientific update*. Abridged English/French Version. Marseille: IRD éditions, 2018.

Moon, Iris and Richard Taws (eds). *Time, Media, and Visuality in Post-Revolutionary France*. London: Bloomsbury, 2021.

Moriceau, Jean-Marc. *Histoire du méchant loup: la question des attaques sur l'homme en France, XVe-XXe siècle*. Paris: Pluriel, 2016.

Moriceau, Jean-Marc. *Les Couleurs de nos campagnes, 1880–1960*. Paris: Les Arènes, 2020.

Moriceau, Jean-Marc, Roger Calmès, and Philippe Madeline (eds). *Autour de Camembert: de l'an mille à l'an 2000. Quatre années de recherches interdisciplinaires*. Caen: Presses universitaires de Caen, 1999.

Mornet, Daniel. *Le Sentiment de la nature en France de J.-J. Rousseau à Bernardin de Saint-Pierre*. Paris: Hachette, 1907.

Neveux, Hugues. 'Un paysage rural d'Ile-de-France au xviiie siècle: Saint-Brice vers 1760–1780'. In *Paris et ses campagnes sous l'Ancien Régime*, edited by Michel Balard, Jean-Claude Hervé, and Nicole Lemaitre. Paris: Éditions de la Sorbonne, 1994.

Noël, Michel. *L'Homme et la forêt en Languedoc-Roussillon. Histoire et économie des espaces boisés*. Perpignan: Presses universitaires de Perpignan, 1996.

O'Gorman, Emily, William San Martín, Mark Carey, and Sandra Swart (eds). *The Routledge Handbook of Environmental History*. London: Routledge, 2024.

Ord, Toby. *The Precipice. Existential Risk and the Future of Humanity*. London: Bloomsbury, 2020.

Parrinello, Giacomo and Renaud Bécot. 'Regional Planning and the Environmental Impact of Coastal Tourism: The Mission Racine for the Redevelopment of Languedoc-Roussillon's Littoral'. *Humanities* 8 (2019), article 13; https://doi.org/10.3390/h8010013.

Passarrius, Olivier, Aymat Catafau, and Michel Martzluff (eds). *Archéologie d'une montagne brûlée: Massif de Rodès, Pyrénées-Orientales*. Perpignan: Éditions Trabucaire, 2009.

Pearson, Chris. *Scarred Landscapes. War and Nature in Vichy France.* Basingstoke: Palgrave Macmillan, 2008.

Pearson, Chris. *Mobilizing Nature: The Environmental History of War and Militarization in Modern France.* Manchester: Manchester University Press, 2016.

Pike, Robert. *Silent Village: Life and Death in Occupied France.* Cheltenham: The History Press, 2021.

Pitte, Jean-Robert. *Histoire du paysage français. De la Préhistoire à nos jours,* vol. 2, *Le Profane: du 16e siècle à nos jours.* Paris: Tallandier, 1983.

Plack, Noelle L. *Common Land, Wine and the French Revolution. Rural Society and Economy in Southern France, c1789–1820.* Farnham, Surrey and Burlington, VT: Ashgate, 2009.

Pons, Gilbert (ed.). *Le Paysage: sauvegarde et création.* Seyssel: Champ Vallon, 1999.

Pooley, William G. *Body and Tradition in Nineteenth-Century France. Félix Arnaudin and the Moorlands of Gascony, 1870–1914.* Oxford: Oxford University Press, 2019.

Postel-Vinay, Gilles. 'À la recherche de la Révolution économique dans les campagnes (1789–1815)'. *Revue économique* 6 (1989): 1015–45.

Reverdy, Georges. *Les Travaux publics en France 1817–1847 – Trente années glorieuses.* Paris: Presses de l'École nationale des ponts et chaussées, 2003.

Robb, Graham. *The Discovery of France.* London: Picador, 2007.

Rogers, Susan Carol. *Shaping Modern Times in Rural France: The Transformation and Reproduction of an Aveyronnais Community.* Princeton, NJ: Princeton University Press, 1991.

Rogers, Susan Carol. 'Which Heritage? Nature, Culture, and Identity in French Rural Tourism'. *FHS* 25 (2002): 475–503.

Rougier de la Bergerie, J.-B. *Mémoire et observations sur les abus des défrichemens et la destruction des bois et forêts; avec un projet d'organisation forestière.* Auxerre: An IX.

Saiello, Émilie Beck, Laurent Châtel and Élisabeth Martichou (eds). *Écrire et peindre le paysage en France et en Angleterre, 1750–1850.* Rennes: Presses universitaires de Rennes, 2021.

Sargos, Jacques. *Histoire de la forêt landaise. Du désert à l'âge d'or.* Bordeaux: L'Horizon Chimérique, 1998.

Schama, Simon. *Landscape and Memory.* New York: Vintage, 1995.

Sebald, W. G. ('Max'). *The Rings of Saturn.* Trans. M. Hulse. London: The Harvill Press, 1998.

Seddon, George. *Sense of Place: A Response to an Environment.* Perth: University of Western Australia Press, 1972.

Seddon, George. *Landprints. Reflections on Place and Landscape.* Cambridge: Cambridge University Press, 1997.

Segalla, Spencer. *Empire and Catastrophe: Decolonization and Environmental Disaster in North Africa and Mediterranean France since 1954.* Lincoln, NE: University of Nebraska Press, 2020. Open Access: http://library.oapen.org/handle/20.500.12657/37329.

Shaffer, John W. *Family and Farm: Agrarian Change and Household Organization in the Loire Valley 1500–1900.* Albany, NY: SUNY Press, 1983.

Shapiro, Gilbert and John Markoff. *Revolutionary Demands: A Content Analysis of the Cahiers de Doléances of 1789.* Stanford, CA: Stanford University Press, 1998.

Soboul, Albert. *Problèmes paysans de la Révolution (1789–1848).* Paris: François Maspero, 1976.

Soulet, Jean-François. *Les Pyrénées au XIXe siècle,* 2 vols. Toulouse: Privat, 1987.

Steffen, Will, Paul J. Crutzen, and John R. McNeill. 'The Anthropocene: Are Humans Now Overwhelming the Great Forces of Nature?'. *Ambio* 36, no. 8 (2007): 614–21.

Thabault, Roger. *Mon village: ses hommes, ses routes, son école. 1848–1914, l'ascension d'un peuple*. 1944. Paris: Presses de la Fondation nationale des sciences politiques, 1982.

Thiébault, Stéphanie. *La Forêt. Histoire, usages, représentations et enjeux*. Paris: CNRS, 2023.

Tilly, Charles. *The Vendée*. Cambridge, MA: Harvard University Press, 1964.

Trotignon, Élisabeth. *Il faut sauver nos campagnes*. Paris: Delachaux et Niestlé, 2021.

Trouvé, Claude-Joseph. *États de Languedoc et département de l'Aude*. 2 vols. Paris: Didot, 1818.

Vabre, Sylvie. *Le Sacre du Roquefort. L'Émergence d'une industrie agroalimentaire*. Rennes: Presses universitaires de Rennes, 2015.

Viney, Raymond. 'L'Oeuvre forestière du Second Empire'. *Revue forestière française* 6 (1962): 532–43.

Vivier, Nadine. *Propriété collective et identité communale. Les Biens communaux en France 1750–1914*. Paris: Publications de la Sorbonne, 1998.

Wharton, Edith. *A Motor-Flight through France*. New York: Atlas & Co., 2008.

Whited, Tamara. *Forests and Peasant Politics in Modern France*. New Haven, CT: Yale University Press, 2000.

Whited, Tamara, Jens I. Engels, C. Hoffmann, Hilde Ibsen, and Wybren Verstegen. *Northern Europe. An Environmental History*. Santa Barbara, CA: ABC-Clio, 2005.

Wiens, J. A., M. R. Moss, M. G. Turner and D. J. Mladenoff (eds). *Foundation Papers in Landscape Ecology*. New York: Columbia University Press, 2007.

Williams, Raymond. *The Country and the City*. London: Chatto and Windus, 1973.

Woronoff, Denis (ed.). *Révolution et espaces forestiers*. Paris: L'Harmattan, 1988.

Wright, Gordon. *Rural Revolution in France; the Peasantry in the Twentieth Century*. Stanford, CA: Stanford University Press, 1964.

Wu, Jianguo. and Richards Hobbs (eds). *Key Topics in Landscape Ecology*. Cambridge: Cambridge University Press, 2007.

Wylie, John. *Landscape*. London & New York: Routledge, 2007.

Young, Arthur. *Travels in France during the Years 1787, 1788 and 1789*. New York: Anchor Books, 1969.

Young, David Bruce. 'A Wood Famine? The Question of Deforestation in Old Regime France'. *Forestry* 49 (1976): 45–56.

INDEX

Gard (department) 4–5, 9, 23, 25, 35, 49,
    53, 62, 121
Gardon (river) 4, 135
Garonne (river) 14, 67, 79, 92, 135
garrigues 9, 13, 14, 21, 22, 33, 35, 42,
    48–9, 65, 71, 149
gas 122, 145
Gascony (region) 68–9, 71, 89, 131, 161
Gaulle, Charles de 100, 112, 121, 127, 132
Genssane, Antoine de 24
geography, geographers 2–3, 7, 13–14,
    73, 74, 92
Gironde (department) 68, *see also*
    Bordeaux
Gordes (Vaucluse) 21–2, 64
Gracq, Julien 4, 159
Grande Peur, see Great Fear
Grasse (Alpes-Maritimes) 54, 153
Great Fear 29–30
Grenoble (Isère) 83, 86, 110, 112–13, 129
Guillaumin, Émile 4, 93

Haute-Garonne (department) 57, 92, *see
    also* Toulouse
Hautes-Pyrénées (department) 57
Haute-Vienne (department) 111, *see
    also* Limousin
hedgerows 14, 15, 19, 37, 47, 74, 76, 112,
    118–20, 147–8, 160, 161, 163, *see
    also bocage*
Hélias, Pierre-Jakez 4, 130–1
Hérault (department) 23, 47, 107–8, 145
herbicides 146–7
holidays 90, 109, 126, *see also* tourism
hunting 30–1, 46, 57–8, 76–7, 90, 118,
    134, 135, 150–1, 159, 161, 186
hydroelectricity 84, 90, 95, 105, 111, 114,
    122, 129, 145, 163

Ille-et-Vilaine (department) 58, 75
industry, *see* manufacturing
Inheritance laws 40
insects, insecticides 95, 120, 121, 150,
    see also pesticides
irrigation 36, 135, 139, 144–5, 153, 159,
    162
Isère (department) 86–7, 95, *see also*
    Grenoble
Italy 38, 128, 150

Jura (department) 53, 91, 110, 164
Jura (mountains) 14, 53, 57, 140

La Grand'Combe (Gard) 53
La Rochelle (Charente-Maritime) 125
Lagrasse (Aude) 23, 36, 38, 49
land clearances 17, 21–2, 24–7, 29, 31–4,
    36–9, 41–3, 45–9, 56, 69, 72, 119,
    134, 139, 147
Landes (department) 68–9, 71, 79, 114
Landes de Gascogne (region) 1, 68–71,
    85, 89, 131, 132, 153, 161
Landes (vegetation) 21, 68–9, 71, 163
landscape
    definitions of 2–4, 89–93, 108–9,
        132, 137–8, 165
    popular attitudes towards 1, 3,
        24–30, 53, 90–3, 104, 108–9, 115,
        129–31, 134, 138–9, 147, 150, 158,
        160
Languedoc (region) 1, 14–15, 19, 22–4,
    33, 42, 47–9, 53, 64–6, 74, 90, 93–5,
    110, 121, 129, 140–1
Laon (Aisne) 53, 100, 101, 140
Larzac (region) 70, 110, 132, 137
Lauragais (region) 13, 20, 135
Le Montat (Lot) 26
Le Roy, Eugène 4, 93
Le Roy Ladurie, Emmanuel 3, 18–19
Lens (Pas-de-Calais) 101, 123
Les Savournins 21–2
Leucate (Aude) 65, 127
Lille (Nord) 51, 126
Limagne (region) 13–14, 104, 119, 162
Limousin (region) 20, 83, 87, 104, 149
Lison (river) 3–4, 89, 91
literature 4, 19, 25, 55, 93, 95–6, 99–100,
    130–1, 159, 162
livestock
    cattle 15, 23, 37, 47, 58, 67, 74, 76,
        87, 95, 101, 107, 120, 129, 135, 150,
        151, 161
    goats 23–4, 42, 46, 48, 64, 68, 71, 84,
        91, 107
    sheep 15, 19, 22–3, 25, 34, 42, 47–9,
        64–5, 67–9, 84, 93–5, 101, 107, 110,
        129, 131, 132, 134, 137, 149, 151,
        164
Lodève (Hérault) 23, 48, 53